D1132114

THE Psalms AND Proverbs

With 31-Day Psalms and
Proverbs Devotionals

DR. BRIAN SIMMONS
LEAD TRANSLATOR OF THE PASSION TRANSLATION®

BroadStreet
PUBLISHING

The Psalms and Proverbs, The Passion Translation®
With 31-Day Psalms and Proverbs Devotionals

Published by BroadStreet Publishing Group, LLC
Savage, Minnesota, USA
BroadStreetPublishing.com

978-1-4245-5557-4

Devotions written by Mark Stibbe with Nathanael White

Cover and interior design by Garborg Design Works, Inc. at garborgdesign.com

Printed in China
19 20 21 22 5 4 3 2

Contents

Psalms

Introduction

AT A GLANCE

Author: Multiple authors, including mostly David, Solomon, the Asaphites, the Kohrites, and Moses.

Audience: Originally Israel, but they speak to humanity in general.

Date: From the Monarchy to Postexilic eras.

Type of Literature: Poems, which reflect several types: wisdom, lament, prayer, praise, blessings, liturgy, and prophetic oracles.

Major Themes: Prayer, praise, wisdom, prophecy, lamentation, and Jesus Christ.

OUTLINE

The Psalms are really five books in one. Moses gave us the five books of the Law called the Pentateuch; David gives us the five books of the Psalms. Each division ends with a doxology that includes the words, "Amen and Amen." The last division ends with Psalm 150 as the doxology, forming an appropriate conclusion to this "Pentateuch of David." These five divisions have been compared to the first five books of the Bible:

Psalms 1–41 (Genesis) — Psalms of man and creation.

Psalms 42–72 (Exodus) — Psalms of suffering and redemption.

Psalms 73–89 (Leviticus) — Psalms of worship and God's house.

Psalms 90–106 (Numbers) — Psalms of our pilgrimage on earth.

Psalms 107–150 (Deuteronomy) — Psalms of praise and the Word.

ABOUT PSALMS

I have loved the Psalms for over forty years. They have been my comfort and joy, leading me to the place where worship flows. When discouraged or downcast, I have never failed to take new strength from reading the Psalms. They charge my batteries and fill my sails. In fact, they seem to grow even more powerful as I grow older. Their thunder stirs me; their sweet melodies move me into the sacred emotions of a heart on fire. The dark rain clouds of grief turn to bright rainbows of hope, just from meditating on David's soul-subduing songs.

The Psalms find the words that express our deepest and strongest emotions, no matter what the circumstances. Every emotion of our hearts is reflected in the Psalms. Reading the Psalms will turn sighing into singing and trouble into triumph. The word *praise* is found 189 times in this book. There is simply nothing that touches my heart like the Psalms. Thousands of years ago my deepest feelings were put to music—this is what we all delightfully discover when reading the Psalms!

A contemporary name for the book of Psalms could be, *Poetry on Fire*! These 150 poetic masterpieces give us an expression of faith and worship. They become a mirror to the heart of God's people in our quest to experience God's presence. Much of Christianity has become so intellectualized that our emotions and artistic creativity are often set aside as unimportant in the worship of God. The Psalms free us to become emotional, passionate, sincere worshipers. It is time to sing the Psalms!

BOOK PROFILE

Purpose

The Psalms are clearly poetic. They are praises placed inside of poetry. Everyone who reads the Psalms realizes how filled with emotion they are! You will never be bored in reading the poetry that spills out of a fiery, passionate heart. These verses contain both poetry and music that touch the heart deeply, enabling you to encounter the heart of God through your emotional and creative senses.

Author & Audience

Most of these poetic masterpieces come to us from David, King of Israel. He wrote them during specific periods of his life when he was on the run from Saul, grateful for the Lord's protection and provision, scared for his future, mournful over his sin, and praising God with uplifted hands. Other authors include David's son Solomon, Moses, the Asaphite temple singers, and Korahite priests.

While they were written during specific periods in the history of Israel—from the monarchy to the postexilic eras—they connect to our own time as much as they reflect their time. So in many ways these poems are written to you and me. The original audience was the children of Israel, but the Psalms reflect the hopes and dreams, fears and failures of humanity in general.

Major Themes

Poetry of Praise: The Psalms are pure praise, inspired by the breath of God. Praise is a matter of life and breath. As long as we have breath we are told to praise the Lord. The Psalms release a flood of God-inspired insights that will lift heaviness off the human heart. The Psalms are meant to do to you what they did to David: They will bring you from your cave of despair into the glad presence of the King who likes and enjoys you.

Poetry of Prayer: The Psalms are prayers. Mixed with intercession, the Psalms become the fuel for our devotional life. Each psalm is a prayer. The early church recited and sang the Psalms regularly. Many contemporary worship songs have been inspired by this book of prayer-poetry!

Poetry of Wisdom: The Psalms unlock mysteries and parables, for in the purest praise is the cryptic language of a wise messenger. The wisdom of God is contained in these 150 keys; you have a key chain with master keys to unlock God's storehouse of wisdom and revelation. It is the "harp" (anointed worship) that releases divine secrets. Read carefully Psalm 49:4 TPT: "I will break open mysteries with my music and my song will release riddles solved."

Poetry of Prophecy: Prophetic insights rest upon the Psalms. David's harp brings revelation and understanding to the people. Singers who tap into the insights of the Psalms will bring forth truths in their songs, which will break the hearts of people and release divine understanding to the church. The prophets must become musicians, and the musicians must become prophets for the key of David to be given to the church.

Poetry of Christ: As with every part of the Old Testament, we are called to read the Psalms in two ways: 1) as the original audience heard them in their ancient Hebrew world; and 2) as the fulfillment of Messianic prophesies, submitting by faith that these poems point to Jesus Christ. Therefore, at one level, these poems are all about him. There are 150 Psalms and each of them reveals a special and unique aspect of the God-Man, Christ Jesus. We could say every Psalm is messianic in that they find their fulfillment in Christ. Looking backwards in light of Christ's revelation, we see they all point to our Lord Jesus, whom God has chosen as King over all.

Since these songs are all about Jesus, one of the keys to

understanding the Psalms is to look for Jesus within its pages. Luke 24:44 TPT says: "This is what I told you while I was still with you: Everything must be fulfilled that is written about me in the Law of Moses, the Prophets and the Psalms." There are many secrets about Jesus waiting to be discovered here!

So without further introduction, I present to you, *Poetry on Fire*. And may the Holy Spirit fill you with joy and revelation as you read it.

Psalms

POETRY ON FIRE

BOOK 1

THE GENESIS PSALMS

Psalms of man and creation

1 The Tree of Life [a]

1 What delight comes to those [b] who follow God's ways! [c]
They won't walk in step with the wicked,
nor share the sinner's way,
nor be found sitting in the scorner's seat.
2 Their pleasure and passion is remaining true to the Word of
"I Am,"
meditating day and night in his true revelation of light. [d]
3 They will be standing firm like a flourishing tree
planted by God's design, [e]

---

a Although we cannot be sure, it is possible that Ezra compiled the Psalms and wrote Ps. 1 as an "introduction" to the Psalter. Others believe it was written by David, or even Jeremiah.

b 1:1 The Hebrew text is actually "that One," and refers prophetically to the Lord Jesus Christ, our Tree of Life. Every one of us who belongs to "that One" can also walk in the light of this psalm.

c Ps. 1 is the contrast of those who follow God's ways and those who choose their own path. Read through this psalm with the purpose of learning how to live with God in first place.

d 1:2 Or "Torah."

e 1:3 Or "transplanted." That is, God planted our lives from where we

deeply rooted by the brooks of bliss;
bearing fruit in every season of their lives.
They are never dry, never fainting,
ever blessed, ever prosperous.[a]
4 But how different are the wicked.
All they are is dust in the wind—
driven away to destruction!
5 The wicked will not endure the day of judgment,
for God will not defend them.
Nothing they do will succeed or endure for long,
for they have no part with those who walk in truth.
6 But how different it is for the righteous!
The Lord embraces their paths as they move forward
while the way of the wicked lead only to doom.

2 The Coronation of the King

Act I – The Nations Speak

1 How dare the nations plan a rebellion.
Their foolish plots are futile![b]
2 Look at how the power brokers of the world
rise up to hold their summit,
as the rulers scheme and confer together
against Yahweh and his Anointed King, saying:
3 "Let's come together and break away from the Creator.
Once and for all let's cast off these controlling chains
of God and his Christ!"[c]

---

were into a place of blessing. See Ps. 92:13–14.

a 1:3 The metaphors found in this verse can be paraphrased as, "No matter what he sets out to do, he brings it to a successful conclusion."

b 2:1 Or "Why are they devising emptiness."

c 2:3 The word found here for *Christ* is the Hebrew word for "Messiah," or "Anointed One."

Act II – God Speaks

4 God-Enthroned[a] merely laughs at them;
the Sovereign One mocks their madness!
5 Then with the fierceness of his fiery anger
he settles the issue[b] and terrifies them to death[c] with these words:
6 "I myself have poured out my King on Zion[d], my holy mountain.[e]"

Act III – The Son Speaks

7 "I will reveal the eternal purpose of God.
For he has decreed over me, 'You are my favored Son.
And as your Father I have crowned you as my King Eternal.
Today I became your Father.
8 Ask me[f] to give you the nations and I will do it,
and they shall become your legacy.
Your domain will stretch to the ends of the earth.
9 And you will shepherd them[g] with unlimited authority,
crushing their rebellion as an iron rod smashes jars of clay!'"

Act IV – The Holy Spirit Speaks

10 Listen to me, all you rebel-kings

---

a 2:4 The Aramaic is *Maryah*, the Aramaic form of YHWH or Lord Jehovah.

b 2:5 Or "In good time he drives them away."

c 2:5 Or "snorts with anger." The Hebrew word *'aph* (fiery anger) is a homonym that also means "nose."

d 2:6 The word *Zion* is found 157 times in the Bible and 38 times in the Psalms.

e 2:6 For the believer today, Zion is not only a place but also a realm where Christ is enthroned. Jesus was "poured out" as a consecrated offering.

f 2:8 Or in the Masoretic text, "Ask wealth of me."

g 2:9 As translated from the Septuagint.

and all you upstart judges of the earth.
Learn your lesson[a] *while there's still time.*
11 Serve and worship the awe-inspiring God.
Recognize his greatness and bow before him,
trembling with reverence in his presence.[b]
12 Fall facedown before him and kiss the Son[c]
before his anger is roused against you.
Remember that his wrath can be quickly kindled!
But many blessings are waiting for all
who turn aside to hide themselves in him!

3 Covered by the Glory

King David's song when he was forced to flee from Absalom, his own son

The Humbling of a King

1 Lord, I have so many enemies, so many who are against me.
2 Listen to how they whisper their slander against me, saying:
"Look! He's hopeless! Even God can't save him from this!"

Pause in his presence[d]

---

a 2:10 Or "Do what is wise."

b 2:11 Or "Rejoice with trembling." The Hebrew word for *rejoice* means "to spin around with excited emotions," or "to twirl."

c 2:12 Or "be ruled by the Son." The Hebrew word for kiss is *nashaq*, and can also mean "to be ruled by" or "be in subjection to (the Son)." Yet another possible translation of this difficult verse is: "be armed with purity."

d This is the Hebrew word *Selah*, a puzzling word to translate. Most scholars believe it is a musical term for pause or rest. It is used a total of seventy-one times in the Psalms as an instruction to the music leader to pause and ponder in God's presence. An almost identical word, *Sela*, means a massive rock cliff. It is said that when *Selah* is spoken that the words are carved in stone in the throne room of the heavens.

The Help of God

3 But *in the depths of my heart I truly know*
that you, Yahweh, have become my Shield;
You take me and surround me with yourself.[a]
Your glory covers me continually.[b]
You lift high my head when I bow low in shame.
4 I have cried out to you, Yahweh, and from your holy
presence.[c]
You send me a Father's help.

Pause in his presence

The Song of Safety

5 So now I'll lie down and sleep like a baby—
then I'll awake in safety for you surround me with your
glory.
6 Even though dark powers prowl[d] around me,
I won't be afraid.

The Secret of Strength

7 *I simply cry out to you:*
"Rise up and help me, Lord! Come and save me!"
And you will slap them in the face,
breaking the power of their words to harm me.[e]
8 *My true Hero comes to my rescue,*

---

a 3:3 Many translations render this: "You are a shield around me." The ancient Hebrew can be translated: "You, O Lord, are my Taker" (Augustine). The implication is that God shields us by taking us into Himself. Jesus Christ is the Taker of humanity, the One who was made flesh. He not only took our nature but He also took our sins that he might take us into glory.

b 3:3 Or "my glory."

c 3:4 Or "from your holy hill."

d 3:6 Or "military troops."

e 3:7 Or "You broke the teeth of the wicked."

for the Lord alone is my Savior.[a]
What a feast of favor and bliss he gives his people!

Pause in his presence

4 An Evening Prayer for Help

For the Pure and Shining One[b]
For the end,[c] *a melody by King David*

1 God, you're my Righteousness, my Champion Defender.
Answer me when I cry for help!
Whenever I was in distress, you enlarged me.[d]
I'm being squeezed again—I need your kindness right away!
Grant me your grace, hear my prayer, and set me free!
2 Listen to me, you elite among men:
How long will you defame my honor[e]
and drag it down into shame?
Will you ever stop insulting me?
How long will you set your heart on shadows,
chasing your lies and delusions?

Pause in his presence

3 May we never forget that the Lord works wonders[f]

---

a 3:8 The Hebrew word used sixty times in the Psalms for deliverance is actually *Yeshuah*, a variant form of the name for *Jesus*. This is pointing us to where our salvation is found.

b The Hebrew word used here, found in the inscription of fifty-four Psalms, is usually rendered as "choirmaster," or "chief director of music." It is taken from the root word for shining or brilliant (i.e. purity, holiness). Another way to translate "choirmaster" is "the shining one," or "the one who glitters from afar." Jesus Christ is the chief musician of all eternity who sings in the midst of his people (Heb. 12:2).

c As translated from the Septuagint. The Hebrew is "stringed instruments" or "smiting."

d 4:1 Or "you created room for me."

e 4:2 Or "my Glorious One."

f 4:3 There is considerable variation in possible translations from different

for every one of his devoted lovers.
And this is how I know that he will answer my every prayer.
4 Tremble in awe before the Lord, and do not sin against him.
Be still upon your bed and search your heart before him.[a]

Pause in his presence

5 Bring to Yahweh the sacrifice of righteousness and put your trust in him.
6 Lord, prove them wrong when they say, "God can't help you!
Let the light of your radiant face
break through and shine upon us!
7 The intense pleasure you give me
surpasses the gladness of harvest time,
even more than when the harvesters
gaze upon their ripened grain
and when their new wine overflows.
8 Now, because of you, Lord, I will lie down in peace and sleep comes at once,
for no matter what happens, I will live unafraid!

---

manuscripts. Some manuscripts read, "the Lord sets apart a faithful one for himself." Another possible translation is "the Lord has revealed to me his marvelous love."

a 4:4 Or "Meditate on your bed and repent (lament)." It is always wise at the end of every day to cleanse our heart in God's grace and mercy.

5 Song of the Clouded Dawn

For the Pure and Shining One
For her who receives the inheritance[a] *by King David*

Morning Watch

1 Listen, Yahweh, to my passionate prayer![b]
Can't you hear my groaning?
2 Don't you hear how I'm crying out to you?
My King and my God, consider my every word,
for I am calling out to you.
3 At each and every sunrise you will hear my voice
as I prepare my *sacrifice of* prayer to you.[c]
Every morning I lay out the pieces of my life on the altar[d]
and wait *for your fire to fall upon my heart.*[e]

Making It Right

4 I know that you, God, are never pleased with lawlessness,

---

a The Hebrew word used here is *Neliloth* or flutes. It can also be translated "inheritances." The early church father Augustine translated this: "For her who receives the inheritance," meaning the church of Jesus Christ. The Father told the Son in Ps. 2 to ask for his inheritance; here we see it is the church that receives what Jesus asks for. We receive our inheritance of eternal life through the cross and resurrection of the Son of God. The Septuagint reads, "For the end," also found in numerous inscriptions of the Psalms.

b 5:1 Or "My words—give them a hearing, Lord!"

c 5:3 The Hebrew word for prepare is *'arak*, a priestly term for lighting the altar fire, preparing a sacrifice, and laying it out in order upon the altar to be consumed.

d 5:3 The Hebrew uses the word *'arak*, which is a priestly term for setting the altar fire and preparing a sacrifice and laying it out in order upon the altar to be consumed.

e 5:3 Implied in the concept of preparing the morning sacrifice. The Aramaic text states, "At dawn I shall be ready and shall appear before you." The Hebrew can also be translated, "I'll be on the watchtower (for the answer to come)." See Ps. 59:16, 88:13; and Hab. 2:1.

and evil ones will never be invited as guests in your house.
5 Boasters collapse, unable to survive your scrutiny,
for your hatred of evildoers is clear.
6 You will make an end of all those who lie.
How you hate their hypocrisy and despise all who love violence!

Multitude of Mercy

7 But I know that you will welcome me into your house,
for I am covered by your covenant of mercy and love.
So I come to your sanctuary[a] with deepest awe
to bow in worship and adore you.
8 Yahweh, lead me in the pathways of your pleasure
just like you promised me you would.
Or else my enemies will conquer me.
Smooth out your road in front of me,
straight and level so that I will know where to walk.

Multitude of Sins

9 For you can't trust anything they say.
Their hearts are nothing but deep pits of destruction,
drawing people into their darkness with their speeches.[b]
They are smooth-tongued deceivers who flatter with their words.
10 Declare them guilty, O God!
Let their own schemes be their downfall!
Let the guilt of their sins collapse on top of them,
for they rebel against you.

Multitude of Blessings

11 But let them all be glad,

---

a 5:7 Or "I come to the temple of your holiness."
b 5:9 Or "their throat is an open grave."

those who turn aside to hide themselves in you.
May they keep shouting for joy forever!
Overshadow them in your presence as they sing and rejoice,
then every lover of your name will burst forth with endless joy.
12 Lord, how wonderfully you bless the righteous.
Your favor wraps around each one and covers them
under your canopy of kindness and joy.

6 A Cry for Healing [a]

For the Pure and Shining One
A song for the end sung for the new day by King David

1 No Lord! Don't condemn me.
Don't punish me in your fiery anger.
2 Please deal gently with me;
show me mercy for I'm sick and frail.
I'm fading away with weakness.
Heal me, for I'm falling apart.
3 How long until you take away this pain in my body and in my soul?
Lord, I'm trembling in fear!
4 Turn to me and deliver my life
because I know you love and desire
to have me as your very own.
5 How can I be any good to you dead?
For those who are in the graveyards sing no songs.
In the darkness of death who remembers you?
How could I bring you praise if I'm buried in a tomb?
6 I'm so exhausted and worn-out with my weeping.
I endure weary, sleepless nights filled with moaning,
soaking my pillow with my tears.

---

a Ps. 6 is a part of the daily prayer ritual of religious Jews.

7 My eyes of faith won't focus anymore, for sorrow fills my heart.
There are so many enemies who come against me!
8 Go away! Leave me, all you workers of wickedness!
For the Lord has turned to listen to my thunderous cry.
9 Yes! The Lord *my Healer* has heard all my pleading
and has taken hold of my prayers and answered them all.
10 Now it's my enemies who have been shamed.
Terror-stricken, they will turn back again,
knowing the bitterness of sudden disgrace!

7 Song for the Slandered Soul

A passionate song to the Lord to the tune of "Breaking the Curse of Cush, the Benjamite" by King David

1 O Lord my God, I turn aside to hide my soul in you.
I trust you to save me from all those
who pursue and persecute me.
2 Don't leave me helpless!
Don't let my foes fall upon me like fierce lions with teeth bared.
Can't you see how they want to rip me to shreds,
dragging me away to tear my soul to pieces?
3 Lord, if I were doing evil things, that would be different,
for then I would be guilty, deserving all of this.
4 If I wronged someone at peace with me,
if I betrayed a friend, repaying evil for good,
or if I have unjustly harmed my enemy,
5 Then it would be right for you
to let my enemy pursue and overtake me.
In fact, let them grind me into the ground.
Let them take my life from me and drag my dignity in the dust!

Pause in his presence

6 Now Lord, let your anger arise against the anger of my enemies.
Awaken your fury and stand up for me!
Decree that justice be done against my foes.
7 Gather all the people around you.
Return to your place on high to preside over them
and once more occupy the throne of judgment.
8 You are the Exalted One who judges the people,
so vindicate me publicly and restore my honor and integrity.
Before all the people declare me innocent!
9 Once and for all, end the evil tactics of the wicked!
Reward and prosper the cause of the righteous,
for you are the righteous God, the Soul-Searcher,
who looks deep into every heart
to examine the thoughts and motives.
10 God, your wrap-around presence
is my protection, and my defense.
You bring victory to all who reach out for you.
11 Righteousness is revealed every time you judge.
Because of the strength of your forgiveness,[a]
your anger does not break out every day
even though you are a righteous Judge.
12–13 Yet if the wicked do not repent,
you will not relent with your wrath;
slaying them with your shining sword.
You are the Conqueror with an arsenal of lethal weapons
that you've prepared for them.
You have bent and strung your bow,
making your judgment-arrows shafts of burning fire.
14–15 Look how the wicked conceive their evil schemes.
They go into labor with their lies and give birth to trouble.

---

a 7:11 As translated from the Septuagint.

They dig a pit for others to fall into,
not knowing that they will be the very ones
that will fall into their own pit of failure.
16 For you, God, will see to it that every pit-digger
who works to trap and harm others
will be trapped and harmed by their own treachery.
17 But I will give all my thanks to you, Lord,
for you make everything right in the end.
I will sing my highest praise to the God of the Highest
Place![a]

8 God's Splendor

For the Pure and Shining One
Set to the melody of "For the Feast of Harvest"[b] *by King David*

1 Lord, your name is so great and powerful!
People everywhere see your splendor.
Your glorious majesty streams from the heavens,
filling the earth with the fame of your name!
2 You have built a stronghold by the songs of babies.
Strength rises up with the chorus of singing children.
This kind of praise has the power to shut Satan's mouth.
Childlike worship will silence[c]
the madness of those who oppose you.
3 Look at the splendor of your skies,
your creative genius glowing in the heavens.
When I gaze at your moon and your stars
mounted like jewels in their settings,

---

a 7:17 Or "to Adonai Elyon."
b This inscription in the Septuagint is, "To the director over the wine vats."
c 8:2 There may be a vast difference between the glory of the heavens and the little mouths of children and babies, yet by both the majestic name of the Lord is revealed. It is amazing that perfected praises do not rise to God from the cherubim or seraphim, but from the children and babies, the weakest of humanity.

I know you are the Fascinating Artist who fashioned it all!
But when I look up and see
such wonder and workmanship above,
I have to ask you this question:
4 *Compared to all this cosmic glory,*[a]
why would you bother with puny, mortal man
or be infatuated with Adam's sons?
5 Yet what honor you have given to man,
created only a little lower than Elohim,[b]
crowned like kings and queens[c] with glory and
magnificence.
6 You have delegated to them
mastery over all you have made,
making everything subservient to their authority,
placing earth itself under the feet of your image-bearers.[d]
7–8 All the created order and every living thing
of the earth, sky, and sea—
the wildest beasts and all the sea creatures,
everything is in submission *to Adam's sons*.
9 Lord, your name is so great and powerful.
People everywhere see your majesty!
What glory streams from the heavens,
filling the earth with the fame of your name!

---

a 8:4 David looked away from the darkness of earth and saw the divine order of the universe. This psalm is meant to join the earth to the heavens, and to bring the heavenly glory into the earth, making the heavens and the earth one.

b 8:5 This is the same Hebrew word used for the Creator God in Gen. 1:1.

c 8:5 The concept of kings and queens is implied in the text by the word *crowned*.

d 8:6 The Septuagint translation of 8:5–7 is quoted in Heb. 2:6–8. Today, all things are not yet under our feet. Even mosquitoes still come to defeat us. But there will be a time of restoration because of Christ's redemption, when everything will rest beneath our authority. See Isa. 11:6–9, 65:25; Matt. 19:28; & Rev. 20:4–6.

9 Triumphant Thanks

For the Pure and Shining One

To the tune of "The Secrets of the Son"[a] *by King David*

1 Lord, I will worship you with extended hands
as my whole heart explodes with praise!
I will tell everyone everywhere about your wonderful
works
and how your marvelous miracles exceed expectations!
2 I will jump for joy and shout in triumph
as I sing your song and make music for the Most High God.
3 For when you appear, I worship
while all of my enemies run in retreat.
They stumble and perish before your presence.
4 For you have stood up for my cause
and vindicated me when I needed you the most.
From your righteous throne you have given me justice.
5 With a blast of your rebuke nations are destroyed.
You obliterated their names forever and ever.
6 The Lord thundered and our enemies have been cut off,
vanished in everlasting ruins.
All their cities have been destroyed—
even the memory of them has been erased.
7 But the Lord of eternity, our mighty God, lives and reigns
forever!
He sits enthroned as King ready to render his verdicts
and judge all with righteousness.
8 He will issue his decrees of judgment,
deciding what is right for the entire world,
dispensing justice to all.
9 All who are oppressed may come to you as a

---

a As translated by Augustine, an early church father. The Hebrew is "to the death of the Son."

shelter in the time of trouble, a perfect hiding place.
10 May everyone who knows your mercy
keep putting their trust in you,
for they can count on you for help no matter what.
O Lord, you will never, no never, neglect those
who come to you.
11 Listen everyone! Sing out your praises to the God
who lives and rules within Zion!
Tell the world about all the miracles he has done!
12 He tracks down killers and avenges bloodshed,
but he will never forget the ones forgotten by others,
hearing every one of their cries for justice.
13 So now, O Lord, don't forget me.
Have mercy on me.
Take note of how I've been humiliated
at the hands of those who hate me.
Bring me back again from the brink, from the very gates of death.
14 Save me! Bring me to the spiritual gates of Zion[a]
so I can bring you the shout of praise you deserve.
15 For the godless nations get trapped
in the very snares they set for others.
The hidden trap they set for the weak
has snapped shut upon themselves—guilty!
16 The Lord is famous for this: his justice will punish the wicked.
While they are digging a pit for others,
they are actually setting the terms for their own judgment.
They will fall into their own pit.

Consider the truth of this and pause in his presence[b]

---

a 9:14 Or "Daughter Gates of Zion."

b 9:16 The Hebrew word *Higayon* means to consider the truth of the matter.

17 Don't forget this: all the wicked will one day
fall into the darkness of death's domain and remain there,
including the nations that forget God and reject his ways.
18 He will not ignore forever all the needs of the poor
for those in need shall not always be crushed.
Their hopes shall be fulfilled, *for God sees it all*!
19 Lord, won't you now arise to judge and
punish the nations who defy you?
Aren't you fed up with their rebellion?
20 Make them tremble in fear before your presence.
Place a lawgiver over them.
Make them know that they are only puny, frail humans
who must give account to you!

Pause in his presence

10 The Cry of the Oppressed [a]

1 Lord, you seem so far away when evil is near!
Why do you stand so far off as though you don't care?
Why have you hidden yourself when I need you the most?
2 The arrogant in their elitist pride persecute the poor and helpless.
May you pour out upon them
the very evil they've planned against others!
3 How they brag and boast of their cravings, exalting the greedy.
They congratulate themselves as they despise you.
4 These arrogant ones, so smug and secure,
in their delusion the wicked boast, saying:
"God doesn't care about what we do.

---

a It is likely that Ps. 9 and 10 were originally one psalm. Eight Hebrew manuscripts unite them as well as the Aramaic, Septuagint, and the Latin Vulgate. The Catholic Bible is based on the Latin Vulgate and therefore has a different numbering for the Psalms.

There's nothing to worry about!
Our wealth will last a lifetime."
5 So seemingly successful are they in their schemes,
prosperous in all their plans and scoffing at any restraint.
6 They boast that neither God nor men will bring them down.
They sneer at all their enemies saying in their hearts,
"We'll have success in all we do
and never have to face trouble"—
never realizing that they are speaking this in vain.
7 Their mouths spout out cursing, lies, and threats.
Only trouble and turmoil come from all their plans.
8–9 Like beasts lurking in the shadows of the city
they crouch silently in ambush for the people to pass by.
Pouncing on the poor, they catch them in their snare
to murder their prey in secret
as they plunder their helpless victims.
10 They crush the lowly as they fall beneath their brutal blows,
watching their victims collapse in defeat!
11 Then they say to themselves,
"The Lofty One is not watching while we do this.
He doesn't even care! We can get away with it!"
12 Now is the time to arise, Lord! Crush them once and for all!
Don't forget the forgotten and the helpless.
13 How dare the wicked think they'll escape judgment,
believing that you would not
call them to account for all their ways.
Don't let the wicked get away with their contempt of you!
14 Lord, I know you see all that they're doing,
noting their each and every deed.
You know the trouble and turmoil they've caused.
Now punish them thoroughly for all that they've done!
The poor and helpless ones trust in you, Lord,
for you are famous for being the Helper of the fatherless.
I know you won't let them down.

15 Break the power of the wicked, and all their strong-arm
tactics.
Search them out and destroy them
for the evil things they've done.
16 You, Lord, are King forever and ever!
You will see to it that all the nations perish from your land.
17 Lord, you know and understand all the hopes of the humble
and will hear their cries and comfort their hearts,
helping them all!
18 The orphans and the oppressed will be terrified no longer,
for you will bring them justice, and no one will trouble
them.

11 Song of the Steadfast

For the Pure and Shining One by King David

1–2 Lord, *don't you hear*
what my well-meaning friends keep saying to me:
"Run away while you can!
Fly away like a bird to hide in the mountains for safety.
For your enemies have prepared a trap for you!
They plan to destroy you with their slander and deceitful
lies.
Can't you see them hiding
in their place of darkness and shadows?
They're set against you and all those who live upright lives."
But don't they know, Lord,
that I have made you my only Hiding Place?
Don't they know that I always trust in you?
3 What can the righteous accomplish
when truth's pillars are destroyed and law and order
collapse?
4 *Yet the Eternal One is never shaken—*[a]

---

a 11:4 This is an implied contrast made explicit from the text. This psalm

he is still found in his temple of holiness
reigning as Lord and King over all.
He is closely watching everything that happens.
And with a glance, his eyes examine every heart.[a]
For his heavenly rule will prevail over all.
5 He will test both the righteous *and the wicked,*
exposing each heart.
God's very soul detests those who love to resort to violence.
6 He will rain down upon them judgment for their sins.
A scorching wind will be their portion and lot in life.
7 But remember this: the Righteous Lord loves
what is right and just, and every godly one
will come into his presence and gaze upon his face!

12 Song for the New Day

For the Pure and Shining One
A song of smiting sung for the new day by King David[b]

1 Help, Lord! Save us! For godly ones are swiftly disappearing.
Where are the dependable, principled ones?
They're a vanishing breed!
2 Everyone lies, everyone flatters, and everyone deceives.
Nothing but empty talk, smooth talk, and double-talk.
Where are the truthful?
3–4 I know the Lord will not deal gently with people like that!

---

shows the contrast between what can be shaken and what is unshakable.

a 11:4 The actual Hebrew is "his eyelids." Some see the "eyelid" as the lid of the ark of covenant, which was the mercy seat.

b The events surrounding this psalm could be the killing of the priests by Saul in 1 Sam. 22:17–19. Saul ordered the death of "eighty-five men who wore the linen ephod." The killing rampage continued until an entire community of priests had been slaughtered with their women and children. This great evil marked David from that day forward. The inscription found in the Septuagint is "The Eighth Psalm of David."

You will destroy every proud liar who says: "We lie all we
want.
Our words are our weapons, and we won't be held
accountable.
Who can stop us?"
May the Lord cut off their twisted tongues
and seal their lying lips.
May they all be silenced—those that boast and brag with
their
high-minded talk about doing whatever they want.
5 But the Lord says, "Now I will arise!
I will defend the poor,
those who were plundered, the oppressed,
and the needy who groan for help.
I will arise to rescue and protect them!"
6 For every word God speaks is sure and every promise pure.
His truth is tested, found to be flawless, and ever faithful.
It's pure as sterling silver, refined seven times in a crucible
of clay.[a]
7–8 Lord, you will keep us forever safe,
out of the reach of the wicked.
Even though they strut and prowl,
tolerating and celebrating what is worthless and vile,
you will still lift up those who are yours!

---

a 12:6 The clay furnace is the heart of man. We are the earthen vessel inside which God has placed his flawless words. His words test us, they try us, and they refine us, seven times over, until purified and assimilated into our spirits. The fire of testing purifies us as vessels to carry the Word within our hearts.

13 Prayer Turns Depression into Delight [a]

For the Pure and Shining One by King David

1 I'm hurting, Lord—will you forget me forever? [b]
How much longer, Lord?
Will you look the other way when I'm in need? [c]
2 How much longer must I cling to this constant grief?
I've endured this shaking of my soul.
So, how much longer will my enemy have the upper hand?
It's been long enough!
3 Take a good look at me, God, and answer me!
Breathe your life into my spirit.
Bring light to my eyes in this pitch-black darkness
or I will sleep the sleep of death.
4 Don't let my enemy proclaim, "I've prevailed over him."
For all my adversaries will celebrate when I fall.
5 Lord, I have always trusted in your kindness, *so answer me*.
I will yet celebrate with passion and joy
when your salvation [d] lifts me up.
6 I will sing my song of joy to you, the Most High,
for in all of this you have strengthened my soul.

---

a Some believe David composed this shortly after being anointed to be the King of Israel. David knew greatness was his destiny, but he struggled with the persecution and challenges that came before his exaltation. In the wilderness David trusts and prays his way out.

b 13:1 This is the psalm that describes the journey from self to God, from despair to delight, from feeling abandoned to feeling affirmed. It begins with pain and ends with praise. Moaning gives way to music. We each can take comfort in what David experienced.

c 13:1 David feels as though God is hiding his face from his cries. David is left alone to wrestle with his doubts, feeling as though his patience can hold on no longer. Have you ever been there?

d 13:5 The term for *salvation* is *yeshu'sh*, which is nearly identical to *Jesus, our Salvation*. Our Savior plans blessings and hope for each of us as we trust in him.

My enemies say that I have no Savior,
but I know that I have one in you!

14 God Looks Down from Heaven [a]

For the Pure and Shining One by King David

1 Only the withering soul [b] would say to himself,
"There is no God."
Anyone who thinks like this is corrupt and callous,
depraved and detestable, devoid of what is good.
2 The Lord looks down in love,
bending over heaven's balcony,
looking over all of Adam's sons and daughters.
He's looking to see if there is anyone who acts wisely,
any who are searching for God and wanting to please him.
3 But no, everyone has wandered astray,
walking stubbornly toward evil.
Not one is good; he can't even find one.
4 Look how they live in luxury while exploiting my people!
Won't these workers of wickedness ever learn?
They don't ever even think of praying to God.
5 But just look at them now, in panic, trembling with terror.
For the Lord is on the side of the generation of loyal lovers.
6 The Lord is always the safest place for the poor
when the workers of wickedness oppress them.
7 How I wish their time of rescue were already here
and that God would appear,
arising from the midst of his Zion-people

---

a With few differences, Ps. 14 and Ps. 53 are nearly identical. Ps. 14 is practical; Ps. 53 is prophetic. Ps. 14 deals with the past, Ps. 53 with the future.

b 14:1 Or "fool." The word for *fool* comes from a Hebrew word meaning withering. If we make no room for God, we have a withered heart; our moral sense of righteousness is put to sleep, and the noble aspirations of the heart shrivel up and die.

to save and restore his very own.
Then what gladness and joy will break forth
when the Lord rescues Israel!

15 Living in the Shining Place [a]

A poetic song by King David

1 Lord, who dares to dwell with you?
Who presumes the privilege of being close to you,
living next to you in your shining place of glory? [b]
Who are those who daily dwell in the life of the Holy
Spirit? [c]
2 They are passionate and wholehearted,
always sincere and always speaking the truth—
for their hearts are trustworthy.
3 They refuse to slander [d] or insult others;
they'll never listen to gossip or rumors,
nor would they ever harm another with their words.
4 They will speak out passionately against evil and evil workers
while commending the faithful ones who follow after the
truth.
They make firm commitments and follow through,
even at great cost.

---

a Perhaps David's prophetic minstrels sang this song of instruction as they laid the ark to rest in David's tent. It is a song that reveals who will dwell in God's holy presence and who will live with him in heaven's glory. It actually is a description of Zion's perfect Man, Christ Jesus, and all those who are transformed into his image (Rom. 8:29).

b 15:1 The Hebrew word for *sanctuary* is taken from a root word for "shining place."

c 15:1 This psalm gives us David's Sermon on the Mount. If we will dwell in the Holy Place, there must first be a holy place in our spirit where God dwells. God's guests must submit to the holiness that lives there. There is etiquette for God's house revealed in this psalm.

d 15:3 The Hebrew word for slander, *ragal*, means to spy on someone and look for evil to use against them.

5 They never crush others with exploitation or abuse
and they would never be bought with a bribe
against the innocent.
They will never be shaken; they will stand firm forever.

16 The Golden Secret

A precious song, engraved in gold, by King David[a]

1 Keep me safe, O mighty God.
I run for dear life to you, my Safe Place.
2 So I said to the Lord God,
"You are my Maker, my Mediator, and my Master.
Any good thing you find in me has come from you."[b]
3 *And he said to me*, "My holy lovers are wonderful,
my majestic ones, my glorious ones,
fulfilling all my desires."
4 Yet, there are those who yield to their weakness,[c]
and they will have troubles and sorrows unending.
I never gather with such ones,[d]
nor give them honor in any way.
5 Lord, I have chosen you alone as my inheritance.
You are my prize, my pleasure, and my portion.
I leave my destiny *and its timing* in your hands.[e]

---

a The Hebrew word used in the inscription is *michtam*. There are many variations of translation for this word. Here are the major ones: *golden, graven, a permanent writing, precious, hidden, or jewel*. The Septuagint renders this: "a sculptured writing of gold"; other translations call it a "golden poem." Perhaps the most accepted translation of *michtam* is "engraved in gold." This speaks of the divine nature engraved into our hearts by the Word. A new humanity is now stamped with God-life, engraved in his golden glory.

b 16:2 The Aramaic text states, "My goodness is found in your presence."

c 16:4 As translated from the Septuagint.

d 16:4 As translated from the Septuagint.

e 16:5 Implied in the text. The Aramaic reads, "You are restoring my

6 Your pleasant path leads me to pleasant places.
I'm overwhelmed by the privileges
that come with following you,
for you have given me the best!
7 The way you counsel and correct me makes me praise you
more,
for your whispers in the night give me wisdom,
showing me what to do next.
8 Because you are close to me and always available,
my confidence will never be shaken,
for I experience your wrap-around presence every moment.
9 My heart and soul explode with joy—full of glory!
Even my body will rest confident and secure.
10 For you will not abandon me to the realm of death
nor will you allow your Holy One to experience
corruption.[a]
11 For you bring me a continual revelation of resurrection life,
the path to the bliss that brings me face-to-face with you.[b]

17 A Cry for Justice

A priestly prayer by King David

1 Listen to me, Lord.
Hear the passionate prayer of this honest man.
It's my piercing cry for justice!
My cause is just and my need is real.
I've done what's right and my lips speak truth.
2 Lord, I always live my life before your face,
so examine and exonerate me.
Vindicate me and show the world I'm innocent.

---

inheritance to me."

a 16:10 Or "the pit." This is likely a metaphor for Sheol.

b 16:11 There is no Hebrew word for *presence*. When the Psalmist wanted to speak of God's presence, he used the Hebrew word for face.

3 For in a visitation of the night
you inspected my heart and refined my soul in fire
until nothing vile was found in me.
I've wanted my words and my ways to always agree.
4 Following your Word has kept me from wrong.
Your ways have molded my footsteps, keeping me
from going down the forbidden paths of the destroyer.
5 My steps follow in the tracks of your chariot wheels,
always staying in their path,
never straying from your way.
6 You will answer me, God; I know you always will,
like you always do as you listen with love to my every
prayer.
7 Magnify the marvels of your mercy to all who seek you.[a]
Make your Pure One wonderful to me,[b]
like you do for all those who turn aside
to hide themselves in you.
8 Protect me from harm;
keep an eye on me like you would a child[c]
reflected in the twinkling of your eye.
Yes, hide me within the shelter of your embrace,
under your outstretched wings.[d]
9 Protect me there from all my foes.
For there are many who surround my soul
to completely destroy me.
10 They are pitiless, heartless—hard as nails,
swollen with pride and filled with arrogance!

---

a 17:7 As translated from the Septuagint.
b 17:7 As translated from the Aramaic.
c 17:8 Or "daughter."
d 17:8 This could also be a reference to the mercy seat, where sacred blood was sprinkled in the Holy of Holies. There the golden cherubim overshadowed all who entered the divine chamber (Ex. 25:18–20).

11 See how they close in on me,
waiting for the chance to throw me to the ground.[a]
12 They're like lions eager to tear me apart,
like young and fearless lions lurking in secret,
so ferocious and cruel—ready to rip me to shreds.
13 Arise, God, and confront them!
Challenge them with your might![b]
Free me from their clutches and rescue me from their rage.
14 Throw them down to the ground,
these who live for only this life on earth.
Thrust them out of their prosperity
and into their portion in eternity,
leaving their wealth and wickedness behind!
15 As for me, because I am innocent I will see[c] your face
until I see you for who you really are.
Then I will awaken with your form and be fully satisfied,[d]
fulfilled in the revelation of your glory in me!

---

a 17:11 This is what they did to Jesus. They threw him to the ground and nailed him to the cross.

b 17:13 The word used here is *sword*. An alternative translation would be, "Rescue my soul from the wicked one, who is your sword." The wicked are sometimes God's tools to execute his judgments (Isa. 10:5; Jer. 51:20).

c 17:15 The Hebrew word for gaze, *chaza*, means "to see a vision."

d 17:15 The Aramaic can be translated, "I will be satisfied when your faith is awakened."

18 I Love You, Lord

Praises sung to the Pure and Shining One by King David, his servant,[a] composed when the Lord rescued David from all his many enemies, including from the brutality of Saul[b]

1 Lord, I passionately love you and I'm bonded to you![c]
I want to embrace you,[d] for now you've become my Power!
2 You're as real to me as bedrock beneath my feet,
like a castle on a cliff, my forever firm Fortress,
my Mountain of hiding, my Pathway of escape,
my Tower of rescue where none can reach me.
My secret Strength and Shield around me,
you are Salvation's Ray of Brightness shining on the hillside,[e]
always the Champion of my cause.
3 So all I need to do is to call to you,
singing to you, the praiseworthy God.

---

a This magnificent poem is so important to the Holy Spirit that it appears twice in the Bible. You will find it again in 2 Sam. 22.

b Or "the paw of Saul." He was like a beast that chased David until his death.

c 18:1 David doesn't employ the common Hebrew word for love, *'ahav*, but instead uses the Hebrew word for pity or mercy. How could David have mercy for God? The word he uses, *raham*, is the word used for a mother who loves and pities her child so much it manifests with a deep love and emotional bond. This concept, although difficult to convey in English, is brought forth as David is saying, "I love you passionately and my life is forever bonded to you!"

d 18:1 The Hebrew word used here for "love" is not the usual word to describe love. It is a fervent and passionate word that carries the thought of embrace and touch. It could actually be translated, "Lord, I want to hug you!" Haven't you ever felt like that?

e 18:2 The Hebrew word for "horn" (i.e., horn of my salvation) comes from a root word meaning ray of brightness or hillside. The translator has chosen to include both concepts in the translation.

And when I do, I'm safe and sound in you.
4–5 For when the ropes of death wrapped around me
and terrifying torrents of destruction overwhelmed me,[a]
taking me to death's door, to doom's domain,
6 I cried out to you in my distress, the delivering God,
and from your temple-throne you heard my troubled cry.
My sobs came right into your heart
and you turned your face to rescue me.[b]
7 The earth itself shivered and shook.
It reeled and rocked before him.
As the mountains trembled, they melted away!
For his anger was kindled, burning on my behalf.
8 Fierce flames leapt from his mouth,
erupting with blazing, burning coals as smoke
and fire encircled him.
9–10 He stretched heaven's curtain open and came to my
defense.
Swiftly he rode to earth as the stormy sky was lowered.
He rode a chariot of thunderclouds amidst thick darkness,
a cherub, his steed, as he swooped down,
soaring on the wings of spirit-wind.
11 Wrapped and hidden in the thick-cloud darkness,
his thunder-tabernacle surrounded him.
He hid himself in mystery-darkness;
the dense rain clouds were his garments.
12 Suddenly the brilliance of his presence broke through
with lightning bolts and with a mighty storm from
heaven—

---

a 18:4–5 Or "waves of Sheol (death) engulfed me." See 2 Sam. 22:5.

b 18:6 This scene is a poetic portrayal not only of how God answered David's prayer, but also a picture of the sufferings of a greater Son of David, Jesus, who hung on the cross with cries of agony. God heard him and shook the planet as thick clouds covered the sun.

like a tempest dropping coals of fire.
13 The Lord thundered, the great God above every god
spoke with his thunder-voice from the skies.
What fearsome hailstones and flashes of fire were before
him!
14 He released his lightning-arrows, and routed my foes.
See how they ran and scattered in fear!
15 Then with his mighty roar he laid bare the foundations of
the earth,
uncovering the secret source of the sea.
The hidden depths of land and sea were exposed
by the hurricane-blast of his hot-breath.
16 He then reached down from heaven,
all the way from the sky to the sea.
He reached down into my darkness to rescue me!
He took me out of my calamity and chaos
and drew me to himself,
taking me from the depths of my despair!
17 Even though I was helpless in the hands
of my hateful, strong enemy,[a]
you were good to deliver me.
18 When I was at my weakest, my enemies attacked—
but the Lord held on to me.
19 His love broke open the way
and he brought me into a beautiful broad place.[b]
He rescued me—because his delight is in me![c]
20 He rewarded me for doing what's right and staying pure.

---

a 18:17 Death is our strong enemy. Only through Christ are we delivered from its grip.

b 18:19 This could be the throne room of heaven.

c 18:19 Here in verses 16–19 you can see the glorious resurrection of Christ as the Father reached down and kissed the Son with life and love. Read it again and think of Christ in the tomb being raised by the Father.

21 I will follow his commands and never stop.
I'll not sin by ceasing to follow him no matter what.
22 For I've kept my eyes focused on his righteous words
and I've obeyed everything that he's told me to do.
23 I've done my best to be blameless and to follow all his ways,
keeping my heart pure.
24 I've kept my integrity by surrendering to him.
And so the Lord has rewarded me with his blessing.
This is the treasure I discovered
when I kept my heart clean before his eyes.
25 Lord, it is clear to me now that how we live
will dictate how you deal with us.[a]
Good people will taste your goodness, Lord.
And to those who are loyal to you,
you love to prove that you are loyal and true.
26 And for those who are purified, they find you always pure.
But you'll outwit the crooked and cunning with your craftiness.
27 To the humble you bring heaven's deliverance.
But the proud and haughty you disregard.
28 God, all at once, you turned on a floodlight for me!
You are the revelation light in my darkness,
and in your brightness I can see the path ahead.
29 With you as my strength I can crush an enemy horde
advancing through every stronghold that stands in front of me.
30 What a God you are! Your path for me has been perfect!
All your promises have proven true.
What a secure shelter for all those
who turn to hide themselves in you!
You are the wrap-around God giving grace to me.[b]

---

a 18:25 This is a summary of the passage, implied in the text.
b 18:30 The Hebrew word used here for *shield* means to wrap around in

31 Could there be any other god like you?
You are the only God to be worshiped,
for there is not a more secure foundation
to build my life upon than you.
32 You have wrapped me in power,
and now you've shared with me your perfection.
33 Through you I ascend to the highest peaks of your glory
to stand in the heavenly places, strong and secure in you.
34 You've trained me with the weapons of warfare-worship;
now I'll descend down into battle with power
to chase and conquer my foes.
35 You empower me for victory with your wrap-around
presence.
Your power within makes me strong to subdue,
and by stooping down in gentleness
you strengthened me and made me great!
36 You've set me free from captivity
and now I'm standing complete, ready to fight some more!
37 I caught up with my enemies and conquered them,
and didn't turn back until the war was won!
38 I pinned them to the ground and broke them to pieces.
I finished them once and for all; they're as good as dead.
39 You've placed your armor upon me
and defeated my enemies, making them bow low at my
feet.
40 You've made them all turn tail and run,
for through you I've destroyed them all!
Forever silenced they'll never taunt me again.
41 They shouted for help but not one dares to rescue them.
They shouted to God but he refused to answer them.
42 So I pulverized them to powder and cast them to the wind.
I swept them away like dirt on the floor.

---

protection. God himself is our shield of grace.

43 You gave me victory on every side,
for look how the nations come to serve me.
Even those I've never heard of come and bow at my feet.
44 As soon as they heard of me they submitted to me.
Even the rebel foreigners obey my every word.
45 Their rebellion fades away as they come near;
trembling in their strongholds
they come crawling out of their hideouts.
Cringing in fear before me, their courage is gone.
46 The Almighty is alive and conquers all!
Praise is lifted high to the unshakable God!
Towering over all, my Savior-God is worthy to be praised!
47 Look how he pays back harm to all who harm me,
subduing all the people who come against me.
48 He rescues me from my enemies;
he lifts me up high and keeps me out of reach,
far from the grasp of my violent foe.
49 This is why I thank God with high praises!
I will sing my song to the Highest God,
so all among the nations will hear me.
50 You have appointed me king and rescued me
time and time again with your magnificent miracles.
You've been merciful and kind to me, your anointed one.
This favor will be forever seen upon your loving servant,
David,
and to all my descendants!

19 God's Witnesses

For the Pure and Shining One
A poem of praise by King David, his loving servant

God's Story in the Skies

1 God's splendor is a tale that is told;

his testament is written in the stars.[a]
Space itself speaks his story every day
through the marvels of the heavens.
His truth is on tour in the starry-vault of the sky,
showing his skill in creation's craftsmanship.
2 Each day gushes out its message[b] to the next,
night with night whispering its knowledge to all.
3 Without a sound, without a word, without a voice being heard,
4 Yet all the world can see its story.
Everywhere its gospel[c] is clearly read so all may know.
5 What a heavenly home God has set for the sun,
shining in the superdome of the sky!
See how he leaves his celestial chamber each morning,
radiant as a bridegroom ready for his wedding,
like a day-breaking champion eager to run his course.
6 He rises on one horizon, completing his circuit on the other,
warming lives and lands with his heat.

God's Story in the Scriptures

7 God's Word is perfect in every way;
how it revives our souls!
His laws lead us to truth,
and his ways change the simple into wise.
8 His teachings make us joyful and radiate his light;
his precepts are so pure!
His commands, how they challenge us to keep close to his heart!

---

a 19:1 Or "The heavens are continually rehearsing the glory of God."
b 19:2 Or "speaks its prophecy."
c 19:4 Literal translation from the Aramaic. There are many who believe that constellations (Heb. *mazzarot*) of the sky bring us the revelation of the gospel of Jesus Christ. A message is being given without words, sound, or a voice. See Job 38:31–33.

The revelation-light of his Word makes my spirit shine
radiant.
9 Everyone of the Lord's commands are right;
following them brings cheer.[a]
Nothing he says ever needs to be changed.
10 The rarest treasures of life are found in his truth.
That's why I prize God's Word like others prize the finest
gold.
Nothing brings the soul such sweetness
as seeking his living words.
11 For they warn us, his servants,
and keep us from following the wicked way,
giving a lifetime guarantee:
Great success to every obedient soul!
12 *Without this revelation light,*
how would I ever detect the waywardness of my heart?[b]
Lord, forgive my hidden flaws whenever you find them.
13 Keep cleansing me, God,
and keep me from my secret, selfish sins;
may they never rule over me!
For only then will I be free from fault
and remain innocent of rebellion.
14 So may the words of my mouth, my meditation-thoughts,
and every movement of my heart be always pure and
pleasing,
acceptable before your eyes,
my only Redeemer, my Protector-God.[c]

---

a 19:9 As translated from the Septuagint. The Hebrew is, "The fear of the Lord is clean."

b 19:12 The word *waywardness* is taken from the Hebrew word for errors.

c 19:14 Or "my rock (of protection)."

20 A Song of Trust

For the Pure and Shining One
For the end times by King David[a]

1 In your day of danger may the Lord answer and deliver you!
May the name of the God of Grace[b] set you safely on high!
2 May supernatural help be sent from his sanctuary!
May he support you from Zion's fortress!
3 May he remember every gift you have given him,
and celebrate every sacrifice of love you have shown him.
Pause in his presence
4 May God give you every desire of your heart
and carry out your every plan *as you go to battle.*
5 When you succeed, we will celebrate and shout for joy.
Flags will fly when victory is yours!
Yes, God will answer your prayers and we will praise him!
6 I know God gives me all that I ask for
and brings victory to his anointed king.
My deliverance cry will be heard in his holy heaven.
Through his mighty hand miracles will manifest
through his saving strength.
7 Some find their strength in their weapons and wisdom,
but my miracle deliverance can never be won by men.
Our boast is in the Lord our God who
makes us strong and gives us victory!
8 Our enemies will not prevail; they will only collapse and
perish in defeat while we will rise up, full of courage.
9 Give victory to our king, O God!
The day we call on you, give us your answer!

---

a The inscription for Ps. 20–22 is "For the End Times," as translated from the Septuagint.

b 20:1 The name used for *God* here is "The God of Jacob." Jacob was one transformed by God's grace, changed from a schemer who took from others, into Israel, God's prince.

21 Through Your Strength

For the end time, to the Pure and Shining One
King David's poem of praise

1 Lord, because of your strength the king is strong.
Look how he rejoices in you![a]
He bursts out with a joyful song because of your victory!
2 For you have given him his heart's desire,
anything and everything he asks for.
You haven't withheld a thing from your betrothed one.

Pause in his presence

3 Rich blessings overflow with every encounter with you,
and you placed a royal crown of gold upon his head.
4 He wanted resurrection—you have given it to him and more!
The days of his blessing stretch on one after another,
forever!
5 You have honored him and made him famous.
Glory garments are upon him,
and you surround him with splendor and majesty.
6 Your victory heaps blessing after blessing upon him.
What joy and bliss he tastes, rejoicing before your face!
7 For the king trusts endlessly in you,
and he will never stumble, never fall.
Your forever-love never fails and holds him firm.
8 Your almighty hands have captured your foes.
You uncovered all who hate you and you seized them.
9–10 When you appear before them,
unveiling the radiance of your face,
they will be consumed by the fierce fire of your presence.
Flames will swallow them up.
They and their descendants
will be destroyed by an unrelenting fire.

---

a 21:1 Think of this song as a praise song to Jesus, our true King.

[11] We will watch them fail,
for these are ones who plan their evil schemes against the Lord.
[12] They will turn and run at the sight of your judgment-arrow
aimed straight at their hearts.
[13] Rise up and put your might on display!
By your strength we will sing and praise your glorious power!

22 A Prophetic Portrait of the Cross[a]

For the Pure and Shining One
King David's song of anguish, to the tune of "The Deer at the Dawning of the Day"[b]

[1] God, my God!
Why would you abandon me now?[c]
[2] Why do you remain distant,
refusing to answer[d] my tearful cries in the day
and my desperate cries for your help in the night?
I can't stop sobbing.
Where are you, my God?
[3] Yet, I know that you are most holy; it's indisputable.
You are God-Enthroned, surrounded with songs,
living among the shouts of praise of your princely people.

---

a There were thirty-three distinct prophecies from this psalm that were fulfilled when Jesus was on the cross.

b This could be an amazing picture of Christ giving birth at the cross to a generation of his seed. They are like children of God born in the dawning of that resurrection morning.

c 22:1 When Jesus quoted these words dying on the cross, he was identifying himself as the One David wrote about in this psalm. It is a breathtaking portrayal of what Jesus endured through his suffering for us. The psalm ends with another quotation of Jesus on the cross: "It is finished!"

d 22:2 David uses poetic nuance here, for the word *answer* ('*anah*) is also a Hebrew homonym for affliction.

4 Our fathers' faith was in you—
through the generations they trusted and believed in you
and you came through.
5 Every time they cried out to you in their despair,
you were faithful to deliver them;
you didn't disappoint them.
6 But look at me now; I am like a woeful worm,
crushed, and I'm bleeding crimson.[a]
I don't even look like a man anymore.
I've been abused, despised, and scorned by everyone!
7 Mocked by their jeers, despised with their sneers—
as all the people poke fun at me, spitting their insults.
8 Saying, "Is this the one who trusted in God?
Is this the one who claims God is pleased with him?
Now let's see if your God will come to your rescue!
We'll just see how much he delights in you!"
9 Lord, you delivered me safely from my mother's womb.
You are the One who cared for me ever since I was a baby.
10 Since the day I was born, I've been placed in your custody.
You've cradled me throughout my days.
I've trusted in you and you've always been my God.
11 So don't leave me now, stay close to me!
For trouble is all around me and there's no one else to
help me.
12 I'm surrounded by many violent foes;
mighty forces of evil are swirling around me
that want to break me to bits and destroy me.[b]

---

a 22:6 The Hebrew word for *worm* is *tola*, which is also the word for *crimson* or *scarlet*. *Tola* was a certain worm in the Middle East that, when crushed, bled a crimson color so strong it was used as a dye for garments. Jesus was not saying he is a despised worm, but that he will bleed as he is crushed for our sins.

b 22:12 Many translations have here "strong bulls of Bashan." The root word for *bull* means to break or destroy. The word *Bashan*, although

13 Curses pour from their mouths!
They're like ravenous, roaring lions tearing their prey.
14 Now I'm completely exhausted, I'm spent.
Every joint of my body has been pulled apart.
My courage has vanished and
my inward parts have melted away.
15 I'm so thirsty and parched—dry as a bone.
My tongue sticks to the roof of my mouth.
And now you've left me in the dust for dead.
16 They have pierced my hands and my feet.
Like a pack of wild dogs they tear at me,
swirling around me with their hatred.
They gather around me like lions
to pin[a] my hands and feet.
17 All my bones stick out.
Look at how they all gloat over me and stare!
18 With a toss of the dice they divide my clothes among
themselves,
gambling for my garments!
19 Lord, my God, please don't stay far away.
For you are my only might and strength.
Won't you come quickly to my rescue?
20 Give me back my life.
Save me from this violent death.
Save my precious one and only[b]

---

known as a fertile land northeast of the Sea of Galilee, is also a word for serpent. These represent the many demonic spirits who came against the Son of God as he was being crucified.

a 22:16 Or "to maul" or "to pierce."

b 22:20 Or "unique," or, "darling." We are that *one and only* child and "unique darling" here in this psalm. See also Song 6:9. On the cross, Jesus—like a deer giving birth at the dawning light (see inscription of Ps. 22)—cared less that his body was being torn apart, and more for our protection and salvation. He prayed for us as he faced the death of the cross.

from the power of these demons![a]
21 Save me from all the power of the enemy,
from this roaring lion raging against me
and the power of his dark horde.
22 I will praise your name before all my brothers;
as my people gather I will praise you in their midst.[b]
23 Lovers of Yahweh, praise him!
Let all the true seed of Jacob glorify him with your praises.
Stand in awe of him all you princely people,
the offspring of Israel!
24 For he has not despised my cries of deep despair.
He's my First Responder to my sufferings,
and he didn't look the other way when I was in pain.
He was there all the time, listening to the song of the
afflicted.
25 You're reason for my praise;
it comes from you and goes to you.
I will keep my promise to praise you
before all who fear you
among the congregation of your people.
26 I will invite the poor and broken
and they will come and eat until satisfied.
Bring Yahweh praise and you will find him.
Your hearts will overflow with life forever!
27 From the four corners of the earth,
the peoples of the world will remember
and return to the Lord.

---

a 22:20 The Hebrew text uses the word *dogs*, which implies evil spirits who were bent on destroying Jesus on the cross. The Hebrew word for *dog* is taken from a root word meaning to attack.

b 22:22 Between verse 21 and verse 22 the glorious resurrection of Jesus takes place. The music is elevated to a higher key as victory is sounded forth. "My people gather" is a reference to the church that was birthed through his resurrection glory. (See also verse 25.)

Every nation will come and worship him.
28 For the Lord is King of all who takes charge of all the
nations.
29 There they are! They're worshiping!
The wealthy of this world will feast in fellowship with him
right alongside the humble of heart,
bowing down to the dust, forsaking their own souls.
They will all come and worship this worthy King!
30 His *spiritual* seed[a] shall serve him.
Future generations will hear from us
about the wonders of the Sovereign Lord.
31 His generation yet to be born will glorify him.
And they will all declare: "It is finished!"

23 The Good Shepherd

David's poetic praise to God[b]

1 The Lord is my Best Friend and my Shepherd.[c]
I always have more than enough.
2 He offers a resting place for me in his luxurious love.[d]

---

a 22:30 Jesus, our crucified Savior, had no natural offspring. These are the sons and daughters that were birthed by the work of the cross.

b Most scholars conclude that Ps. 23 was written by David when he was a young shepherd serving his father, Jesse, while he was keeping watch over sheep near Bethlehem. He was most likely sixteen or seventeen years old. The other psalm that he wrote when but a young lad was Ps. 19. Those are two good psalms to memorize and meditate upon if you want to have the heart of the giant killer.

c 23:1 The word most commonly used for *shepherd* is *ra'ah* which is also the Hebrew word for "best friend." The translation includes both meanings.

d 23:2 The Greek word for love is *agape*, which is a merging of two words and two concepts. *Ago* means to lead like a shepherd, and *pao* is a verb which means "to rest." Love is our Shepherd leading us to the place of true rest in his heart.

His tracks take me to an oasis of peace, the quiet brook of bliss.
3 That's where he restores and revives my life.[a]
He opens before me pathways to God's pleasure,
and leads me along in his footsteps of righteousness[b]
so that I can bring honor to his name.
4 Lord, even when your path takes me through
the valley of deepest darkness,
fear will never conquer me, for you already have!
You remain close to me and lead me through it all the way.
Your authority is my strength and my peace.[c]
The comfort of your love takes away my fear.
I'll never be lonely, for you are near.
5 You become my delicious feast
even when my enemies dare to fight.
You anoint me with the fragrance of your Holy Spirit;[d]
you give me all I can drink of you until my heart overflows.
6 So why would I fear the future?
For your goodness and love pursue me all the days of my life.
Then afterwards—when my life is through,
I'll return to your glorious presence to be forever with you!

---

a 23:3 Or "He causes my life (or soul, Heb. *nephesh*) to return." So often life drains out of us through our many activities, but David found that God restores our well being by pursuing what pleases God and resting in him.

b 23:3 Or "circular paths of righteousness." It is a common trait for sheep on the hillsides of Israel to circle their way up higher. They eventually form a path that keeps leading them higher. This is what David is referring to here. Each step we take following our Shepherd will lead us higher, even though it may seem we are going in circles.

c 23:4 Or "Your rod and your staff, they comfort me."

d 23:5 The word *oil* becomes a symbol of the Holy Spirit.

24 The Glorious King

David's poetic praise to God[a]

1 God claims the world as his!
Everything and everyone belongs to him!
2 He's the One who pushed back oceans
to let the dry ground appear,
planting firm foundations for the earth.
3 Who, then, ascends into the presence of the Lord?[b]
And who has the privilege of entering into God's Holy Place?
4 Those who are clean—whose works and ways are pure,
whose hearts are true and sealed by the truth,
those who never deceive, whose words are sure.
5 They will receive the Lord's blessing
and righteousness given by the Savior-God.
6 They will stand before God,
for they seek the pleasure of God's face,[c] the God of Jacob.

Pause in his presence

7 So wake up, you living gateways!
Lift up your heads, you ageless doors of destiny!
Welcome the King of Glory,
for he is about to come through you.
8 You ask, "Who is this Glory-King?"
The Lord, armed and ready for battle,
the Mighty One, invincible in every way!
9 So wake up, you living gateways, and rejoice![d]
Fling wide, you ageless doors of destiny!

---

a The Septuagint adds "for the Sabbath."

b 24:3 Or "hill of the Lord."

c 24:6 The Hebrew is plural ("faces").

d 24:9 The Hebrew text says, "lift up your heads," which is a figure of speech for rejoicing. We are the living gateways who rejoice as the Lord draws near to us from his temple.

Here he comes; the King of Glory is ready to come in.
10 You ask, "Who is this King of Glory?"
He's the Lord of Victory, armed and ready for battle,
the Mighty One, the invincible Commander of heaven's hosts!
Yes, he is the King of Glory!

Pause in his presence

25 Don't Fail Me, God! [a]

King David's poetic praise to God

1 Forever I will lift up my soul into your presence, Lord.
2 Be there for me, God, for I keep trusting in you.
Don't allow my foes to gloat over me or
the shame of defeat to overtake me.
3 For how could anyone be disgraced
when they've entwined their hearts with you?
But they will all be defeated and ashamed
when they harm the innocent.
4 Lord, direct me throughout my journey
so I can experience your plans for my life.
Reveal the life-paths that are pleasing to you.
5 Escort me along the way; take me by the hand and teach me.
For you are the God of my increasing salvation;
I have wrapped my heart into yours! [b]
6–7 Forgive my failures as a young man,

---

a Ps. 25–39 are fifteen poetic songs of bringing pure worship before God. Ps. 25–29 speak of our confidence to worship God. Ps. 30–34 point us to receiving life eternal from our Hero-God. And the last five, Ps. 35–39, bring us to the importance of personal purity and holiness before God as we worship him in truth.

b 25:5 The Hebrew word most commonly translated as *wait* (wait upon the Lord) is *qavah,* which also means to tie together by twisting, or entwine, or wrap tightly. This is a beautiful concept of waiting upon God, not as something passive, but entwining our hearts with him and his purposes.

and overlook the sins of my immaturity.
Give me grace, Lord! Always look at me
through your eyes of love—
your forgiving eyes of mercy and compassion.
When you think of me, see me as one you love and care for.
How good you are to me!
8 When someone turns to you,
they discover how easy you are to please—so faithful and true!
Joyfully you teach them the proper path,
even when they go astray.
9 Keep showing the humble your path,
and lead them into the best decision.
Bring revelation light that trains them in the truth.
10 All the ways of the Lord are loving and faithful for those who follow the ways of his covenant.
11 For the honor of your name, Lord,
never count my sins and forgive them all—
lift their burden off of my life![a]
12 But still one question remains:
How do I live in the holy fear of God?
Show me the right path to take.
13 Then prosperity and favor will be my portion,
and my descendants will inherit all that is good.
14 There's a private place reserved for the lovers of God
where they sit near him and receive
the revelation-secrets of his promises.[b]
15 Rescue me, Lord, for you're my only Hero.

---

a 25:11 The Hebrew word used here for *forgive* or *pardon* is a rare word only used twice in the Old Testament and comes from a root word meaning to "lift off a burden."

b 25:14 Or "covenant."

16 Sorrows fill my heart as I feel helpless, mistreated—
I'm all alone, and in misery!
Come closer to me now, Lord, for I need your mercy.
17 Turn to me, for my problems seem to be going from bad to worse.
Only you can free me from all these troubles!
18 Until you lift this burden, the burden of all my sins,
my troubles and trials will be more than I can handle.
Can't you feel my pain?
19 Vicious enemies hate me.
There are so many, Lord. Can't you see?
20 Will you protect me from their power against me?
Let it never be said that I trusted you
and you didn't come to my rescue.
21 Your perfection and faithfulness are my bodyguards,
for you are my hope and I trust in you as my only protection.
22 Zealously, God, we ask you
to come save Israel from all her troubles,
for you provide the ransom price for your people![a]

26 Declare Me Innocent

King David's poetic praise to God

1 You be my Judge and declare me innocent!
Clear my name, for I have tried my best to keep your laws
and to trust you without wavering.
2 Lord, you can scrutinize me.
Refine my heart and probe my every thought.

---

a Ps. 25 is an acrostic psalm—that is, in the Hebrew text every verse begins with a progressive letter of the alphabet. It is considered a poetic device of Hebrew literature. Go back through the psalm and notice how almost every verse begins with the next letter of our English alphabet. See if you can find them. (*X* was not included.)

Put me to the test and you'll find it's true.
3 I will never lose sight of your love for me.
Your faithfulness has steadied my steps.
4 I won't keep company with tricky, two-faced men,
nor will I go the way of those who defraud with hidden motives.
5 I despise the sinner's hangouts, refusing to even enter them.
You won't find me walking among the wicked.
6–7 When I come before you, I'll come clean,[a]
approaching your altar with songs of thanksgiving,
singing the songs of your mighty miracles.
8 Lord, I love your home, this place of dazzling glory,
bathed in the splendor and light of your presence!
9 Don't treat me as one of these scheming sinners
who plot violence against the innocent.
10 Look how they devise their wicked plans;
holding the innocent hostage for ransom.
11 I'm not like them, Lord—not at all.
Save me, redeem me with your mercy,
for I have chosen to walk only in what is right.
12 I will proclaim it publicly in every congregation,
and because of you, Lord,
I will take my stand on righteousness alone!

27 Fearless Faith

David's poetic praise to God before he was anointed king[b]

1 The Lord is my Revelation Light to guide me along the way;[c]
he's the Source of my salvation to defend me every day.
I fear no one!
I'll never turn back and run from you, Lord,

---

a 26:6–7 Or "I wash my hands in innocence."
b Inscription from the Septuagint.
c 27:1 See also John 1:5, 9, and 1 John 1:5.

surround and protect me.
2 When evil ones come to destroy me,
they will be the ones who turn back.
3 My heart will not be afraid even if an army rises to attack.
I know that you are there for me so I will not be shaken.
4 Here's the one thing I crave from God,
the one thing I seek above all else:
I want the privilege of living with him every moment in his house,[a]
finding the sweet loveliness of his face,
filled with awe, delighting in his glory and grace.
I want to live my life so close to him
that he takes pleasure in my every prayer.
5–6 In his shelter in the day of trouble, that's where you'll find me,
for he hides me there in his holiness.
He has smuggled me into his secret place
where I'm kept safe and secure—
out of reach from all my enemies.
Triumphant now, I'll bring him my offerings of praise,
singing and shouting with ecstatic joy!
Yes, listen and you can hear
the fanfare of my shouts of praise to the Lord!
7 God, hear my cry! Show me your grace.
Show me mercy, and send the help I need!
8 Lord, when you said to me, "Seek my face,"
my inner being responded:
I'm seeking your face with all my heart.
9 So don't hide yourself, Lord, when I come to find you.[b]

---

a 27:4 There was not yet a temple built when David wrote this psalm. He is saying that he longs to be surrounded with God's presence, enclosed and encircled with holiness.

b 27:9 The Septuagint is "Don't overlook me."

You're the God of my salvation;
how can you reject your servant in anger?
You've been my only hope,
so don't forsake me now when I need you!
10 My father and mother abandoned me. I'm like an orphan!
But you took me in and made me yours.[a]
11 Now teach me all about your ways and tell me what to do.
Make it clear for me to understand
for I am surrounded by waiting enemies.
12 Don't let them defeat me, Lord.
You can't let me fall into their clutches!
They keep accusing me of things I've never done
while they plot evil against me.
13 Yet, I totally trust you to rescue me one more time,
so that I can see once again how good you are while I'm still alive!
14 Here's what I've learned through it all:
Don't give up; don't be impatient;
be entwined as one with the Lord.[b]
Be brave, courageous, and never lose hope.
Yes, keep on waiting—for he will never disappoint you!

28 My Strength and Shield

David's poetic praise to God

1 I'm pleading with you, Lord, help me![c]
Don't close your ears to my cry, for you're my Defender.
If you continue to remain aloof and refuse to answer me,

---

a 27:10 Every child needs four things: acceptance, focused attention, guidance, and protection. All four of these emotional needs are met by God (verses 7–14).

b 27:14 Or "wait upon the Lord." See Ps. 25:5 footnote.

c 28:1 This psalm was likely written when David was exiled because of the rebellion of his son, Absalom. He was not longing and looking for his throne, but for God's throne (verse 2).

I might as well give up and die.
2 Can't you see me turning toward your mercy seat
as I lift my hands in surrendered prayer?
Now, Lord, please listen to my cry.
3 Don't allow me to be punished along with the wicked—
these hypocrites who speak sweetly to their neighbor's face
while holding evil against them in their hearts.
4 Go ahead and punish them as they deserve.
Let them be paid back for all their evil plans
in proportion to their wickedness.
5 Since they don't care anything about you
nor about the great things you've done,
take them down like an old building being demolished,
never again to be rebuilt.
6 But may your name be blessed and built up!
For you have answered my passionate cry for mercy.
7 You are my Strength and my Shield from every danger.
When I fully trust in you, help is on the way.
I jump for joy and burst forth with ecstatic, passionate praise!
I will sing songs of what you mean to me!
8 You will be the Inner Strength of all your people,
the Mighty Protector of all,
the Saving Strength for all your anointed ones.
9 Keep protecting and cherishing your chosen ones;
in you they will never fall.
Like a Shepherd going before us, keep leading us forward,
forever carrying us in your arms!

29 The Glory-God Thunders!

King David's poetic praise to God for the last days
The Feast of Tabernacles[a]

1 Proclaim his majesty all you mighty champions,
you sons of Almighty God,
giving all the glory and strength back to him!
2 Be in awe before his majesty.
Be in awe before such power and might!
Come worship wonderful Yahweh arrayed in all his splendor,
bowing in worship as he appears in all his holy beauty.
Give him the honor due his name!
Worship him wearing the glory-garments
of your holy, priestly calling!
3–4 The voice of the Lord echoes through the skies and seas.
The Glory-God reigns as he thunders in the clouds.
So powerful is his voice, so brilliant and bright,
how majestic as he thunders over the great waters![b]
5 His tympanic thunder topples the strongest of trees.[c]
His symphonic sound splinters the mighty forests.
6 Now he moves Zion's[d] mountains by the might of his voice,[e]

---

a The additional words of the inscription are found in the Septuagint. Ps. 29 is one of the loveliest poems ever written. It is pure and unrestrained praise. The name *Yahweh* (Jehovah) is found eighteen times in eleven verses. David was a prophetic seer, and this psalm can properly be interpreted to speak of God's majesty revealed in the last days.

b 29:3–4 The sea (great waters) is often a term used in the Bible to symbolize the "sea of humanity." See Isa. 57:20 and Rev. 17:15.

c 29:5 Trees in the Bible are symbols used for men. The strongest of men are toppled and bowed down when the Glory-God speaks.

d 29:6 Or "Sirion" (Mt. Hermon), an ancient term for Mount Zion. See Ps. 133.

e 29:6 The "voice of the Lord" is used seven times (the seven thunders) in this psalm.

shaking the snowy peaks with his earsplitting sound!
7 The lightning-fire flashes, striking as he speaks.
8 God reveals himself when he makes the fault lines quake,
shaking deserts, speaking his voice.
9 God's mighty voice makes the deer to give birth.[a]
His thunderbolt voice lays the forest bare.
In his temple all fall before him with each one shouting,
"Glory, glory, the God of glory!"[b]
10 Above the furious flood,[c] the Enthroned One reigns,
the King-God rules with eternity at his side.
11 This is the One who gives his strength and might to his people.
This is the Lord giving us his kiss of peace.[d]

30 He Healed Me

King David's poetic praise to God

A song for the Feast of Dedication of the dwelling place

1 Lord, I will exalt you and lift you high,
for you have lifted me up on high!
Over all my boasting, gloating enemies,
you made me to triumph.
2 O Lord, my healing God,

---

a 29:9 Or "God's mighty voice makes the oaks to whirl."

b 29:9 The Septuagint reads, "Those who give him glory he carries to his house."

c 29:10 The Hebrew word for flood is found thirteen times in the Bible and is always used in connection to man's rebellion and turning away from God. Thirteen is the Biblical number signifying apostasy. Sitting as king, he rules even over the dark flood of evil to make it end.

d 29:11 In Jewish synagogues this psalm is read on the first day of the feast of Pentecost. The Christian Church was born on Pentecost two thousand years ago when the mighty "storm" of the Spirit came into the upper room. See Acts 2. The last word of this psalm is peace. It begins with a storm, but God brings his people peace even in the midst of storms.

I cried out for a miracle and you healed me!
3 You brought me back from the brink of death,
from the depths below.
Now here I am, alive and well, fully restored!
4 O sing and make melody, you steadfast lovers of God.
Give thanks to him every time you reflect on his holiness!
5 I've learned that his anger lasts for a moment,
but his loving favor lasts a lifetime![a]
We may weep through the night,
but at daybreak it will turn into shouts of ecstatic joy.
6–7 I remember boasting, "I've got it made!
Nothing can stop me now!
I'm God's favored one; he's made me steady as a mountain!"
But then suddenly, you hid your face from me.
I was panic-stricken and became so depressed.
8 Still I cried out to you, Lord God, I shouted out for mercy, saying:
9 "What would you gain in my death,
if I were to go down to the depths of darkness?
Will a grave sing your song?
How could death's dust declare your faithfulness?"
10 So hear me now, Lord; show me your famous mercy.
O God, be my Savior and rescue me!
11 Then he broke through and transformed all my wailing
into a whirling dance of ecstatic praise!
He has torn the veil and lifted from me
the sad heaviness of mourning.
He wrapped me in the glory-garments of gladness.
12 How could I be silent when it's time to praise you?
Now my heart sings out loud, bursting with joy—

---

a 30:5 The Septuagint says, "There is wrath in his anger but life in his will [promise]."

a bliss inside that keeps me singing,
"I can never thank you enough!"

31 How Great Is Your Goodness

For the Pure and Shining One
A song of poetic praise by King David

1 I trust you, Lord, to be my Hiding Place.
Don't let me down.
Don't let my enemies bring me to shame.
Come and rescue me for you are the only God
who always does what is right.
2 Rescue me quickly when I cry out to you.
At the sound of my prayer may your ear be turned to me.
Be my strong Shelter and Hiding Place on high.
Pull me into victory and breakthrough.
3–4 For you are my high Fortress where I'm kept safe.
You are to me a stronghold of salvation.
When you deliver me out of this peril,
it will bring glory to your name.
As you guide me forth I'll be kept safe
from the hidden snares of the enemy—
the secret traps that lie before me—
for you have become my Rock of Strength.
5 Into your hands I now entrust my spirit.[a]
O Lord, the God of faithfulness,
you have rescued and redeemed me.
6 I despise these deceptive illusions,
all this pretense and nonsense;
for I worship only you.
7 In mercy you have seen my troubles
and you have cared for me;

---

a 31:5 This was quoted by Jesus as he was dying on the cross. See Matt. 27:50.

even during this crisis in my soul I will be radiant with joy,
filled with praise for your love and mercy.
8 You have kept me from being conquered by my enemy;
you broke open the way to bring me to freedom,[a]
into a beautiful, broad place.[b]
9 O Lord, help me again! Keep showing me such mercy.
For I am in anguish, always in tears,
and I'm worn-out with weeping.
I'm becoming old because of grief; my health is broken.
10 I'm exhausted! My life is spent with sorrow,
my years with sighing and sadness.
Because of all these troubles, I have no more strength.
My inner being[c] is so weak and frail.
11 My enemies say, "You are nothing!"
Even my friends and neighbors hold me in contempt!
They dread seeing me
and they look the other way when I pass by.
12 I am totally forgotten, buried away like a dead man,
discarded like a broken dish thrown in the trash.
13 I overheard their whispered threats, the slander of my enemies.
I'm terrified as they plot and scheme to take my life.
14 I'm desperate, Lord! I throw myself upon you,
for you alone are my God!
15 My life, my every moment, my destiny—it's all in your hands.
So I know you can deliver me
from those who persecute me relentlessly.
16 Let your shining face shine on me.

---

a 31:8 This is a picture of the stone rolled away from the tomb of Jesus.

b 31:8 This could be the throne room where Jesus ascended after his death.

c 31:10 The Hebrew text says, "My bones grow weak." Bones in the Bible are symbols of our inner being.

Let your undying love and glorious grace
save me from all this gloom.
17 As I call upon you, let my shame and disgrace
be replaced by your favor once again.
But let shame and disgrace fall instead upon the wicked—
those going to their own doom,
drifting down in silence to the dust of death.
18 At last their lying lips will be muted in their graves.
For they are arrogant, filled with contempt and conceit
as they speak against the godly.
19 Lord, how wonderful you are!
You have stored up so many good things for us,
like a treasure chest heaped up and spilling over with
blessings—
all for those who honor and worship you!
And everybody knows what you can do
for those who turn and hide themselves in you.
20 So, hide all your beloved ones
in the sheltered, secret place before your face.
Overshadow them by your glory-presence.
Keep them from these accusations, the brutal insults of evil
men.
Tuck them safely away in the tabernacle where you dwell.
21 The name of the Lord is blessed and lifted high!
For his marvelous miracle of mercy protected me
when I was overwhelmed by my enemies.
22 I spoke so hastily when I said, "The Lord has deserted me."
For in truth, you did hear my prayer and came to rescue
me.
23 Listen to me all you godly ones: Love the Lord with passion!
The Lord protects and preserves all those who are loyal to
him.
But he pays back in full all those who reject him in their
pride.

24 So cheer up! Take courage all you who love him!
Wait for him to break through for you, all who trust in him!

32 Forgiven

A poem of insight and instruction by King David [a]

1 How happy and fulfilled are those
whose rebellion has been forgiven,[b]
those whose sins are covered *by blood*!
2 How blessed and relieved are those
who have confessed their corruption[c] to God!
For he wipes their slates clean
and removes hypocrisy from their hearts.
3 Before I confessed my sins, I kept it all inside;
my dishonesty devastated my inner life,
causing my life to be filled with frustration,
irrepressible anguish, and misery.
4 The pain never let up, for your hand of conviction
was heavy on my heart.
My strength was sapped, my inner life dried up
like a spiritual drought within my soul.

Pause in his presence

---

a David wrote this psalm after he seduced the wife of his most loyal soldier, then had him killed to try to keep her pregnancy a secret. This sin with Bathsheba brought great disgrace to David, yet he finds complete forgiveness in God's mercy. The apostle Paul chose the first two verses of Ps. 32 to support the important doctrine of salvation by grace through faith. See Rom. 4:5–8. This was Saint Augustine's favorite psalm. He had it written on the wall near his bed before he died so he could meditate upon it.

b 32:1 The Hebrew word for *forgiven* means lifted off. Sin's guilt is a burden that must be lifted off our souls. The Septuagint says, "because they have not hidden their sins."

c 32:2 David uses three Hebrew words to describe sin in these first two verses: *rebellion*, *sins* (failures, falling short), and *corruption* (crookedness, the twisting of right standards).

5 Then I finally admitted to you all my sins,
refusing to hide them any longer.
So I said, "My life-giving God,
I'll openly acknowledge my evil actions."
And you forgave me!
All at once the guilt of my sin washed away
and all my pain disappeared!

Pause in his presence

6 This is what I've learned through it all:
Every believer should confess their sins to God;
do it every time God has uncovered you
in the time of exposing.
For if you do this, when sudden storms of life overwhelm,
you'll be kept safe.[a]
7 Lord, you are my secret Hiding Place,
protecting me from these troubles,
surrounding me with songs of gladness!
Your joyous shouts of rescue release my breakthrough.

Pause in his presence

8–9 I hear the Lord saying, "I will stay close to you,
instructing and guiding you along the pathway for your life.
I will advise you along the way
and lead you forth with my eyes as your guide.
So don't make it difficult, don't be stubborn
when I take you where you've not been before.
Don't make me tug you and pull you along.
Just come with me!"
10 So my conclusion is this:
Many are the sorrows and frustrations
of those who don't come clean with God.
But when you trust in the Lord for forgiveness,
his wrap-around love will surround you.

---

a 32:6 Prov. 2:13 is a good commentary on this verse.

11 So celebrate the goodness of God!
He shows this kindness to everyone who is his!
Go ahead—shout for joy,
all you upright ones who want to please him!

33 A Song of Praise

Poetic praise by King David[a]

1 It's time to sing and shout for joy!
Go ahead all you redeemed ones, do it!
Praise him with all you have,
for praise looks lovely on the lips of God's lovers.
2 Play the guitar as you lift your praises loaded with thanksgiving.
Sing and make joyous music with all you've got inside.
3 Compose new melodies[b] that release new praises to the Lord.
Play his praises on instruments
with the anointing and skill he gives you.
Sing and shout with passion; make a spectacular sound of joy—
4 For God's Word is something to sing about!
He is true to his promises; his Word can be trusted;
and everything he does is so reliable and right.
5 The Lord loves seeing justice on the earth.
Anywhere and everywhere you can find his faithful, unfailing love!
6 All he had to do was speak by his Spirit-Wind command
and God created the heavenlies.

---

a Most manuscripts have no inscription for this psalm. However, ancient Qumran evidence suggests this is the original inscription that was later omitted.

b 33:3 There are seven new songs mentioned in the Bible. Six are in the Psalms (33:3, 40:3, 96:1, 98:1, 144:9, 149:1) and one in Isaiah (42:10).

Filled with galaxies and stars,
the vast cosmos he wonderfully made.
7 His voice scooped out the seas.
The ocean depths he poured into vast reservoirs.
8 Now, with breathtaking wonder,
Let everyone worship Yahweh, this awe-inspiring
Creator. 9 Words he breathed and worlds were birthed,
"Let there be" and there it was—
Springing forth the moment he spoke.
No sooner said than done!
10 With his breath he scatters the schemes of nations who
oppose him;
they will never succeed.
11 His destiny-plan for the earth stands sure.
His forever-plan remains in place and will never fail.
12 Blessed and prosperous is that nation who has God as their
Lord!
They will be the people he chooses for his own.
13–15 The Lord looks over us from where he rules in heaven.
Gazing into every heart from his lofty dwelling place,
he observes all the peoples of the earth.
The Creator of our hearts considers and examines
everything we do.
16 Even if a king has the best equipped army,
it would never be enough to save him.
Even if the best warrior went to battle,
he could not be saved simply by his strength alone.
17 Human strength and the weapons of man
are such false hopes for victory;
they may seem mighty but they will always disappoint.
18 The eyes of the Lord are upon
even the weakest worshipers who love him—
those who wait in hope and expectation
for the strong, steady love of God.

19 God will deliver them from death,
even the certain death of famine, with no one to help.
20 The Lord alone is our radiant hope
and we trust in him with all our hearts.
His wrap-around presence will strengthen us.
21 As we trust, we rejoice with an uncontained joy
flowing from Yahweh!
22 So let your love and steadfast kindness overshadow us
continually—for we trust and we wait upon you!

34 God's Goodness

A song by King David composed after his escape from the king when he pretended to be insane

1 Lord! I'm bursting with joy over what you've done for me!
My lips are full of perpetual praise.
2 I'm boasting of you and all your works,
so let all who are discouraged take heart.
3 Join me everyone! Let's praise the Lord together.
Let's make him famous!
Let's make his name glorious to all.
4 So listen to my testimony: I cried to God in my distress
and he answered me! He freed me from all my fears!
5 Gaze upon him, join your life with his, and joy will come.
Your faces will glisten with glory.
You'll never wear that shame-face again.
6 When I had nothing—desperate and defeated,
I cried out to the Lord and he heard me,
bringing his miracle-deliverance when I needed it most.[a]

---

a 34:6 David wrote this psalm at perhaps the lowest point in his life. He was alone. He had to part from Jonathan, his dearest friend. He was being chased by Saul and his paid assassins. Now he had run to hide in the cave of Adullam ("their prey"). Yet the beautiful sounds of praise were heard echoing in his cavern. This is a lesson for all of us: we praise our way out of our difficulties into his light.

7 The angle of the Lord stooped down to listen as I prayed,
encircling me, empowering me, and showing me how to
escape.
He will do this for everyone who fears God.
8 Drink deeply of the pleasures of this God.[a]
Experience for yourself the joyous mercies he gives
to all who turn to hide themselves in him.
9 Worship in awe and wonder, all you who've been made holy!
For all who fear him will feast with plenty.
10 Even the strong and the wealthy[b] grow weak and hungry,
but those who passionately pursue the Lord
will never lack any good thing.
11 Come, children of God, and listen to me.
I'll share the lesson I've learned of fearing the Lord.[c]
12–13 Do you want to live a long, good life,
enjoying the beauty that fills each day?
Then never speak a lie or allow wicked words
to come from your mouth.
14 Keep turning your back on every sin,
and make "peace" your life motto.
Practice being at peace with everyone.[d]

---

a 34:8 Many translations read, "Taste and see." The Hebrew root word for *see* is taken from a word that means,to drink deeply.

b 34:10 Following the ancient versions (Septuagint, Syriac, and Vulgate), this phrase is translated "rich ones." Modern translations read "young lions."

c 34:12–13 See 1 Peter 3:10–12.

d 34:14 Twice the Hebrew uses the word *shalom*. This word means much more than peace, it is wholeness, wellness, well-being, safe, happy, friendly, favor, completeness, to make peace, peace offering, secure, to prosper, to be victorious, to be content, tranquil, quiet, and restful. The pictographic symbols for the word *shalom* (*shin, lamed, vav, mem*), actually reads, "Destroy the authority that binds to chaos." The noun *shalom* is derived from the verbal root *shalam* which means "to restore," in the sense of replacing or providing what is needed in order to make

15 The Lord sees all we do;
he watches over his friends day and night.
His godly ones receive the answers they seek
whenever they cry out to him.
16 But the Lord has made up his mind to oppose evildoers
and to wipe out even the memory of them
from the face of the earth.
17 Yet when holy lovers of God cry out
to him with all their hearts,
the Lord will hear them and come to rescue them
from all their troubles.
18 The Lord is so close to all whose hearts are crushed by pain,
and he is always ready to restore the repentant one.
19 Even when bad things happen to the good and godly ones,
the Lord will save them and not let them be defeated
by what they face.
20 God will be your bodyguard to protect you
when trouble is near.
Not one bone will be broken.
21 But the wicked commit slow suicide.
For they hate and persecute the lovers of God.
Make no mistake about it,
God will hold them guilty and punish them;
they will pay the penalty!
22 But the Lord has paid for the freedom of his servants,
and he will freely pardon those who love him.
He will declare them free and innocent
when they turn to hide themselves in him.

---

someone or something whole and complete. So *shalom* is used to describe one who has been provided all that is needed to be whole and complete and break off all authority that would attempt to bind us to chaos.

35 Rescue Me

A poetic song by King David[a]

Part One – David, a Warrior

1 O Lord, fight for me! Harass the hecklers, accuse my
accusers.
Fight those who fight against me.
2–3 Put on your armor, Lord; take up your shield and protect me.
Rise up, mighty God! Grab your weapons of war
and block the way of the wicked who come to fight me.
Stand for me when they stand against me!
Speak over my soul: "I am your strong Savior!"[b]
4 Humiliate those who seek my harm. Defeat them all!
Frustrate their plans to defeat me and drive them back.
Disgrace them all as they have devised their plans to
disgrace me.
5 Blow them away like dust in the wind,
with the Angel of Almighty God driving them back!
6 And make the road in front of them nothing but slippery
darkness,
with the Angel of the Lord behind them chasing them
away!
7 For though I did nothing wrong to them, they set a trap for
me,
wanting me to fall and fail.
8 Surprise them with your ambush, Lord,
and catch them in the very trap they set for me.

---

a This is the first of seven Psalms in which David cried out for vengeance upon his enemies (Ps. 52, 58, 59, 69, 109, and 137).

b 35:2–3 The Aramaic word used here is found thirty-three times in the Psalms, and is clearly *Savior*. Although a New Testament concept, David had a deep understanding almost one thousand years before the Savior was born that God would become his Savior. The Hebrew word for *Savior*, *Yasha*, is very similar to the name *Jesus*, *Yeshua*.

Let them be the ones to fail and fall into destruction!
9 And then my fears will dissolve into limitless joy;
my whole being will overflow with gladness
because of your mighty deliverance.
10 Everything inside of me will shout it out:
"There's just no one like you, Lord!"
For look at how you protect the weak and helpless
from the strong and heartless who oppress them.

Part Two – David, a Witness

11 They are malicious men, hostile witnesses of wrong.
They rise up against me, accusers appearing out of nowhere.
12 When I show them mercy, they bring me misery.
I'm forsaken and forlorn, like a motherless child.
13 I even prayed over them when they were sick.
I was burdened and bowed low with fasting
and interceded for their healing,
and I didn't stop praying.
14 I grieved for them, heavyhearted,
as though they were my dearest family members
or my good friends who were sick,
nearing death, needing prayer.
15 But when I was the one who tripped up and stumbled,
they came together only to slander me,
rejoicing in my time of trouble, tearing me to shreds
with their lies and betrayal.
16 These nameless ruffians,
mocking me like godless fools at a feast—
how they delight in throwing mud on my name.
17 God, how long can you just stand there doing nothing?
Now is the time to act.
Rescue me from these brutal men,
for I am being torn to shreds by these "beasts"

who are out to get me.
Save me from their rage, their cruel grasp.
18 For then I will praise you wherever I go.[a]
And when everyone gathers for worship,
I will lift up your praise with a shout
in front of the largest crowd I can find!

Part Three – David, a Worshiper

19 Don't let those who fight me for no reason be victorious.
Don't let them succeed, these heartless haters
who come against me with their gloating sneers.
20 They are the ones who would never seek peace as friends,
for they are ever devising deceit against the innocent ones
who mind their own business.
21 They open their mouths with ugly grins,
gloating with glee over my every fault.
"Look," they say, "we caught him red-handed!
We saw him fall with our own eyes!"
22 But my caring God, you have been there all along.
You have seen their hypocrisy.
God, don't let them get away with this.
Don't walk away without doing something.
23 Now is the time to awake! Rise up, Lord!
Vindicate me, my Lord and my God!
24 You have every right to judge me, Lord,
according to your righteousness,
but don't let them rejoice over me when I stumble.
25–26 Let them all be ashamed of themselves,
humiliated when they rejoice over my every blunder.
Shame them, Lord, when they say, "We saw what he did.
Now we have him right where we want him.

---

a 35:18 The Septuagint says, "My only child, I will save you from the lions."

Let's get him while he's down!"
Make them look ridiculous when they exalt themselves
over me.
May they all be disgraced and dishonored!
27 But let all my true friends shout for joy,
all those who know and love what I do for you.
Let them all say, "The Lord will be glorified through it all!
God will still bless his servant!"
28 Then I won't be able to hold it in—
everyone will hear my joyous praises all day long!
Your righteousness will be the theme of my glory-song of
praise!

36 The Blessing of the Wise

A poetic song by King David, the servant of the Lord

1 The rebellion of sin speaks as an oracle of God,
speaking deeply to the conscience of wicked men.[a]
Yet they are still eager to sin,
for the fear of God is not before their eyes.
2 See how they flatter themselves,
unable to detect and detest their sins.
They are crooked and conceited,
convinced they can get away with anything.
3 Their wicked words are nothing but lies.
Wisdom is far from them.
Goodness is both forgotten and forsaken.
4 They lay awake at night to hatch their evil plots,
always planning their schemes of darkness,
and never once do they consider the evil of their ways.
5 But you, O Lord, your mercy-seat love is limitless,
reaching higher than the highest heavens.
Your great faithfulness is so infinite,

---

a 36:1 Or "the heart of the wicked is rebellious to the core."

stretching over the whole earth.
6 Your righteousness is unmovable,
just like the mighty mountains.
Your judgments are as full of wisdom
as the oceans are full of water.
Your tender care and kindness leave no one forgotten,
not a man nor even a mouse.
7 O God, how extravagant is your cherishing love!
All mankind can find a hiding place[a]
under the shadow of your wings.
8 All may drink of the anointing[b] from the abundance of your
house!
All may drink their fill from the delightful springs of Eden.[c]
9 To know you is to experience a Flowing Fountain,
drinking in your life, springing up to satisfy.
In the light of your holiness we receive the light of
revelation.[d]
10 Lord, keep pouring out your unfailing love
on those who are near you.
Release more of your blessings to those who are loyal to
you.
11 Don't let these proud boasters trample me down;
don't let them push me around
by the sheer strength of their wickedness.

---

a 36:7 Or "They will be satisfied (or watered) in the abundance of your house."

b 36:8 The Hebrew word for *abundance* is actually *butterfat* or *oil*. It is a symbol of the anointing of the Holy Spirit.

c 36:8 Or "Eden's rivers of pleasure." The garden of Eden had flowing rivers of delight. Eden means *pleasure*. The Hebrew word used here is the plural form of Eden, *Edens*.

d 36:9 See John 1:4.

12 There they lie in the dirt, these evil ones,
thrown down to the ground, never to arise again!

37 A Song of Wisdom

Poetic praise by King David[a]

1 Don't follow after the wicked ones or be jealous of their wealth.
Don't think for a moment they're better-off than you.
2 They *and their short-lived success*
will soon shrivel up and quickly fade away
like grass clippings in the hot sun.
3 Keep trusting in the Lord and do what is right in his eyes.
Fix your heart on the promises of God and you will be secure,
feasting on his faithfulness.
4 Make God the utmost delight and pleasure of your life,[b]
and he will provide for you what you desire the most.
5 Give God the right to direct your life,[c]
and as you trust him along the way
you'll find he pulled it off perfectly!
6 He will appear as your Righteousness,[d]
as sure as the dawning of a new day.
He will manifest as your Justice,
as sure and strong as the noonday sun.
7 Quiet your heart in his presence and pray;
keep hope alive as you long for God to come through for you.

---

a Ps. 37 is an acrostic psalm with every other verse beginning with a successive letter of the Hebrew alphabet.

b 37:4 The word *delight* actually means to be soft or tender.

c 37:5 The Hebrew uses the word *commit*, which means "to roll over your burdens on the Lord."

d 37:6 The Hebrew verb found here is also used for giving birth. Perhaps this is a reference to the birth of Christ, our Righteousness.

12 Meanwhile my enemies are out to kill me,
plotting my ruin, speaking of my doom
as they spend every waking moment
planning on how to finish me off.
13–14 I'm like a deaf man who no longer hears.
I can't even speak up, and words fail me;
I have no argument to counter their threats.
15 Lord, the only thing I can do is wait and put my hope in
you.
I wait for your help, my God.
16 So hear my cry and put an end to their strutting in pride,
who gloat when I stumble in pain.
17 I'm slipping away and on the verge of a breakdown,
with nothing but sorrow and sighing.[a]
18 I confess all my sin to you; I can't hold it in any longer.
My agonizing thoughts punish me for my wrongdoing;
I feel condemned as I consider all I've done.
19 My enemies are many.
They hate me and persecute me,
though I've done nothing against them to deserve it.
20 I show goodness to them and get repaid evil in return.
And they hate me even more when I stand for what is right.
21 So don't forsake me now, Lord!
Don't leave me in this condition.
22 God, hurry to help me, run to my rescue!
For you're my Savior and my only hope!

---

a 38:17 The Septuagint reads, "I am prepared for all of their whips—prepared to suffer."

39 A Cry for Help

For the Pure and Shining One
A song of praising by King David[a]

1–2 Here's my life motto, the truth I live by:
I will guard my ways for all my days.
I will speak only what is right, guarding what I speak.
Like a watchman guards against an attack of the enemy,
I'll guard and muzzle my mouth
when the wicked are around me.
I will remain silent and will not grumble,
or speak out of my disappointment.
But the longer I'm silent my pain grows worse!
3–4 My heart burned with a fire within me,
and my thoughts eventually boiled over
until they finally came rolling out of my mouth.
"Lord, help me to know how fleeting my time on earth is.
Help me to know how limited is my life
and that I'm only here but for a moment more.
5 What a brief time you've given me to live![b]
Compared to you my lifetime is nothing at all!
Nothing more than a puff of air, I'm gone so swiftly.
And so too are the grandest of men;
They are nothing but a fleeting shadow!"

Pause in his presence

6 We live our lives like those living in shadows.[c]
All our activities and energies are spent for things that pass away.

---

a The Hebrew inscription includes the name *Jeduthun*, which can be translated praising.

b 39:5 Interestingly, the Hebrew word for *short* in this verse is "a handbreadth," or the span of a man's hand. Our life's duration is compared to a mere six-inch span!

c 39:6 Or "like phantoms going to and fro."

We gather, we hoard, we cling to our things,
only to leave them all behind for who knows who.
7 And now, God,[a] I'm left with one conclusion.
My only hope is to hope in you alone!
8 Save me from being overpowered by my sin;
don't make me a disgrace before the degenerate!
9 Lord, I'm left speechless and I have no excuse,
so I'll not complain any longer.
Now I know you're the One who is behind it all.
10 But I can't take it much longer.
Spare me these blows from your discipline-rod.
For if you are against me, I will waste away to nothing.
11 No one endures when you rebuke and discipline us for our sins.
Like a cobweb is swept away with a wave of the hand,
you sweep away all that we once called dear.
How fleeting and frail our lives!
We're nothing more than a puff of air.

Pause in his presence

12 Lord, listen to all my tender cries.
Read my every tear, like liquid words that plead for your help.
I feel all alone at times, like a stranger to you
passing through this life just like all those before me.
13 Don't let me die without restoring
joy and gladness to my soul.
May your frown over my failure
become a smile over my success.

---

a 39:7 The Aramaic is *Maryah*, the Aramaic form of YHWH or Lord Jehovah.

40 A Joyful Salvation

For the Pure and Shining One

A song of poetic praise by King David

1 I waited and waited and waited some more;
patiently, knowing God would come through for me.
Then, at last, he bent down and listened to my cry.
2 He stooped down to lift me out of danger
from the desolate pit I was in,
out of the muddy mess I had fallen into.
Now he's lifted me up into a firm, secure place
and steadied me while I walk along his ascending path.
3 A new song for a new day rises up in me
every time I think about how he breaks through for me!
Ecstatic praise pours out of my mouth until
everyone hears how God has set me free.
Many will see his miracles;
they'll stand in awe of God and fall in love with him!
4 Blessing after blessing comes to those who love and trust the Lord.
They will not fall away,
for they refuse to listen to the lies of the proud.
5 O Lord, our God, no one can compare with you.
Such wonderful works and miracles are all found with you!
And you think of us all the time
with your countless expressions of love—
far exceeding our expectations!
6 It's not sacrifices that really move your heart.
Burnt offerings, sin offerings—that's not what brings you joy.
But when you open my ears and speak deeply to me,

I become your willing servant, your prisoner of love for life.[a]
7 So I said: "Here I am! I'm coming *to you as a sacrifice,*[b]
for in the prophetic scrolls of your book
you have written about me.
8 I delight to fulfill your will, my God,
for your living words are written upon the pages of my heart."
9 I tell everyone everywhere the truth of your righteousness.
And you know I haven't held back in telling the message to all.
10 I don't keep it a secret, or hide the truth.
I preach of your faithfulness and kindness,
proclaiming your extravagant love to the largest crowd I can find!
11 So Lord, don't hold back your love or withhold
your tender mercies from me.
Keep me in your truth and let your compassion overflow to me
no matter what I face.
12 Evil surrounds me; problems greater than I can solve
come one after another.
Without you, I know I can't make it.
My sins are so many!
I'm so ashamed to lift my face to you.
For my guilt grabs me and stings my soul
until I am weakened and spent.
13 Please, Lord! Come quickly and rescue me!

---

a 40:6 The Septuagint is "a body you have prepared for me." The Hebrew says, "You have pierced my ear." This is a Hebraic reference to being a bond servant whose ear has been pierced by his master to signify a desire to serve for life. See Ex. 21:1–6, Isa. 50:5, and Heb. 10:5.

b 40:7 Implied in the context. See Heb. 10:5–7.

Take pleasure in showing me your favor and restore me.
14 Let all who seek my life be humiliated!
Let them be confused and ashamed, God.
Scatter those who wish me evil, they just want me dead.
15 Scoff at every scoffer and cause them all to be utter failures.
Let them be ashamed and horrified by their complete defeat.
16 But let all who passionately seek you
erupt with excitement and joy over what you've done!
Let all your lovers rejoice continually in the Savior[a] saying:
"How great and glorious is our God!"
17 Lord, in my place of weakness and need, I ask again:
Will you come and help me?
I know I'm always in your thoughts.
You are my true Savior and Hero,
so don't delay to deliver me now for you are my God.

41 I Need You, Lord

King David's poetic song for the Pure and Shining One

1 God always blesses those who are kind to the poor and helpless.
They're the first ones God helps
when they find themselves in any trouble.
2 The Lord will preserve and protect them.
They'll be honored and esteemed[b]
while their enemies are defeated.
3 When they are sick, God will restore them,
lying upon their bed of suffering.
He will raise them up again and restore them back to health.
4 So *in my sickness* I say to you,

---

a 40:16 This verse contains the root word for *Yeshua* in Hebrew.
b 41:2 Or "they will be blessed in the land."

"Lord, be my Kind Healer.
Heal my body and soul; heal me, God!
For I have confessed my sins to you."[a]
5 But those who hate me wish the worst for me, saying,
"When will he die and be forgotten?"
6 And when these "friends" come to visit me
with their pious sympathy and their hollow words
and with hypocrisy hidden in their hearts—
I can see right through it all.
For they come merely to gather gossip about me,
using all they find to mock me with malicious hearts of slander.
7 They are wicked whisperers who imagine the worst for me,
repeating their rumors, saying:
8 "He got what he deserved; it's over for him!
The spirit of infirmity[b] is upon him and
he'll never get over this illness."
9 Even my ally, my friend, has turned against me.
He was one I totally trusted with my life,
sharing supper with him,[c]
and now he shows me nothing but betrayal and treachery.
He has sold me as an enemy.[d]
10 So Lord, please don't desert me when I need you!
Give me grace and get me back on my feet
so I can triumph over them all.
11 Then I'll know you're pleased with me

---

a 41:4 Or "For I have sinned against you."

b 41:8 Or "a thing of Belial," or, "an affliction from the abandoned one."

c 41:9 In the culture of that day, sharing a meal together was a sign of covenant friendship.

d 41:9 The Hebrew literally reads, "He lifted up his heel against me." This is a powerful figure of speech meaning he was sold as an enemy and was treated treacherously. This verse was quoted, in part, by Jesus at the Last Supper (John 13:18).

when you allow me to taste of victory over all my foes.
12 Now stand up for me and don't let me fall,
for I've walked with integrity.
Keep me before your face forever.
13 Everyone praise the Lord God of Israel, always and forever!
For he is from eternity past
and will remain for the eternity to come.
That's the way it will be forever!
Faithful is our King! Amen![a]

BOOK 2

THE EXODUS PSALMS

Psalms of suffering and redemption

42 A Cry for Revival[b]

For the Pure and Shining One

A contemplative poem for instruction by the prophetic singers of Korah's clan[c]

1 I long to drink of you, O God,
drinking deeply from the streams of pleasure
flowing from your presence.
My longings overwhelm me for more of you![d]

---

a 41:13 Some scholars believe this last verse was added as a "doxology of praise," marking the end of the first book of Psalms. The word *Amen* means "Faithful is our King!"

b Ps. 42 and 43 were originally composed as one psalm and later made into two.

c Korah was the great-grandson of Levi. The sons of Korah were a family of Levitical singers. David chose them to preside over the music of the tabernacle-tent on Mount Zion.

d 42:1 The literal Hebrew is "as the deer pants for the riverbank (or water's edge)." The translation takes the metaphor of a hunted deer and

2 My soul thirsts, pants, and longs for the Living God.
I want to come and see the face of God.
3 Day and night my tears keep falling
and my heart keeps crying for your help
while my enemies mock me over and over, saying,
"Where is this God of yours? *Why doesn't he help you?*"
4 So I speak over my heartbroken soul,
"Take courage. Remember when you used to be
right out front leading the procession of praise
when the great crowd of worshipers
gathered to go into the presence of the Lord?
You shouted with joy as the sound of passionate
celebration
filled the air and the joyous multitude of lovers
honored the festival of the Lord!"
5 So then, my soul, why would you be depressed?
Why would you sink into despair?
Just keep hoping and waiting on God, your Savior.
For no matter what, I will still sing with praise,
for living before his face is my saving grace!
6 But here I am depressed and downcast.
Yet I will still remember you as I ponder the place
where your glory streams down from the mighty
mountaintops, lofty and majestic—*the mountains of your awesome presence.*[a]
7 My deep need calls out to the deep kindness of your love.
Your waterfall of weeping sent waves of sorrow
over my soul, carrying me away,

---

puts it into terms that transfer the meaning into today's context. David is describing the passion and longing he has that is yet unfulfilled.

a 42:6 The Hebrew text contains *Mount Hermon* and *Mount Mizar*, considered to be sacred mountains in the Hebrew culture. *Hermon* means lofty and majestic. *Mizar* means littleness.

cascading over me like a thundering cataract.
8 Yet all day long God's promises of love pour over me.
Through the night I sing his songs,
for my prayer to God has become my life.
9 I will say to God, "You are my Mountain of Strength;
how could you forget me?
Why must I suffer this vile oppression of my enemies—
these heartless tormentors who are out to kill me?"
10 Their wounding words pierce my heart
over and over while they say,
"Where is this God of yours?"
11 So I say to my soul,
"Don't be discouraged. Don't be disturbed.
For I know my God will break through for me."
Then I'll have plenty of reasons to praise him all over again.
Yes, living before his face is my saving grace!

43 Light and Truth

For the Pure and Shining One by the
prophetic singers of Korah's clan[a]
A contemplative poem for instruction

1 God, clear my name.
Plead my case against the unjust charges
of these ungodly workers of wickedness.
Deliver me from these lying degenerates.
2 For you are where my strength comes from[b] and my
Protector,
so why would you leave me now?
Must I be covered with gloom
while the enemy comes after me gloating with glee?

---

a Although there is no inscription for this psalm, it was originally part of Ps. 42.

b 43:2 Or "God of my strength."

3 Pour into me the brightness of your daybreak!
Pour into me your rays of revelation-truth!
Let them comfort and gently lead me onto the shining path,
showing the way into your burning presence,
into your many sanctuaries of holiness.
4 Then I will come closer to your very altar
until I come before you, the God of my ecstatic joy!
I will praise you with the harp that plays in my heart,
to you, my God, my magnificent God!
5 Then I will say to my soul,
"Don't be discouraged; don't be disturbed,
for I fully expect my Savior-God to break through for me.
Then I'll have plenty of reasons to praise him all over again."
Yes, living before his face is my saving grace!

44 Wake Up, Lord, We're in Trouble

For the Pure and Shining One by the prophetic singers of Korah's clan
A contemplative poem for instruction

The Past

1–2 God, we've heard about all the glorious miracles
you've done for our ancestors in days gone by.
They told us about the ancient times, how by your power
you drove out the ungodly nations from this land,
crushing all their strongholds, and giving the land to us.
Now the people of Israel cover the land
from one end to the other,
all because of your grace and power!
3 Our forefathers didn't win these battles by their own strength
or their own skill or strategy.
But it was through the shining forth of your radiant-presence

and the display of your mighty power.
You loved to give them victory,
for you took great delight in them.
4 You are my God, my King!
It's now time to decree majesties for Israel![a]
5 Through your glorious name and your awesome power
we can push through to any victory and defeat every enemy.
6 For I will not trust in the weapons of the world;[b]
I know they will never save me.
7 Only you will be our Savior from all our enemies.
All those who hate us you have brought to shame.
8 So now I constantly boast in you.
I can never thank you enough!

Pause in his presence

The Present

9 But you have turned your back on us; you walked off and left us!
You've rejected us, tossing us aside in humiliating shame.
You don't go before us anymore in our battles.
10 We retreat before our enemies in defeat,
for you are no longer helping us.
Those who hate us have invaded our land
and plundered our people.
11 You have treated us like sheep in the slaughter pen,
ready to be butchered.
You've scattered us to the four winds.
12 You have sold us as slaves for nothing!
You have counted us, your precious ones, as worthless.
13 You have caused our neighbors to despise and scorn us.

---

a 44:4 Or "Jacob."
b 44:6 Or "bow and sword."

All that are around us mock and curse us.
14 You have made us the butt of their jokes.
Disliked by all, we are the laughingstock of the people.
15–16 There's no escape from this constant curse, this humiliation!
We are despised, jeered, overwhelmed by shame,
and overcome at every turn
by our hateful and heartless enemies.
17 Despite all of this, we have not forgotten you;
we have not broken covenant with you.
18 We have not betrayed you; our hearts are still yours.
Our steps have not strayed from your path.
19 Yet you have crushed us,
leaving us in this wilderness place *of misery and desperation.*[a]
With nowhere else to turn,
death's dark door seems to be the only way out.
20–21 If we had forsaken your holy name, wouldn't you know it?
You'd be right in leaving us.
If we had worshiped before other gods,
no one would blame you for punishing us.
God, you know our every heart-secret.
You know we still want you!
22 Because of you we face death threats every day.
Like martyrs we are dying daily!
We are seen as lambs lined up to be slaughtered as sacrifices.

The Future

23 So wake up, Lord God!
Why would you sleep when we're in trouble?
Are you forsaking us forever?
24 You can't hide your face any longer from us!

---

a 44:19 Or "in this place of jackals."

How could you forget our agonizing sorrow?
25 Now we lay facedown, sinking into the dust of death,
the quicksand of the grave.
26 Arise, awake, and come to help us, O Lord.
Let your unfailing love save us from this sorrow!

45 The Wedding Song

For the Pure and Shining One by the prophetic singers of Korah's clan
A contemplative song of instruction for the Loved One
To the melody of "Lilies"[a]

1 My heart is on fire, boiling over with passion.
Bubbling up within me are these beautiful lyrics
as a lovely poem to be sung for the King!
Like a river bursting its banks, I'm overflowing with words,
spilling out into this sacred story.[b]

His Royal Majesty

2 Beautiful! Beautiful! Beyond the sons of men![c]
Elegant grace pours out through every word you speak.[d]
Truly, God has anointed you, his Favored One for eternity!
3 Now strap your lightning-sword of judgment upon your side,
O Mighty Warrior, so majestic!
You are full of beauty and splendor as you go out to war!
4 In your glory and grandeur go forth in victory!

---

a Lilies in the Bible are metaphors of God's precious people. See Song 2:1–2, Hos. 14:5, and Luke 12:27–28. Many believe this was the wedding song composed for Solomon as he married the princess of Egypt. But the language is so lofty and glorious that we see One greater than Solomon in its verses. This is a song of the wedding of Jesus and his Bride, the church.

b 45:1 The Hebrew is literally, "my tongue is the pen of a skillful (inspired) scribe."

c 45:2 Or "You are the most wonderful and winsome of all men."

d 45:2 See John 6:68 and 7:46.

Through your faithfulness and meekness
the cause of truth and justice will stand.
Awe-inspiring miracles are accomplished by your power,
leaving everyone dazed and astonished!
5 Your wounding leaves men's hearts defeated
as they fall before you broken.
6 Your glory-kingdom, O God, endures forever,
for you are enthroned to rule with a justice-scepter in your hand!
7 You are passionate for righteousness and you hate lawlessness.
This is why God, your God,
crowns you with bliss above your fellow-kings.
He has anointed you, more than any other,
with his oil of fervent joy,
the very fragrance of heaven's gladness.
8 Your royal robes release the scent of suffering love for your bride;[a]
the odor of aromatic incense is upon you.[b]
From the pure and shining place[c] such lovely music
that makes you glad is played for your pleasure.

Her Royal Majesty

9 The daughters of kings, women of honor,
are maidens in your courts.
And standing beside you,

---

a 45:8 The Hebrew word *myrrh* is taken from a root word that means suffering. Jewish Rabbis refer to myrrh as "tears from a tree," a symbol of suffering love.

b 45:8 The text reads, "aloes and cassia." They both are equated with the anointing spice, the incense burned in the Holy Place.

c 45:8 Or "from the ivory palaces." This is an obvious reference to the Holy Place, as our High Priest comes from the chamber of glory to be with us. The word *ivory* is taken from a Hebrew word for white and glistening.

glistening in your pure and golden glory,
is the beautiful bride-to-be![a]
10 Now listen, daughter, pay attention, and forget about your past.
Put behind you every attachment to the familiar,
even those who once were close to you!
11 For your Royal Bridegroom is ravished by your beautiful brightness.
Bow in reverence before him, for he is your Lord!
12 Wedding presents pour in from those of great wealth.[b]
The royal friends of the Bridegroom shower you with gifts.
13 As the princess-bride enters the palace,
how glorious she appears within the holy chamber,
robed with a wedding dress embroidered with pure gold!
14 Lovely and stunning she leads the procession with all her bridesmaids[c]
as they come before you, her Bridegroom-King.
15 What a grand, majestic entrance!
A joyful, glad procession as they enter the palace gates!
16 Your many sons will one day be kings, just like their Father.
They will sit on royal thrones all around the world.
17 I will make sure the fame of your name
is honored in every generation as all the people praise you,
giving you thanks forever and ever!

46 God on Our Side!

For the Pure and Shining One by the prophetic singers of Korah's clan
A poetic song to the melody of "Hidden Things"[d]

1 God, you're such a safe and powerful place to find refuge!

---

a 45:9 Or "queen."
b 45:12 The Hebrew text is literally "the daughter of Tyre." This was symbolic of the merchants of the earth, those possessing great wealth.
c 45:14 Or "virgins." See Rev. 14:1–4 and 2 Cor. 11:2.
d As translated in the Septuagint. Other versions read, "for the Maidens."

You're a proven help in time of trouble—
more than enough and always available whenever I need you.
2 So we will never fear
even if every structure of support[a] were to crumble away.
We will not fear even when the earth quakes and shakes,
moving mountains and casting them into the sea.
3 For the raging roar of stormy winds and crashing waves
cannot erode our faith in you.

Pause in his presence

4 God has a constantly flowing river whose sparkling streams
bring joy and delight to his people!
His river flows right through the city of God-Most-High,
into his holy dwelling places.[b]
5 God is in the midst of his city,[c] secure and never shaken.
At daybreak his help will be seen with the appearing of the dawn.
6 When the nations are in uproar with their tottering kingdoms,
God simply raises his voice
and the earth begins to disintegrate before him!
7 *Here he comes*!
The Commander!
The mighty Lord of Angel-Armies is on our side!
The God of Jacob fights for us!

Pause in his presence

Ps. 46 is known as one of the Songs of Zion. The others are psalms 48, 76, 84, 87, and 122. These are psalms which praise Jerusalem as God's dwelling place.

a 46:2 Or "earth itself."

b 46:4 The plural "dwelling places" points to believers today. Each believer is now the holy dwelling place of God. God's river flows into us and through us.

c 46:5 This is a reference to Jerusalem, but today God calls his church a *city* on a hill.

8–9 Everyone look!
Come and see the breathtaking wonders of our God.
For he brings *both* ruin *and revival.*
And he's the One who makes conflicts to end
throughout the earth,
breaking and burning every weapon of war.
10 Surrender your anxiety![a]
Be silent and stop your striving and you will see that I am God.
I am the God above all the nations,
and I will be exalted throughout the whole earth.
11 Here he stands!
The Commander!
The Mighty Lord of Angel-Armies is on our side!
The God of Jacob fights for us!

Pause in his presence

47 The King of All the Earth

For the Pure and Shining One by the prophetic singers of Korah's clan
A poetic song

1 Go ahead and celebrate!
Come on and clap your hands everyone!
Shout to God with the raucous sounds of joy!
2 The Lord God Most High is astonishing, awesome beyond words!
He's the formidable and powerful King over all the earth.
3 He's the One who conquered the nations before us
and placed them all under our feet.
4 He's marked out our inheritance ahead of time,
putting us in the front of the line, honoring those he loves.[b]

Pause in his presence

---

a 46:10 The Septuagint reads, "relax."
b Or "the pride of Jacob." The Septuagint says: "the beauty of Jacob."

5 God arises with the earsplitting shout of his people!
God goes up with a trumpet blast!
6 Sing and celebrate! Sing some more, celebrate some more!
Sing your highest song of praise to our King!
7 For God is the Triumphant King; the powers of earth are all his.
So sing your celebration songs of highest praise
to the Glorious Enlightened One!
8 Our God reigns over every nation!
He reigns on his holy throne over all.
9 All the nobles and princes,
the loving servants of the God of Abraham,
they all gather to worship.
Every warrior's shield is now lowered
as surrendered trophies before this King.
He has taken his throne, high and lofty exalted over all!

48 Beautiful Zion

A poetic song, for the prophetic singers of Korah's clan

1 There are so many reasons to describe God as wonderful!
So many reasons to praise him with unlimited praise![a]
2 Zion-City is his home; he lives on his holy mountain—
high and glorious, joy-filled and favored.
Zion-Mountain looms in the farthest reaches of the north,[b]
the city of our incomparable King!
3 This is his divine abode, an impenetrable citadel,
for he is known to dwell in the highest place.
4–6 See how the mighty kings united to come against Zion,
yet when they saw God manifest in front of their eyes,

---

a 48:1 This psalm was written to commemorate the defeat of the Assyrian army in the days of King Hezekiah.

b 48:2 Or "the sides of the north," a metaphor to describe God's heavenly home. See also Isa. 14:13.

they were stunned.
Trembling, they all fled away gripped with fear.[a]
Seized with panic, they doubled up in frightful anguish
like a woman in the labor pains of childbirth.
7 Like a hurricane blowing and breaking the invading ships,[b]
God blows upon them and breaks them to pieces.
8 We have heard about these wonders,
and then we saw them with our own eyes.
For this is the city of the Commander of Angel-Armies,
the city of our God, safe and secure forever!

Pause in his presence

9 Lord, as we worship you in your temple,
we recall over and over your kindness to us
and your unending love.
10 The fame of your name echoes throughout the entire world
accompanied with praises!
Your right hand is full of victory.
11 So let the people of Zion rejoice with gladness;
let the daughters of praise leap for joy![c]
For God will see to it that you are judged fairly.
12–13 Circle Zion; count her towers.
Consider her walls; climb her palaces,
and then go and tell the coming generation
of the care and compassion of our God.
14 Yes, this is our God, our great God forever.
He will lead us onward until the end,
through all time, beyond death,
and into eternity!

---

a 48:4–6 This no doubt refers to the night the angel of the Lord descended into the ranks of the Assyrians and killed 185,000 men. See Isa. 37:36.
b 48:7 Or "ships of Tarshish."
c 48:11 Or "the daughters of Judah."

49 Wisdom Better Than Wealth

For the Pure and Shining One
A poetic song by the prophetic singers of Korah's clan

1–2 Listen one and all!
Both rich and poor together, all over the world—
everyone listen to what I have to say!
3 For wisdom will come from my mouth,
words of insight and understanding will be heard
from the musings of my heart.
4 I will break open mysteries with my music,
and my song will release riddles solved.
5 There's no reason to fear when troubling times come,
even when you're surrounded with problems
and persecutors who chase at your heels.[a]
6–7 They trust in their treasures and boast in their riches,
yet not one of them, though rich as a king,
could rescue his own brother from the guilt of his sins.
Not one could give God the ransom price
for the soul of another, let alone for himself!
8–9 A soul's redemption is too costly and precious
for anyone to pay with earthly wealth.
The price to pay is never enough
to purchase eternal life for even one, to keep them out of hell.
10–11 The brightest and best, along with the foolish and senseless,
God sees that they all will die one day,
leaving their houses and wealth to others.
Even though they name streets and lands after themselves,[b]

---

a 49:5 This phrase contains a variant form of the name *Jacob*, which means heel-grabber.
b 49:10–11 Or "they read their names in the ground."

hoping to have their memory endure beyond the grave,
legends in their own minds,
their home address is now the cemetery!
12 The honor of man is short-lived and fleeting.
There's so little difference between man and beast
for both will one day perish.
13 Such is the path of foolish men
and those who quote everything they say,
for they are here today and gone tomorrow!

Pause in his presence

14 A shepherd called "Death" herds them,
leading them like mindless sheep straight to hell.
Yet at daybreak you will find the righteous ruling in their place.
Every trace of them will be gone forever
with all their "glory" lost in the darkness of their doom.
15 But I know the loving God will redeem my soul,
raising me up from the dark power of death,
taking me as his bridal partner.[a]

Pause in his presence

16 So don't be disturbed when you see the rich
surround you with the "glory" of their wealth on full display.
17 For when they die they will carry nothing with them,
and their riches will not follow them beyond the grave.
18–19 Though they have the greatest rewards of this world
and all applaud them for their accomplishments,
they will follow those who have gone before them
and go straight into the realm of darkness
where they never ever see the light again.

---

a 49:15 Or "He will offer his hand to me in marriage."

20 So this is the way of mortal man—
honored for a moment, yet without eternal insight
like a beast that will one day perish.

50 God Has Spoken

A poetic song of Asaph, the gatherer[a]

1 The God of gods, the mighty Lord himself, has spoken!
He shouts out over all the people of the earth
in every brilliant sunrise and every beautiful sunset,
saying, "Listen to me!"
2 God's glory-light shines out of the Zion-realm[b]
with the radiance of perfect beauty.
3 With the rumble of thunder he approaches;
He will not be silent, for he comes with an earsplitting sound!
All around him are furious flames of fire,
and preceding him is the dazzling blaze of his glory.
4 Here he comes to judge his people!
He summons his court with heaven and earth as his jury, saying:
5 "Gather all my lovers,
my godly ones whose hearts are one with me—
those who have entered into my holy covenant
by sacrifices upon the altar."
6 And the heavens declare his justice:
"God himself will be their Judge,
And he will judge them with righteousness!"

Pause in his presence

---

a Asaph's name means gatherer. Like David, Asaph was anointed with the spirit of prophecy and wrote twelve psalms (Ps. 50 and 73–83).

b 50:2 The Aramaic text can be translated, "Out of Zion God has shown a glorious crown."

7 Listen to me, O my people! Listen well, for I am your God!
I am bringing you to trial and here are my charges.[a]
8 I do not rebuke you for your sacrifices,
which you continually bring to my altar.
9 Do I need your young bull or goats from your fields
as if I was hungry?
10–11 Every animal of field and forest belongs to me, the Creator.
I know every movement of the birds in the sky,
and every animal of the field is in my thoughts.
The entire world and everything it contains is mine.
12–13 If I were hungry do you think I would tell you?
For all that I have created, the fullness of the earth, is mine.
Am I fed by your sacrifices? Of course not!
14 Why don't you bring me the sacrifices I desire?
Bring me your true and sincere thanks,
and show your gratitude by keeping your promises to me,
the Most High.
15 Honor me by trusting in me in your day of trouble.
Cry aloud to me, and I will be there to rescue you.
16 And now I speak to the wicked. Listen to what I have to say to you!
What right do you have to presume to speak for me
and claim my covenant promises as yours?
17 For you have hated my instruction, and disregarded my words,
throwing them away as worthless!
18 You forget to condemn the thief or adulterer.
You are their friend, running alongside them into darkness!
19–20 The sins of your mouth multiply evil!
You have a lifestyle of lies,

---

a 50:7 This summons to judgment is not against the heathen nations, but against God's people. See 1 Peter 4:17.

devoted to deceit as you speak against others,
even slandering those of your own household!
21 All this you have done and I kept silent,
so you thought that I was just like you, sanctioning evil.
But now I will bring you to my courtroom
and spell out clearly my charges before you!
22 This is your last chance; my final warning! Your time is up!
Turn away from all this evil, or *the next time you hear from me it will be when* I am coming to pass sentence upon you.
I will snatch you away and no one will be there
to help you escape my judgment!
23 The life that pleases me is a life lived in the gratitude of grace,
always choosing to walk with me in what is right.
This is the sacrifice I desire from you!
If you do this, more of my salvation will unfold for you!

51 Pardon and Purity

For the Pure and Shining One
A prayer of confession when the prophet Nathan exposed King David's adultery with Bathsheba[a]

David's Confession

1–2 God, give me mercy from your fountain of forgiveness!
I know your abundant love is enough to wash away my guilt.
Because your compassion is so great,
take away this shameful guilt of sin.
Forgive the full extent of my rebellious ways,

---

a This psalm is based on the incident that is recorded in 2 Sam. 12–13. This is a psalm of confession that has been sung for ages. Imagine composing a song about your failure and making it public for all time. David was not so much concerned about what the people thought, but what God thought. He wanted to be clean before God.

and erase this deep stain on my conscience.[a]
3–4 For I'm so ashamed.
I feel such pain and anguish within me
I can't get away from the sting of my sin against you, Lord!
Everything I did, I did right in front of you, for you saw it all.
Against you, and you above all, have I sinned.
Everything you say to me is infallibly true
and your judgment conquers me.
5 Lord, I have been a sinner from birth,
from the moment my mother conceived me.
6 I know that you delight to set your truth deep in my spirit.[b]
So come into the hidden places of my heart
and teach me wisdom.

David's Cleansing

7 Purify my conscience! Make this leper clean again![c]
Wash me in your love until I am pure in heart.[d]
8 Satisfy me in your sweetness, and my song of joy will return.
The places within me you have crushed
will rejoice in your healing touch.[e]

---

a 51:1–2 Or "Wash me." David uses the Hebrew word *kabas* which is used for washing clothes, not bathing. David is asking for his royal robes to be cleansed from the stains of his actions and publicly restored.

b 51:6 The Hebrew word *bat-ṭūhôt,* although difficult to translate, can mean "something that is covered over, hidden, or concealed." You could paraphrase this as, "You desire light in my darkness," or "You want truth to expose my secrets."

c 51:7 The Hebrew text contains the word *hyssop*. This was a bushy plant used for sprinkling blood on a healed leper to ceremonially cleanse him for the worship of God. See Lev. 14:3–7 and Num. 19.

d 51:7 Or "Wash me with the snow from above so I can be whitened."

e 51:9 In this beautiful verse, the "broken places" are literally "broken bones." Our bones speak allegorically of our inner being, our emotional strength.

9 Hide my sins from your face;[a]
erase all my guilt by your saving grace.
10 Create a new, clean heart within me.[b]
Fill me with pure thoughts and holy desires, ready to please you.[c]
11 May you never reject me!
May you never take from me your Sacred Spirit!

David's Consecration

12 Let my passion for life be restored,
tasting joy[d] in every breakthrough you bring to me.
Hold me close to you with a willing spirit
that obeys whatever you say.
13 Then I can show to other guilty ones
how loving and merciful you are.
They will find their way back home to you,
knowing that you will forgive them.
14 O God, my saving God,
deliver me fully from every sin,
even the sin that brought blood-guilt.[e]
Then my heart will once again be thrilled to sing

---

a 51:9 David was not just ashamed of what others would think, but that he had been seen by God. True remorse has no thought about reputation, but righteousness.

b 51:10 The word used for *create* takes us back to Gen. 1, and it means to create from nothing. David now knows he had no goodness without God placing it within him. David wanted a new creation heart, not just the old one changed.

c 51:10 Or "renew a reliable spirit in my inner being."

d 51:12 The Hebrew word for *joy* comes from two Hebrew roots, one means "bright" and the other means "lily (whiteness)." David wanted to taste a joy that was bright, pure, and beautiful as a lily.

e 51:14 Or simply "blood." David could be asking God to spare his life from death (Lit. "blood," that is, deliverance from death because of his sin).

the passionate songs of joy and deliverance!
15 Lord God, unlock my heart, unlock my lips,
and I will overcome with my joyous praise!
16 For the source of your pleasure is not in my performance
or the sacrifices I might offer to you.
17 The fountain of your pleasure is found
in the sacrifice of my shattered heart before you.
You will not despise my tenderness
as I humbly bow down at your feet!
18 Because you favor Zion, do what is good for her.
Be the protecting wall around Jerusalem.
19 And when we are fully restored,
you will rejoice and take delight
in every offering of our lives
as we bring our sacrifices of righteousness before you in love![a]

52 The Fate of Cynics

For the Pure and Shining One

A song of instruction by King David composed when Doeg, the Edomite, betrayed David to Saul, saying: "David has come to the house of Ahimilech!"[b]

1 You call yourself a mighty man, a big shot?
Then why do you boast in the evil you have done?
Yet God's loyal love will protect me and carry the day!
2 Listen, O deceiver, trickster of others:

---

a 51:19 Or "Then they will offer up bulls on your altar."

b For this episode in David's life, see 1 Sam. 21:1–9; 22:9–23. The Edomites, although close relatives to the Hebrews, were bitter enemies to God's people. In spite of Doeg's lineage, he became a high ranking official in Saul's kingdom. Herod the Great, who slaughtered the babes of Bethlehem, was an Edomite. At the time David wrote this psalm, Saul had already attempted to kill him sixteen times. Ahimilech, the caretaker of the sword of Goliath, was a descendant of Eli.

Your words are wicked, harming and hurting all who hear
them!
3 You love evil and hate what is good and right.
You would rather lie than tell the truth.

Pause in his presence

4 You love to distort, devour, and deceive,
using your sly tongue to spin the truth.
5 But the Almighty will strike you down forever!
He will pull you up by your roots
and drag you away to the darkness of death.

Pause in his presence

6 The godly will see all this and will be awestruck.
Then they will laugh at the wicked, saying,
7 "See what happens to those great in their own eyes
who don't trust in the Most High to save them!
Look how they trusted only in their wealth
and made their living from wickedness."[a]
8 But I am like a flourishing olive tree, *anointed* in the house of
God.[b]
I trust in the unending love of God;
his passion toward me is forever and ever.
9 Because it is finished[c]
I will be praising you forever and giving you thanks!
Before all your godly lovers I will proclaim your beautiful
name!

---

a 52:2 Or "and was strong in his destruction."

b 52:8 The olive tree was the source of the sacred anointing oil.

c 52:9 Or "You have acted (finished it)." The words "It is finished" were the last words of Jesus on the cross.

53 The Wickedness of the World

For the Pure and Shining One
A contemplative song of instruction to the tune of "The Dancings of Mourning"[a]

1 Only the withering soul would say to himself,[b]
"There's no God for me!"
Anyone who thinks like that is corrupt and callous;
depraved and detestable, they are devoid of what is good.
2 The Lord looks down in love, bending over heaven's balcony.
God looks over all of Adam's sons and daughters,
looking to see if there are any who are wise with insight—
any who search for him, wanting to please him.
3 But no, all have wandered astray, walking stubbornly toward evil.
Not one is good; he can't even find one!
4 Look how they live in luxury while exploiting my people.
Won't these workers of wickedness ever learn!
They never even think of praying to God.
5 Soon, unheard-of terror will seize them while in their sins.
God himself will one day scatter the bones
of those who rose up against you.[c]

---

a Or "The Dance of Mourning." This could have been a footnote to Ps. 52 instead of an inscription for Ps. 53. If so, read Ps. 52 and imagine the dancing that broke loose when David and his mighty men knew that Doeg had been judged by God for his murderous betrayal.

b 53:1 The word for *fool* comes from a Hebrew word meaning "withering." If we make no room for God, we have a withered heart; and our moral sense of righteousness is put to sleep, and the noble aspirations of the heart shrivel up and die. Ps. 53 clearly speaks of the downfall of those who oppose Israel. Ps. 14 and Ps. 53 are nearly similar psalms. Ps. 14 deals with God's verdict, while Ps. 53 speaks of God's vengeance. If God says it once, it is to believed. If he says it twice, it demands our utmost attention!

c 53:5 This could refer to the scattering of the armies of Sennacherib in

Doomed and rejected they will be put to shame,
for God has despised them!
6 Oh, I wish our time of rescue were already here.
Oh, that God would come forth now—[a]
arising from the midst of his Zion-people
to save and restore his very own.
What gladness and joy will break forth
when the Lord has rescued Israel!

54 Defend Me

For the Pure and Shining One, David's contemplative song of instruction
A song of derision[b] when the Ziphites betrayed David to Saul, saying: "David is hiding among us, come and get him!"

1 God, deliver me by your mighty name!
Come with your glorious power and save me!
2 Listen to my prayer; turn your ears to my cry!
3 These violent men have risen up against me;
heartless, ruthless men[c] who care nothing about God—
they seek to take my life.

Pause in his presence

4 But the Lord God has become my divine Helper!.
He leans into my heart and lays his hands upon me![d]

---

the days of Hezekiah. See 2 Kings 18–19.

a This is considered to be an ecphonesis, a rhetorical literary device that amplifies the emotion of the text. It is equivalent to an emotional outburst! Clearly, this is a passionate psalm.

b The Hebrew word used here and translated in some versions as *stringed instrument* can also be rendered *a song of mocking*. This is a psalm for anyone who feels betrayed, rejected, and in a difficult situation with no one at your side.

c 54:3 Or "foreigners."

d 54:4 The word used here is *uphold* or *sustain*. It comes from a root word that means to lean upon or to lay hands upon. The translation uses both concepts in this verse.

5 God will see to it that those who sow evil will reap evil.
So Lord, in your great faithfulness, destroy them once and for all!
6 Lord, I will offer myself freely, and everything I am I give to you.
I will worship and praise your name, O Lord,
for it is precious to me.
7 Through you I'm saved—rescued from every trouble.
I've seen with my eyes the defeat of my enemies.
I've triumphed over them all!

55 Betrayed

To the Pure and Shining One
King David's song of derision, for instruction

1 God, listen to my prayer!
Don't hide your heart from me when I cry out to you!
2–3 Come close to me and give me your answer.
Here I am, moaning and restless.
I'm preoccupied with the threats of my enemies
and crushed by the pressure of their opposition.
They surround me with trouble and terror.
In their fury they rise up against me in an angry uproar.
4 My heart is trembling inside my chest
as the terror of death seizes me.
5 Fear and dread overwhelm me. I shudder before the horror I face.
6 I say to myself, "If only I could fly away from all of this!
If only I could run away to the place of rest and peace.
7 I would run far away where no one could find me,
escaping to a wilderness retreat."

Pause in his presence

8 I will hurry off to hide in the higher place,
into my Shelter, safe from this raging storm and tempest.
9 God, confuse them until they quarrel with themselves.

Destroy them with their own violent strife and slander!
They have divided the city with their discord.
10 Though they patrol the walls night and day against invaders,
the real danger is within the city!
It's the misery and strife in the heart of its people.
11 Murder is in their midst.
Wherever you turn you find trouble and ruin.
12 It wasn't an enemy who taunted me.
If it was my enemy, filled with pride and hatred,
then I could have endured it. I would have just run away.
13 But it was you, my intimate friend—one like a brother to me.
It was you, my advisor,[a] the companion
I walked with and worked with!
14 We once had sweet fellowship with each other.
We worshiped in unity as one,
celebrating together with God's people.[b]
15 Now desolation and darkness come upon you.
May you and all those like you descend into the pit of destruction!
Since evil has been your home, may evil now bury you alive!
16 But as for me, I will call upon the Lord to save me, and I know he will!
17 Every evening I will explain my need to him.
Every morning I will move my soul toward him.
Every waking hour I will worship only him,
and he will hear and respond to my cry.

---

a 55:13 The Greek word in the Septuagint can be translated as a seer (prophet).

b 55:14 David is speaking of Ahithophel who had once been his friend and advisor, only to betray him. This is foreshadowing of what happened between Jesus and Judas.

18 Though many wish to fight and the tide of battle turns against me,
by your power I will be safe and secure;
peace will be my portion.
19 God himself will hear me!
God-Enthroned through everlasting ages,
the God of Unchanging Faithfulness,
he will put them in their place,
all those who refuse to love and revere him!

Pause in his presence

20 I was betrayed by my friend, though I live in peace with him.
While he was stretching out his hand of friendship,
he was secretly breaking every promise he had ever made to me!
21 His words were smooth and so charming.
Yet his heart was disloyal and full of hatred—
his words so soft as silk while all the time scheming my demise.
22 So here's what I've learned through it all:
Leave all your cares and anxieties at the feet of the Lord,
and measureless grace will strengthen you.
23 He will watch over his lovers,
never letting them slip or be overthrown.
He will send all my enemies to the pit of destruction.
Murderers, liars, and betrayers will face an untimely death.
My life's hope and trust is in you, and you'll never fail to rescue me!

56 Trusting in God

For the Pure and Shining One
King David's golden song of instruction composed when the Philistines captured him in Gath To the tune "The Oppression of the Princes to Come" [a]

1 Lord, show me Your kindness and mercy,
for these men oppose and oppress me all day long.
2 Not a day goes by but that somebody harasses me.
So many in their pride trample me under their feet. [b]
3 But in the day that I'm afraid, I lay all my fears before you
and trust in you with all my heart.
4 What harm could a man bring to me?
With God on my side I will not be afraid of what comes.
The roaring praises of God fill my heart,
and I will always triumph as I trust his promises.
5 Day after day cruel critics distort my words;
constantly they plot my collapse.
6 Lurking in the dark, waiting, spying on my movements in secret
to take me by surprise, ready to take my life.
7 They don't deserve to get away with this!
Look at their wickedness, their injustice, Lord!
In your fierce anger cast them down to defeat!
8 You've kept track of all my wandering and my weeping.
You've stored my many tears in your bottle—not one will be lost.
For it is all recorded in your book of remembrance. [c]
9 The very moment I call to you for a Father's help
the tide of battle turns and my enemies flee!

---

a Or "the distant dove of silence."
b 56:2 The Septuagint says, "they war with me in the high places."
c 56:8 See also Mal. 3:16.

This one thing I know: God is on my side!
10 I trust in the Lord. And I praise him!
I trust in the Word of God. And I praise him!
11 What harm could man do to me?
With God on my side I will not be afraid of what comes.
My heart overflows with praise to God and for his promises.
I will always trust in him.
12 So I'm thanking you with all my heart,
with gratitude for all you've done.
I will do everything I've promised you, Lord.
13 For you have saved my soul from death
and my feet from stumbling
so that I can walk before the Lord
bathed in his life-giving light.

57 Triumphant Faith

To the Pure and Shining One
King David's golden song of instruction composed when he hid from Saul
in a cave[a]
To the tune "Do Not Destroy"

1 Please God, show me mercy!
Open your grace-fountain for me,
for you are my soul's true Shelter.
I will hide beneath the shadow of your embrace,
under the wings of your cherubim
until this terrible trouble is past.
2 I will cry out to you, the God of the highest heaven,
the mighty God, who performs all these wonders for me.
3 From heaven he will *send a Father's help to* save me.

---

a This incident is recorded in 1 Sam. 24.

He will trample down those who trample me.

Pause in his presence

For he will always show me love
by his gracious and constant care.
4 I am surrounded by these fierce and brutal men.
They are like lions just wanting to tear me to shreds.
Why must I continue to live among these seething terrorists,
breathing out their angry threats and insults against me?
5 Lord God, be exalted as you soar throughout the heavens.
May your shining glory be seen in the skies!
Let it be seen high above over all the earth!
6 For they have set a trap[a] for me.
Frantic fear has me overwhelmed.
But look! The very trap they set for me
has sprung shut upon themselves instead of me!

Pause in his presence

7 My heart, O God, is quiet and confident.
Now I can sing with passion your wonderful praises!
8 Awake, O my soul, with the music of his splendor-song!
Arise my soul and sing his praises!
My worship will awaken the dawn,
greeting the daybreak with my songs *of light*!
9 Wherever I go I will thank you, my God.
Among all the nations they will hear my praise songs to you.
10 Your love is so extravagant it reaches to the heavens!
Your faithfulness so astonishing it stretches to the sky!
11 Lord God, be exalted as you soar throughout the heavens.
May your shining glory be shown in the skies!
Let it be seen high above all the earth!

---

a 57:6 The Septuagint says, "They have dug a cesspool in front of me."

58 Judge of the Judges

For the Pure and Shining One
King David's golden song of instruction
To the tune "Do Not Destroy"

1–2 God's justice? You high and mighty politicians
know nothing about it!
Which one of you has walked in justice toward others?
Which one of you has treated everyone right and fair?
Not one! You only give "justice" in exchange for a bribe.
For the right price you let others get away with murder.
3–4 Wicked wanderers even from the womb! That's who you
are!
Lying with your words, your teaching is poison.[a]
5 Like cobras closing their ears to the most expert of the
charmers,
you strike out against all who are near.
6 O God, break their fangs;
shatter the teeth of these ravenous lions!
7 Let them disappear like water falling on thirsty ground.
Let all their weapons be useless.
8 Let them be like snails dissolving into the slime.
Let them be cut off, never seeing the light of day!
9 God will sweep them away so fast
that they'll never know what hit them.[b]
10 The godly will celebrate in the triumph of good over evil.
And the lovers of God will trample
the wickedness of the wicked under their feet!

---

a 58:3–4 The Hebrew says "venom of a serpent," which is a clear metaphor for wrong teaching.

b 58:9 The Hebrew here is recognized by nearly every scholar to be one of the most difficult verses in the Psalms to translate.

11 Then everyone will say, "There is a God who judges the
judges";
and "there is a great reward in loving God!"

59 Protect Me

For the Pure and Shining One
King David's song of instruction composed when Saul set an ambush for him
at his home[a]
To the tune "Do Not Destroy"

1 My God, protect me!
Keep me safe from all my enemies for they're coming to
kill me.
Put me in a high place out of their reach—
a place so high that these assassins will never find me.
2 Save me from these murdering men, these bloodthirsty
killers.
3 See how they set an ambush for my life.
They're fierce men ready to launch their attack against me.
O Lord, I'm innocent, *protect me*!
4 I've done nothing to deserve this,
yet they are already plotting together to kill me.
Arise, Lord, see what they're scheming and come and meet
with me.
5 Awaken, O God of Israel!
Commander of Angel-Armies,
arise to punish these treacherous people who oppose you!
Don't go soft on these hardcase killers!

Pause in his presence

6 After dark they came to spy, sneaking around the city,
snarling, prowling like a pack of stray dogs in the night—
7 Boiling over with rage, shouting out their curses,

---

a This incident is recorded in 1 Sam. 19:11–18.

convinced that they'll never get caught.
8 But you, Lord, break out laughing at their plans,
amused by their arrogance, scoffing at their sinful ways.
9 My strength is found when I wait upon you.
Watch over me, God, for you are my Mountain Fortress;
you set me on high!
10 The God of passionate love will meet with me.
My God will empower me to rise in triumph over my foes.
11 Don't kill them; stagger them all with a vivid display of power.
And scatter them with your armies of angels,
O mighty God, our Protector!
Use your awesome power to make them wanderers and vagabonds
and then bring them down.
12 They are nothing but proud, cursing liars.
They sin in every word they speak, boasting in their blasphemies!
13 May your wrath be kindled to destroy them; finish them off!
Make an end of them and their deeds until they are no more!
Let them all know and learn
that God is the Ruler over his people,[a]
the God-King over all the earth!

Pause in his presence

14 Here they come again!
Prowling, growling like a pack of stray dogs in the city
15 Drifting, devouring, and coming in for the kill.
They refuse to sleep until they've eaten their full.
16 But as for me, your strength shall be my song of joy.
At each and every sunrise, my lyrics of your love will fill the air!

---

a 59:13 The Hebrew is literally "God of Jacob."

For you have been my Glory-Fortress,
a Stronghold in my day of distress.
17 O my Strength, I sing with joy your praises.
O my Stronghold, I sing with joy your song!
O my Savior, I sing with joy the lyrics of your faithful love for me!

60 Has God Forgotten Us?

To the Pure and Shining One
King David's poem for instruction[a] *composed when he fought against the Syrians with the outcome still uncertain and Joab turned back to kill 12,000 descendants of Esau in the Valley of Salt*
To the tune of "Lily of the Covenant"

1 God, it seemed like you walked off and left us!
Why have you turned against us?
You have been angry with us.
O Lord, we plead, come back and help us *as a Father.*
2 The earth quivers and quakes before you,
splitting open and breaking apart.
Now come and heal it, for it is shaken to its depths.
3 You have taught us hard lessons
and made us drink the wine of bewilderment.
4 You have given miraculous signs to those who love you.
As we follow you we fly the flag of truth,
and all who love the truth will rally to it.

Pause in his presence

5 Come to your beloved ones and gently draw us out!
For Lord, you save those whom you love.
Come with your might and strength!
6–7 Then I heard the Lord speak in his holy splendor,

---

a Or "According to Shushan Eduth. A Mikhtam of David, to teach." There is no scholary consensus about what Shushan Eduth means. Some have concluded it refers to a specific tune or possibly an instrument, but it remains a mystery.

from his sanctuary I heard the Lord promise:
"In my triumph I will be the One to measure out
the portion of my inheritance to my people,
and I will secure the land as I promised you.
Shechem, Succoth, Gilead, Manasseh;
they are all still mine!" he says.
"Judah will continue to produce kings and lawgivers;
and Ephraim will produce great warriors.
8 Moab will become my lowly servant!
Edom will likewise serve my purposes!
I will lift up a shout of victory over the land of Philistia!
9 But who will bring my triumph into the strong city?
Who will lead me into Edom's fortresses?" [a]
10 Have you really rejected us, refusing to fight our battles?
11 Give us a Father's help when we face our enemies.
For to trust in any man is an empty hope.
12 With God's help we will fight like heroes
and he will trample down our every foe!

61 Prayer For Protection

To the Pure and Shining One
A song for the guitar by King David

1 O God, hear my prayer. Listen to my heart's cry.
2 For no matter where I am, even when I'm far from home,
I will cry out to you for a Father's help.
When I'm feeble and overwhelmed by life,
guide me into your glory where I am safe and sheltered.
3 Lord, you are a paradise of protection to me.
You lift me high above the fray.
None of my foes can touch me
when I'm held firmly in your wrap-around presence!
4 Keep me in this glory.

---

a 60:9 *Edom* is a variant form of the word *Adam*.

Let me live continually under your splendor-shadow,
hiding my life in you forever.

Pause in his presence

5 You have heard my sweet resolutions
to love and serve you, for I am your beloved.
And you have given me an inheritance of rich treasures,
which you give to all your lovers.
6 You treat me like a king, giving me a full and abundant life,
years and years of reigning,[a]
like many generations rolled into one.
7 I will live enthroned with you forever!
Guard me, God, with your unending, unfailing love.
Let me live my days walking in grace and truth before you.
8 And my praises will fill the heavens forever,
fulfilling my vow to make every day a love gift to you!

62 Unshakable Faith

To the Pure and Shining One
King David's melody of love's celebration[b]

1 I stand silently to listen for the One I love,
waiting as long as it takes for the Lord to rescue me.
For God alone has become my Savior.
2 He alone is my Safe Place;
his wrap-around presence always protects me.
For he is my Champion Defender;
there's no risk of failure with God.
So why would I let worry paralyze me,
even when troubles multiply around me?
3 But look at these who want me dead,
shouting their vicious threats at me!

---

a 61:6 Or "add to the days of the king."
b The inscription includes the name *Jeduthun*, which means one who praises.

The moment they discover my weakness
they all begin plotting to take me down.
4 Liars, hypocrites, with nothing good to say.
All of their energies are spent
on moving me from this exalted place.

Pause in his presence

5 I am standing in absolute stillness, silent before the One I love,
waiting as long as it takes for him to rescue me.
Only God is my Savior, and he will not fail me.
6 For he alone is my Safe Place.
His wrap-around presence always protects me
as my Champion Defender.
There's no risk of failure with God!
So why would I let worry paralyze me
even when troubles multiply around me?
7 God's glory is all around me!
His wrap-around presence is all I need,
for the Lord is my Savior, my Hero, and my life-giving strength.
8 Join me, everyone! Trust only in God every moment!
Tell him all your troubles and pour out your heart-longings to him.
Believe me when I tell you—he will help you!

Pause in his presence

9 Before God, all the people of the earth, high or low,
are like smoke that disappears,
like a vapor that quickly vanishes away.
Compared to God they're nothing but vanity, nothing at all!
10 The wealth of the world is nothing to God.
So if your wealth increases, don't be boastful or
put your trust in your money.
And don't you think for a moment that
you can get away with stealing by overcharging others

3 For he's the awe-inspiring God, great and glorious in power!
We've never seen anything like him!
Mighty in miracles, you cause your enemies to tremble.
No wonder they all surrender and bow before you!
4 All the earth will bow down to worship;
all the earth will sing your glories forever!

Pause in his presence

5 Everyone will say: "Come and see the incredible things God has done;
it will take your breath away!
He multiplies miracles for his people!"[a]
6 He made a highway going right through the Red Sea
as the Hebrews each passed through on dry ground,
exploding with joyous excitement over the miracles of God.
7 In his great and mighty power he rules forever,
watching over every movement of every nation.
So beware, rebel lands; he knows how to humble you!

Pause in his presence

8 Praise God, all you peoples.
Praise him everywhere and let everyone know you love him!
9 There's no doubt about it; God holds our lives safely in his hands.
He's the One who keeps us faithfully following him.
10 O Lord, we have passed through your fire;
like precious metal made pure,
you've proved us, perfected us, and made us holy.
11 You've captured us, ensnared us in your net.
Then, like prisoners, you *placed chains around our necks*.[b]
12 You've allowed our enemies to prevail against us.

---

a 66:5 The Septuagint says, "His works are more to be feared than the decisions of men."

b 66:11 Or "you attached suffering to our hips."

We've passed through fire and flood,
yet in the end you always bring us out better than we were before,
saturated with your goodness.[a]
13 I come before your presence with my sacrifice.
I'll give you all that I've promised, everything I have.
14 When I was overcome in my anguish,
I promised to give you my sacrifice.
Here it is! All that I said I would offer you is yours!
15 The best I have to bring, I'll throw it all into the fire
as the fragrance of my sacrifice ascends unto you.[b]

Pause in his presence

16 All you lovers of God who want to please him,
come and listen, and I'll tell you what he did for me.
17 I cried aloud to him with all my heart and he answered me!
Now my mouth overflows with the highest praise.
18 Yet if I had closed my eyes to my sin,
the Lord God would have closed his ears to my prayer.
19 But praises rise to God,
for he paid attention to my prayer and answered my cry to him!
20 I will forever praise this God who didn't close his heart when I prayed
and never said "No" when I asked him for help.
He never once refused to show me his tender love.

67 It's Time to Praise Him

For the Pure and Shining One
A poetic song of praise for guitar

1 God, keep us near your grace-fountain and bless us!

---

a 66:12 Or "You brought us out into a wide-open space [a place of rest]."
b 66:15 The literal Hebrew describes the sacrifice as "burnt offerings of fat beasts and the smoke of rams, bulls, and male goats."

And when you look down on us, may your face beam with
joy!

Pause in his presence

[2] Send us out all over the world so that everyone everywhere
will discover your ways and know who you are
and see your power to save!
[3] Let all the nations burst forth with praise;
let everyone everywhere love and enjoy you!
[4] Then how glad the nations will be when you are their King.
They will sing, they will shout, for you give true justice to
the people.
Yes! You, Lord, are the Shepherd of the nations!

Pause in his presence

[5] No wonder the peoples praise you!
Let all the people praise you more![a]
[6] The harvest of the earth is here!
God, the very God we worship
keeps us satisfied at his banquet of blessings.
[7] And the blessings keep coming!
Then all the ends of the earth will give him
the honor he deserves and be in awe of him!

68 A Song of Triumph

For the Pure and Shining One
David's poetic song of praise

[1] God! Arise with awesome power,
and every one of your enemies will scatter in fear!
[2] Chase them away—all these God-haters.
Blow them away as a puff of smoke.
Melt them away like wax in the fire.
One good look at you and the wicked vanish.
[3] But let all your godly-lovers be glad!

---

a 67:5 The Septuagint says, "Let all the people come to know you."

Yes, let them all rejoice in your presence
and be carried away with gladness.[a]
Let them laugh and be radiant with joy!
4 Let them sing their celebration-songs
for the coming of the Cloud-Rider whose name is Yah![b]
5–6 To the fatherless he is a Father,
to the widow he is a Champion Friend.
To the lonely, he gives a family.
To the prisoner,[c] he leads into prosperity until they each sing for joy.
This is our Holy God in his Holy Place!
But for the rebels there is heartache and despair.[d]
7 O Lord, it was you who marched in front of your people
leading them through the wasteland.

Pause in his presence

8 The earth shook beneath your feet; the heavens filled with clouds
before the presence of the God of Sinai!
The sacred mountain shook at the sight of the face of Israel's God!
9 You, O God, sent the reviving rain upon your weary inheritance,
showers of blessing to refresh it.
10 So there your people settled.
And in your kindness you provided the poor with abundance.
11 God Almighty declares the Word of the gospel with power,[e]

---

a 68:3 As translated from the Septuagint. The Aramaic is: "They rejoice in his sweetness."

b 68:4 More than an abbreviation, the name *Yah* is associated with the God of heaven, the God of highest glory and power.

c 68:5–6 The Septuagint says "the bitter ones."

d 68:6 The Aramaic says "the rebels will dwell among the tombs."

e 68:11 As translated from the Aramaic.

and the warring women of Zion deliver its message:[a]
12 "The conquering legions have themselves been conquered.
Look at them flee!"
Now Zion's women are left to gather the spoils.
13 When you sleep between sharpened stakes,[b]
I see you sparkling like silver and glistening like gold,
covered by the beautiful wings of a dove![c]
14 When the Almighty found a king for himself,
it became white as snow in his shade.[d]
15–16 O huge, magnificent mountain,
you are the mighty Kingdom of God![e]
All the other peaks, though impressive and imposing,
look with envy on you, Mount Zion!
For Zion is the mountain where God has chosen to live
forever.
17 Look! The mighty chariots of God!
Ten thousands upon [ten] thousands,
more than anyone could ever number.
God is at the front,
leading them all from Mount Sinai into his sanctuary
with the radiance of holiness upon him.[f]

---

a 68:11 As translated from the Masoretic text.

b 68:13 The Aramaic word *shaphya* can be translated "sharpened stakes or thorns": an obvious prophecy of the cross and our union with Christ as he was crucified.

c 68:13 As translated from the Aramaic text, this verse contains prophetic hints of Calvary, where Jesus *slept* the sleep of death between the *sharpened stakes* of the cross. The word *you* is plural and points us to our co-crucifixion with Christ.

d 68:14 Every scholar consulted concludes that this verse is difficult, if not impossible to interpret properly and translate accurately. The last words are literally: "snow fell in Zalmon." *Zalmon* (or *Salmon*) was a wooded area and means "shady."

e 68:15 The Septuagint reads "mountain of provision."

f 68:17 The Septuagint says "the Lord sends his provisions from his Holy

18 He ascends into the heavenly heights,
taking his many captured ones with him,
leading them in triumphal procession.
And gifts were given to men, even the once rebellious,
so that they may dwell with Yah.
19 What a glorious God![a]
He gives us salvation over and over,[b]
then daily he carries our burdens![c]

Pause in his presence

20 Our God is a mighty God who saves us over and over!
For the Lord, Yahweh, rescues us
from the ways of death many times.
21 But he will crush every enemy, shattering their strength.
He will make heads roll
for they refuse to repent of their stubborn, sinful ways.
22 I hear the Lord God saying to all the enemies of his people:
"You'd better come out of your hiding places,
all of you who are doing your best to stay far away from me;[d]
don't you know there's no place to hide!
23 For my people will be the conquerors;
they will soon have you under their feet!
they will crush you until there is nothing left!"[e]
24 O God, my King, your triumphal processions
keep moving onward in holiness;

Place on Mount Sinai."

a 68:19 The Aramaic is *Maryah*, the Aramaic form of YHWH or Lord Jehovah.

b 68:19 Salvation is in the plural form in the text (*salvations*).

c 68:19 Or "daily loads us with benefits."

d 68:22 The Hebrew text makes reference to Bashan (a high mountain) and to the depths of the sea. In other words, there's no place to hide.

e 68:23 The Hebrew text is literally: "Your enemies will be food for the dogs."

you're moving onward toward the Holy Place!
25 Leaders in front,[a] then musicians,
with young maidens in between striking their tambourines!
26 And they sing "Let all God's princely people rejoice!
Let all the congregations bring their blessing to God,
saying:
'The Lord of the Fountain! The Lord of the Fountain of
life!
The Lord of the Fountain of Israel!'"
27 Astonishingly, it's the favored youth leading the way.[b]
Princes of praise in their royal robes
and exalted princes are among them
along with princes who have wrestled with God.
28–29 Display your strength, God, and we'll be strong![c]
For your miracles have made us who we are.
Lord, do it again,
and parade from your temple your mighty power.
By your command even kings will bring gifts to you.
30 God, rebuke the beast-life that hides within us![d]
Rebuke those who claim to be "strong ones"[e]

---

a 68:25 As translated from the Septuagint. The Hebrew is "singers in front."

b 68:27 The Hebrew includes the names of four sons of Jacob, representing four tribes. Benjamin, the youngest son, means "son of my right hand," or "the favored one." Judah means "praise." Zebulon's name is the word for "exalted." Naphtali means "obtained by wrestling." Each name speaks of a princely group, and is used here poetically not only for Israel but for all of God's "princely people" in this holy procession of worship.

c 68:28–29 The Great Bible translated by Miles Coverdale (1488–1569) translates this: "Your God has sent forth strength for you."

d 68:30 Literal Hebrew: "Rebuke the beasts in the reeds."

e 68:30 This verse has puzzled scholars, and many conclude that the Hebrew text is nearly incomprehensible with tremendous variations in the translation.

that lurk within the congregation
and abuse the people out of their love for money.
So God scatters the people who are spoiling for a fight.
31 Africa will send her noble envoys to you, O God.
They will come running, stretching out their hands in love to you.
32 Let all the nations of the earth sing songs of praise to Almighty God!
Go ahead all you nations—sing your praise to the Lord!
Pause in his presence
33 Make music for the One who strides the ancient skies.
Listen to his thunderous voice of might split open the heavens.
34 Give it up for God, for he alone has all the strength and power!
Proclaim his majesty! For his glory shines down on Israel.
His mighty strength soars in the clouds of glory.
35 God, we are consumed with awe, trembling before you
as your glory streams from your Holy Place.
The God of power shares his mighty strength with Israel
and with all his people.
God, we give our highest praise to you!

69 A Cry of Distress [a]

To the Pure and Shining One
David's poetic song of praise to the tune "Lilies"

1–2 God, my God, come and save me!
These floods of trouble have risen higher and higher.
The water is up to my neck![b]

---

a Ps. 69 is considered one of the most outstanding messianic psalms, with obvious prophetic references to the sufferings and cross of Jesus Christ. Next to Ps. 22 it is the psalm most often quoted in the New Testament.
b 69:1–2 Or "throat."

I'm sinking into the mud with no place to stand,
and I'm about to drown in this storm.
3 I'm weary, exhausted with weeping.
My throat is dry, my voice is gone, my eyes are swollen with sorrow,
and I'm waiting for you, God, *to come through for me.*
4 I can't even count all those who hate me for no reason.
Many influential men want me silenced,
yet I've done nothing against them.
Must I restore what I never took away?
5 God, my life is an open book to you.
You know every sin I've ever done.
For nothing within me is hidden from your sight!
6 Lord Yahweh of Angel-Armies,
keep me from ever being a stumbling block to others,
to those who love you.
Lord God of Israel, don't let what happens to me
be the source of confusion to those who are passionate for you.
7 Because of my love for you, Lord,
I have been mocked, cursed, and disgraced.
8 Even my own brothers, those of my family,
act as though they don't want anything to do with me.
9 My love for you has my heart on fire!
My passion consumes me for your house!
Nothing will turn me away.
Even though I endure all the insults of those who insult you.
10 When they see me seeking for more of you with weeping[a] and fasting,
they all just scoff and scorn at my passion.
11 When I humble myself with sorrow over my sin,

---

a 69:10 Or "I pour out my soul," or "I wept soul-tears."

it gives them a reason to mock me even more.
12 The leaders, the influential ones—how they scorn my passion for you!
I've become the talk of the town, the theme of drunkards' songs.
13 But I keep calling out to you, Yahweh!
I know you will bend down to listen to me,
for now is the season of favor.
Because of your faithful love for me,
your answer to my prayer will be my sure salvation.
14 Pull me out of this mess! Don't let me sink!
Rescue me from those who hate me and from all this trouble I'm in!
15 Don't let this flood drown me.
Save me from these deep waters
or I'll go down to the pit of destruction.
16–17 Oh, Lord God, answer my prayers!
I need to see your tender kindness, your grace,
your compassion, and your constant love.
Just let me see your face, and turn your heart toward me.
Come running quickly to your servant.
In this deep distress, come and answer my prayer.
18 Come closer as a friend and redeem me.
Set me free so my enemies cannot say that you are powerless.
19 See how they dishonor me in shame and disgrace?
You know, Lord, what I'm going through, and you see it all.
20 I'm heartsick and heartbroken by it all.
Their contempt has crushed my soul.
I looked for sympathy and compassion
but found only empty stares.
21 I was hungry and they gave me bitter food.

I was thirsty and they offered me vinegar.[a]
22 Let their "feasts" turn to ashes!
Let their "peace and security" become their downfall!
23 Make them blind as bats, groping in the dark!
Let them be feeble, trembling continually!
24–25 Pour out your fury on them all!
Consume them with the fire of your anger!
Burn down the walled palace where they live!
Leave them homeless and desolate!
26 For they come against the one you yourself have struck,
and they scorn the pain of those you've pierced.
27 Pile on them the guilt of their sins!
Don't let them ever go free!
28 Leave them out of your list of the living!
Blot them out of your book of life!
Never name them as your own!
29 I am burdened and broken by this pain.
When your miracle rescue comes to me,
it will lift me to the highest place.
30 Then my song will be a burst of praise to you.
My glory-shouts will make your fame even more glorious
to all who hear my praises!
31 For I know, Yahweh, that my praises mean more to you
than all my gifts and sacrifices.
32 All who seek you will see God do this for them,
and they'll overflow with gladness.
Let this revive your hearts, all you lovers of God!
33 For Yahweh does listen to the poor and needy
and will not abandon his prisoners of love.[b]
34 Let all the universe praise him!

---

a 69:21 This was fulfilled with Jesus being offered vinegar on the cross. See Luke 23:36.

b 69:33 Or "those wearing shackles."

The high heavens and everyone on earth praise him!
Let the oceans deep with everything in them, keep it up!
35 God will come to save his Zion-people.
God will build up his cities of Judah,
for there his people will live in peace.
36 All their children will inherit the land,
and the lovers of his name will live there safe and secure!

70 A Cry for Help

To the Pure and Shining One
David's poetic lament to always remember

1 Please Lord! Come quickly and rescue me!
God, show me your favor and restore me.
2 Let all who seek my life be humiliated, confused, and ashamed.
God, send them sprawling, all who wish me evil;
they just want me dead.
3 Scoff at every scoffer and cause them all to be utter failures!
Let them be ashamed and horrified over their complete defeat.
4 But let all who passionately seek you erupt with excitement and joy
over what you've done!
Let all your lovers, who continually rejoice in the Savior,[a]
say aloud: "How great and glorious is our God!"
5 Lord, in my place of weakness and need,
won't you turn your heart toward me and hurry to help me?
For you are my Savior and I'm always in your thoughts.
So don't delay to deliver me now, for you are my God.

---

a 70:4 This verse contains the Hebrew root word for *Yeshua*.

71 The Psalm of Old Age

1 Lord, you are my secure shelter. Don't ever let me down!
2 Let your justice be my breakthrough.
Bend low to my whispered cry
and save me from all my enemies!
3 You're the only place of protection for me.
I keep coming back to hide myself in you,
for you are like a mountain-cliff-fortress where I'm kept safe.
4 Let me escape from these cruel and wicked men
and save me from the evil hands of the evil one.
5 For you are my only hope, Lord!
I've hung onto you, trusting in you all my life.
6–7 It was you who supported me from the day I was born,
loving me, helping me through my life's journey.
You've made me into a miracle;
no wonder I trust you and praise you forever!
Many marvel at my success,
but I know it is all because of you, my mighty Protector!
8 I'm overflowing with your praise for all you've done,
and your splendor thrills me all day long.
9 Now that I'm old, don't set me aside.
Don't let go of me when my strength is spent.
10–11 For all my enemies whisper behind my back.
They're waiting for me to fall so they can finish me off.
They're convinced you've left me
and that you'll never come to my rescue.
They're saying, "Let's get him now! He has no Savior!"
12 O God, stay close to me!
Don't just watch from a distance! Hurry to help me, my God!
13 Cover these accusers of mine with shame and failure!
Destroy them all, for they only want to kill me!

14 No matter what, I'll trust in you to help me.
Nothing will stop me from praising you to magnify your glory!
15 I couldn't begin to count the times you've been there for me.
With the skill of a poet I'll never run out of things to say
of how you faithfully kept me from danger.
16 I will come forth in your mighty strength, O my Lord God.[a]
I'll tell everyone that you alone are the Perfect One.
17 From my childhood you've been my teacher,
and I'm still telling everyone of your miracle-wonders!
18 God, now that I'm old and gray, don't walk away.
Give me grace to demonstrate to the next generation
all your mighty miracles and your excitement
to show them your magnificent power!
19 For your glorious righteousness reaches up to the high heavens.
No one could ever be compared to you!
Who is your equal, O God of marvels and wonders?
20 Even though you've let us sink down with trials and troubles,
I know you will revive us again,
lifting us up from the dust of death.
21 Give us even more greatness than before.
Turn and comfort us once again.
22 My loving God, the harp in my heart will praise you.
Your faithful heart toward us will be the theme of my song.
Melodies and music will rise to you, the Holy One of Israel.
23 I will shout and sing your praises for all you are to me—
Savior, lover of my soul!
24 I'll never stop telling others how perfect you are
while all those who seek my harm slink away ashamed and defeated!

---

a 71:16 Or "I will enter into the manliness of Lord Jehovah."

72 The Righteous King

Solomon's psalm[a]

1 O God, make the king a godly judge like you
and give the king's son the gift of justice too.
2 Help him to give true justice to your people,
honorably and equally to all.
3 Then the mountains of influence will be fruitful,
and from your righteousness
prosperity and peace flow to all the people.
4 May the poor and humble have an advocate with the king.
May he consider the children of the poor
and crush the cruel oppressor.
5 The sun and moon will stop shining
before your lovers will stop worshiping;
for ages upon ages the people will love and adore you!
6 Your favor will fall like rain upon our surrendered lives,[b]
like showers reviving the earth!
7 In the days of his reign the righteous will spring forth
with the abundance of peace and prosperity forevermore.
8 May he subdue and take dominion from sea to sea;
may he rule from the river to the rim.
9 Desert-nomads are bowing at his feet,
every enemy falling facedown, biting the dust!
10 Distant kings will surrender and come with their gifts
from every continent and coastland;
they will offer their tribute to you.[c]

---

a The Septuagint indicates this could be a psalm written by David for his son, Solomon. This royal psalm is a prayer for the king. Read through it as though it is referring to King Jesus—One who is greater than Solomon.

b 72:6 Or "like rain on mown grass."

c 72:10 Included in the Hebrew text are: kings of Tarshish (Spain), and kings of Sheba and Seba (Ethiopia).

11 O King of kings, they will all bow before you.
O King of kings, every nation will one day serve you.
12–13 He will care for the needy and neglected
when they cry to him for help.
The humble and helpless will know his kindness,
for with a father's compassion he will save their souls.
14 They will be rescued from tyranny and torture,
for their lifeblood is precious in his eyes.
15 Long live this King!
May the wealth of the world be laid before him.[a]
May there be ceaseless praise and prayer to him.
May all the blessing be brought to him.
16 Bless us with a bountiful harvest,
with golden grain swaying on the mountain fields!
May the cities be full of praising people, fruitful and filled—
17 So that his name may be honored forever!
May the fame of his name spring forth!
May it shine on, like the sunshine!
In him all will be blessed to bless others,
and may all the people bless the One who blessed them.
18 Praise forever Jehovah God, the God of Israel!
He is the one and only God of wonders,
surpassing every expectation.
19 The blazing glory of his name will be praised forever!
May all the earth overflow with his glory!
Faithful is our King! Amen!
20 This concludes the poetry sung by David, Jesse's son.

---

a 72:15 Or "the gold of Sheba."

BOOK 3

THE LEVITICUS PSALMS

Psalms of worship and God's house

73 God's Justice

Asaph's psalm

1 No one can deny it—God is really good to Israel
and to all those with pure hearts.
But I nearly missed seeing it for myself.
2 Here's my story: I came so close to missing the way.
3 I was stumbling over what I saw with the wicked.
For when I saw the boasters with such wealth and
prosperity,
I became jealous over their smug security.
4–5 Indulging in whatever they wanted, going where they
wanted,
doing what they wanted, and with no care in the world.
No pain, no problems, they seemed to have it made.
They lived as though life would never end.
6 They didn't even try to hide their pride and opulence.
Cruelty and violence is part of their lifestyle.
7 Pampered and pompous, vice oozes from their souls;
they overflow with vanity!
8 They're such snobs—looking down their noses
they even scoff at God!
They are nothing but bullies threatening God's people!
9 Loudmouths with no fear of God, pretending to know it all!
Windbags full of hot air, impressing only themselves!
10 Yet the people keep coming back to listen
to more of their same nonsense.
11 They tell their cohorts, "God will never know.
See, he has no clue of what we're doing."
12 These are the wicked ones I'm talking about!

They never have to lift a finger,
living a life of ease while their riches multiply.
13 Have I been foolish to play by the rules and keep my life pure?
14 Here I am suffering under your discipline day after day.
I feel like I'm being punished all day long.
15 If I had given in to my pain and spoken of what I was really feeling,
it would have sounded like unfaithfulness to the next generation.
16 So when I tried to understand it all, I just couldn't.
It was too puzzling—too much of a riddle to me.
17 But then, one day I was brought into the sanctuaries of God,
and in the light of glory, my distorted perspective vanished.
Now I understood that the destiny of the wicked was near!
18 They're the ones who are on the slippery path,
and God will suddenly let them slide off into destruction
to be consumed with terrors forever!
19 It will be an instant end to all their life of ease;
a blink of the eye and they're swept away by sudden calamity!
They're all nothing more than momentary monarchs—
20 Soon to disappear like a dream when one awakes.
So when the rooster crows,
Lord God, you'll despise their life of fantasies.[a]
21 When I saw all of this, what turmoil filled my heart,
piercing my opinions with your truth.
22 I was so stupid. I was senseless and ignorant,
acting like a brute beast before you, Lord.
23 Yet, in spite of all this, you comfort me by your counsel;
you draw me closer to you.
24 You lead me with your secret wisdom.

---

a 73:20 Or "shadows."

And following you brings me into your brightness and
glory!
25 Whom have I in heaven but you! You're all I want!
No one on earth means as much to me as you.
26 Lord, so many times I fail; I fall into disgrace,
but when I trust in you, I have a strong and glorious
presence
protecting and anointing me. Forever you're all I need!
27 Those who abandon the worship of God will perish.
The false and unfaithful will be silenced, never heard from
again.
28 But I'll keep coming closer and closer to you, Lord Yahweh,
for your name is good to me. I'll keep telling the world of
your awesome works, my faithful and glorious God!

74 We Need You Now

Asaph's poem of instruction

1 Are you really going to leave us, God?
Would you turn your back on us, rejecting your people?
We are yours, your very own.[a]
Will your anger smolder against us forever?
2 Don't forget that we are your beloved ones.
Wrap us back into your heart again, for you chose us.
You brought us out of our slavery and bondage
and made us your favored ones, your Zion-people,
your home on earth.
3 Turn your steps toward this devastation.
Come running to bring your restoring grace to these
ruins,[b]

---

a 74:1 Or "the sheep of your pasture."

b 74:3 This verse reads so differently in the Aramaic: "Lift up your servants with your might above those who take them captive, for those who oppress us are enemies to your holiness."

to what the enemy has done to devastate your Holy Place.
4 They have come into the very midst of your dwelling place,
roaring like beasts, setting up their banners to flaunt their conquest!
5 Now everything is in shambles! They've totally destroyed it.
Like a forest chopped down to the ground,
there's nothing's left!
6 All of the beauty of the craftsmanship
of the inner place has been ruined,
smashed, broken, and shattered![a]
7 They've burned it all to the ground!
They've violated your sanctuary,
the very dwelling place of your glory and your name.
8 They boasted, "Let's completely crush them!
Let's wipe out every trace of this God.
Let's burn up every sacred place where they worship this God."
9 Now we don't see any miraculous signs anymore!
There's no longer a prophet among us
who can tell us how long this devastation will continue!
10 So God, how much longer will you let this go on
and allow these barbarians to blaspheme your name?
Will you stand back and watch them get away with this forever?
11 Why don't you do something?
You have the power to break in,
so why would you hide your great power from us?
Don't hold back! Unleash your might and give them a final blow.

---

a 74:6 This psalm also describes what the enemy of our souls has done spiritually to mar the image of God in the *inner place* of man's spirit. God will fully restore all things, including his image within us, as our hearts become his *Holy Place* on the earth.

12 You have always been, and always will be, my King.
You are the Mighty Conqueror working wonders all over the world.
13 It was you who split the sea in two by your glorious strength.
You smashed the power of Tannin, the sea-god![a]
14 You crushed the might of Leviathan,[b] the great dragon,
then you took the crumbs and fed them to the sharks![c]
15 With your glory you opened up springs and fountains,
then you spoke and the ever flowing springs of Jordan
dried up so we could cross over.
16 You own the day and the night.
Sunlight and starlight call you Creator.
17 The four corners of the earth were formed by your hands,
and every changing season owes its beauty to you.
18 O, Jehovah, don't ever forget how these arrogant enemies,
like fools, have mocked your name.
19 Lord, aren't we your beloved dove that praises you?[d]
Protect us from these wild beasts who want to harm us.
Don't leave us as lambs among wolves!
You can't abandon us after all we've been through!
20 Remember your promises to us,
for darkness covers the land,
giving the violent ones a hiding place.
21 Don't let these insults continue.
Can't you see that we are your downtrodden
and oppressed people?

---

a 74:13 As translated literally from the Hebrew. The Septuagint says, "You've crushed the heads of the dragons in the water [water spirits]."

b 74:14 Leviathan is mentioned six times in Job 41. Leviathan means twisted or coiled, and is considered to be a sea monster. See Gen. 1:21.

c 74:14 The Septuagint says, "You fed them to the black peoples."

d 74:19 As translated from the Septuagint, Syriac, and one Hebrew manuscript.

For who could ever stand before your face
when your fierce anger burns and still live to tell about it.
8 As the earth itself holds its breath in awe before you,
judgment is decreed from heaven.
9 You arise to punish evil and defend the gentle upon the earth.

Pause in his presence

10 You have power to transform man's futile anger into praise.[a]
The fury of your enemies only causes your fame to increase.[b]
11 So you'd better keep every promise you've ever made
to the Awesome One, Jehovah God!
Let everyone bring their extravagant gifts to him alone.
12 He is famous for breaking the spirit of the powers that be.
And the kings of the earth will know him as the Fearsome One!

77 God of Comfort

To the Pure and Shining One
Asaph's poetic song of love's celebration

1 I poured out my complaint to you, God.
I lifted up my voice, shouting out for your help.
2 When I was in deep distress, in my day of trouble,
I reached out for you with hands stretched out to heaven!
Over and over I kept looking for you, God,
but your comforting grace was nowhere to be found.
3 As I thought of you I just moaned: "God, where are you?"[c]

---

a 76:10 Or "the counsel of men will praise you."
b 76:10 The Septuagint reads, "Survivors of your wrath keep your festivals."
c 77:3 Or, "When I am in heaviness (depressed), I will think upon God."

I'm overwhelmed with despair as I wait for your help to
arrive.

Pause in his presence

4 I can't get a wink of sleep until you come and comfort me.
Now I'm too burdened to even pray!
5 My mind wanders thinking of days gone by—
the years long since passed.
6 Then I remembered my worship songs I used to sing
in the night seasons,
and my heart began to fill again with thoughts of you.
So my spirit went out once more in search of you.
7 Would you really walk off and leave me forever, my Lord
God?
Won't you show me your kind favor; delighting in me
again?
8 Has your well of sweet mercy dried up?
Will your promises never come true?
9 Have you somehow forgotten to show me love?
Are you so angry that you've closed
your heart of compassion toward me?

Pause in his presence

10 Lord, what wounds me most is that it's somehow my fault
that
you've changed your heart toward me
and I no longer see the years of the Mighty One
and your right hand of power.[a]
11 Yet I could never forget all your miracles, my God,
as I remember all your wonders of old.
12 I ponder all you've done, Lord, musing on all your miracles.
13 It's here in your presence, in your sanctuary,

---

a 77:10 This difficult verse has a number of alternate translations, including: "Your right hand has changed [or withered]." The implication is that God's power and protection are no longer being seen.

where I learn more of your ways.[a]
For holiness is revealed in everything you do!
Lord, you're the One and Only, the great and glorious God!
14 Your display of wonders, miracles, and power
makes the nations acknowledge you.
15 By your glory-bursts you've rescued us over and over.
Just ask the sons of Jacob or
the sons of Joseph and they will tell you!
And all of us, your beloved ones, know that it's true!

Pause in his presence

16 When the many waters of the Red Sea took one look at you,[b]
they were afraid and ran away to hide—
trembling to its depths!
17 Storm clouds filled with water high in the skies;
cloudbursts and thunderclaps announced your approach.
Lightning-flashes lit up the landscape.
18 Rolling whirlwinds exploded with sonic booms of thunder,
rumbling as the skies shouted out your story
with light and sound and wind.
Everything on earth shook and trembled as you drew near.
19 Your steps formed a highway through the seas
with footprints on a pathway no one even knew was there.[c]
20 You led your people forward by your loving hand,
blessed by the leadership of Moses and Aaron.

78 Lessons from History

Asaph's poetic song of instruction

1 Beloved ones, listen to this instruction.

---

a 77:13 This is an alternative translation.
b 77:16 Although the Red Sea is not mentioned in the verse, it is implied in the context.
c 77:19 This could be a prophecy of Jesus one day walking on water.

Open your heart to the revelation
of this mystery that I share with you.
2 A parable and a proverb are hidden in what I say—
an intriguing riddle from the past.
3–4 We've heard true stories from our fathers about our rich heritage.
We will continue to tell our children
and not hide from the rising generation
the great marvels of our God—
his miracles and power that have brought us all this far.
5 The story of Israel is a lesson in God's ways.
He gave Moses his laws then commanded us to keep them,
and to make them known to all our children.
6 For perpetuity God's ways will be passed down
from one generation to the next, even to those not yet born.
7 In this way, every generation will have a living faith in the laws of life
and will never forget the faithful ways of God.
8 By following his ways they will break the past bondage
of their fickle fathers who were a stubborn, rebellious generation
and whose spirits strayed from the Eternal God.
They refused to love him with all their hearts!
9 Take for an example, the sons of Ephraim;
though they were all equipped warriors, each with weapons,
when the battle began they retreated and ran away in fear.
10 They didn't really believe the promises of God;
they simply refused to trust him and move forward in faith.
11 They forgot his wonderful works and the miracles of the past,
12 Even their exodus from Egypt, the epic miracle of his might.

They forgot the glories of his power at the place of passing over.[a]
13 God split the sea wide open, and
the waters stood at attention on either side
as the people passed on through!
14 By day the moving glory-cloud led them forward.
And all through the night the fire-cloud stood as a sentry of light.
15–16 In the days of desert dryness he split open the mighty rock,
and the waters flowed like a river before their very eyes.
He gave them all they wanted to drink from his living springs.
17 Yet they kept their rebellion alive against God Most High,
and their sins against God continued to be counted.
18 In their hearts they tested God just to get what they wanted,
asking for the food their hearts craved.
19–20 Like spoiled children they grumbled against God himself,
demanding he prove his love by saying,
"Can't God provide for us in this barren wilderness?
Will he give us food, or will he only give us water?
Where's our meal?"
21 Then God heard all their complaining and was furious!
His anger flared up against his people.
22 For they turned away from faith and walked away in fear;
they failed to trust in his power to help them when he was near.
23–24 Still he spoke on their behalf and the skies opened up;
the windows of heaven poured out food,
the mercy bread-manna.
The grain of grace fell from the clouds.

---

a 78:12 Or "the fields of Zoan." *Zoan* means crossing place or place of departure. See also verse 43.

25 Humans ate angels' food—the meal of the mighty ones.
His grace gave them more than enough!
26–27 The heavenly winds of miracle power blew in their favor
and food rained down upon them;
succulent quail quieted their hunger as they ate all they
wanted.
28 Food fell from the skies, thick as clouds;
their provision floated down right in front of their eyes!
29 He gave them all they desired, and they ate to their fill.
30–31 But before they had even finished,
even with their food still in their mouths,
God's fiery anger arose against them
killing the finest of their mighty men.
32 Yet in spite of all this, they kept right on sinning.
Even when they saw God's marvels,
they refused to believe God could care for them.
33 So God cut their lives short with sudden disaster,
with nothing to show for their lives but fear and failure.
34 *When he cared for them they ignored him*,
but when he began to kill them ending their lives in a
moment,
they came running back to God pleading for mercy.
35 They remembered that God, the Mighty One,
was their strong Protector,
the Hero-God who would come to their rescue.
36–37 But their repentance lasted only as long as they were in
danger;
they lied through their teeth to the True God of Covenant.
So quickly they wandered away from his promises,
following God with their words and not their hearts!
Their worship was only flattery.
38 But amazingly, God—so full of compassion—still forgave
them.
He covered over their sins with his love,

refusing to destroy them all.
Over and over he held back his anger,
restraining wrath to show them mercy.
39 He knew that they were made from mere dust—
frail, fragile, and short-lived, here today and gone
tomorrow.
40 How many times they rebelled in their desert days!
How they grieved him with their grumblings.
41 Again and again they limited God, preventing him from
blessing them.
Continually they turned back from him
and wounded the Holy One!
42 They forgot his great love, how he took them by his hand
and *with redemption's kiss* he delivered them from their
enemies.
43 They disregarded all the epic signs and marvels they saw
when they escaped from Egypt's bondage.
They forgot the judgment of the plagues that set them free.
44 God turned their rivers into blood, leaving the people
thirsty.
45 How he sent them vast swarms of filthy flies that sucked
their blood.
He sent hordes of frogs, ruining their lives.
46 And grasshoppers consumed all their crops.
47 And every garden, every orchard
was flattened with blasts of hailstones,
their fruit trees ruined by a killing frost.
48 Even their cattle fell prey, pounded by the falling hail;
their livestock were struck with bolts of lightning.
49 Finally, he unleashed upon them the fierceness of his anger.
Such fury!
He sent them sorrow and devastating trouble
by his mighty band of destroying angels;
messengers of death were dispatched against them!

50–51 He lifted his mercy and let loose his fearful anger
and did not spare their lives.
He released the judgment-plagues to rage through their land.
God struck down in death all the firstborn sons of Egypt—
the pride and joy of each family!
52 Then like a Shepherd leading his sheep, God led his people
out of tyranny, guiding them through the wilderness like a flock.
53 Safely and carefully God led them out with nothing to fear.
But their enemies he led into the sea.
He took care of them there once and for all!
54 Eventually God brought his people to the Holy Land,
to a land of hills that he prepared for them.[a]
55 He drove out and scattered all the peoples occupying the land,
staking out an inheritance, a portion for each of Israel's tribes.
56 Yet for all of this, they still rebelled and refused to follow his ways,
provoking to anger the God Most High.
57–58 Like traitors turning back they forsook him.
They were even worse than their fathers!
They became treacherous deceivers, crooked and corrupt,
and worshiped false gods in the high places,
bringing low the name of God with every idol they erected.
No wonder he was filled with jealousy and furious with anger!
59 Enraged with anger, God turned his wrath on them
and he rejected his people with disgust!

---

a 78:54 The Aramaic reads: "He brought them to the border of his holiness, the mountain possessed by his right hand."

60 God walked away from them and left his dwelling place at
Shiloh,
abandoning the place where he had lived among them.
61 Allowing his emblem of strength, his glory-ark to be
captured,[a]
enemies stole the very source of Israel's power.
62 God vented his rage, allowing his people to be butchered
when they went out to battle,
for his anger was intense against his very own!
63 Their young men fell on the battlefield and never came
back.
Their daughters never heard their wedding songs
since there was no one left to marry!
64 Their priests were slaughtered and their widows were killed
before they had time to weep.
65 Then all at once the Almighty awakened
as though he had been asleep.
Like a mighty man he arose, roaring into action!
66 He blasted into battle driving back every foe,
defeating them in disgrace for time and eternity.
67 He rejected Joseph's family, the tribe of Ephraim.[b]
68 But he chose instead the tribe of Judah
and Mount Zion, which he loves.
69 There he built his towering temple,
strong and enduring as the earth itself.
70 And God also chose his beloved one, David.
He promoted him from caring for sheep
and made him his prophetic servant.

---

a 78:61 Although the ark is not directly mentioned in this text, the obvious implication is that God allowed his "strength" to be stolen as a sign of his judgment.

b 78:67 The place of God's dwelling was moved from the land of Ephraim (Shiloh) to the land of Judah (Jerusalem).

71–72 God prepared David and took this gentle shepherd-king
and presented him before the people
as the one who would love and care for them
with integrity, a pure heart, and the anointing
to lead Israel, his holy inheritance.

79 Prayer in a Time of National Disaster

Asaph's poetic song

1 God, won't you do something?
Barbarians have invaded your inheritance.
Your temple of holiness has been violated,
and Jerusalem has been left in ruins.
2 The corpses of your loving people are lying in the open—
food for the beasts and the birds.
3 The shed blood of your servants has soaked the city
with no one left to bury the dead.
4 Now the nearby nations heap their scorn upon us,
scoffing, mocking us incessantly.
5 How much longer, O Jehovah God, must we endure this?
Does your anger have no end?
Will your jealousy burn like a raging fire?
6 If you're going to pour out your anger,
pour it out on all these nations around us, not on us!
They're the ones that do not love you like we do!
7 See how they've attacked us, consuming the land,
leaving it desolate.
8 Please, God, don't hold the sins of our fathers against us.
Don't make us pay for their sins.
Hurry to our side, and let your tenderhearted mercy
meet us in our need, for we are devastated beyond belief.
9 Our Hero, come and rescue us!
O God of the Breakthrough, for the glory of your name,
come and help us!
Forgive and restore us; heal us and cover us in your love.

10 Why should all the nations sneer at us saying:
"Where is this God of yours?"
Now is the time, Lord.
Show your people and all the world that
you will avenge this slaughter and bloodshed once and for all!
11 Listen, Lord! Hear the sighing of all the prisoners of war,
all those doomed to die. Demonstrate your glory-power
and come and rescue your condemned children!
12 Lord God, take what these mocking masses have done to us
and pay it all back to them seven times over.
13 Then we, your lovers, will forever thank you,
praising your name from generation to generation!

80 Rescue and Restore

For the Pure and Shining One
Asaph's poetic song set to the tune "Your Decrees Are Like Lilies"

1 God-Enthroned, be revealed in splendor
as you ride upon the cherubim!
How perfectly you lead us, a people set free.[a]
Loving Shepherd of Israel—listen to our hearts' cry!
Shine forth from your throne of dazzling light.
2 In the sight of Benjamin, Ephraim, and Manasseh,
stir up your mighty power in full display before our eyes.[b]
Breakthrough and reveal yourself by coming to our rescue.

---

a 80:1 Or "You lead Joseph like a flock." Joseph, as a metaphor, becomes a picture of the saga of God's people once imprisoned and now set free to rule and reign.

b 80:2 The Hebrew text includes the names Ephraim ("doubly fruitful"), Benjamin ("son of my right hand"), and Manassah ("you made me forget"). These three sons of Rachel marched together behind the ark of glory (Num. 2:17–24) and became representatives of all who follow the glory of God. They will be "doubly fruitful," "sons of his right hand," and those who have "forgotten" their lives in Adam.

3 Revive us, O God! Let your beaming face shine upon us
with the sunrise rays of glory;
then nothing will be able to stop us.
4 O God, the Mighty Commander of Angel-Armies,
how much longer will you smolder in anger?
How much longer will you be disgusted with your people
even when they pray?
5 You have fed us with sorrow and grief
and made us drink our tears by the bowlful.
6 You've made us a thorn in the side of all the neighboring
lands,
and now they just laugh at us with their mocking scorn.
7 Come back, come back, O God, and restore us!
You are the Commander of Angel-Armies.
Let your beaming face shine upon us with the sunrise rays
of glory,
and then nothing will be able to stop us!
8–9 Remember how you transplanted us here
like a tender vine from Egypt.
You cleared the land for your vineyard,
evicting the nations from your land and planting us here!
The roots of your vineyard went deep into the soil
and filled the land with fruit.
10–11 Because of your favor on your vineyard,
blessing extended to every mountain of influence.
Through this flourishing vineyard mighty ones were raised
up.
The nations were blessed by your fruitful vineyard of
Israel,[a]

---

a 80:10–11 In this passage the translator has chosen to make explicit the symbols in the text. The vineyard is Israel; the mountains are the high places of influence in culture; the cedars are the mighty and powerful of men; and the sea speaks of the nations ("sea of humanity").

all the way from the Mediterranean to the Euphrates.
12–13 So Lord, why have you broken down
your fence of favor around us?
Trespassers can steal the fruit from off our vines,
and now every wild beast comes
breaking through our wall to ravage us.
You've left us without protection!
14 Come back, come back, O God to restore us!
You are the Commander of Angel-Armies.
Look down from heaven and see our crisis.
Come down and care for your lovely vineyard once again.
15 Nurture our root and our fruit with your loving care.
Raise up the Branch-Man, the Son that you've made strong.
16 Enemies chopped down our vine and set it on fire;
now show them your anger and let them perish by your frown.
17 Strengthen this Branch-Man, the Son of your love,
the Son of Man who dwells at your right hand.
18 Then we will never turn back from you.
Revive us again, that we may trust in you.
19 O God, the Mighty Commander of Angel-Armies,
come back and rescue us!
Let your beaming face shine upon us
with the sunrise rays of glory.
Then nothing will ever stop us again!

81 For the Feast of Tabernacles

For the Pure and Shining One

Asaph's poetic song set to the melody "For the Feast of Harvest"

1 Lord, just singing about you makes me strong!
So I'll keep shouting for joy to Jacob's God, my Champion!
2 Let the celebration begin!
I will sing with drum accompaniment and with the sweet sound

of the harp and guitar strumming.
3 Go ahead! Blow the jubilee trumpet to begin the feast!
Blow it before every joyous celebration and festival.[a]
4 For God has given us these seasons of joy,
days that he decreed for us to celebrate and rejoice.
5 He's given these feasts to remind us of his triumph over
Egypt,
when he went out to wage war against them.
Then I heard the message in an unknown tongue as he said
to me:
6 "I have removed your backbreaking burdens
and have freed your hands from the hard labor and toil.[b]
7 You called out to me in your time of trouble and I rescued
you.
I came down from the realm of the secret place of thunder
where mysteries hide.
I came down to save you.
I tested your hearts at the place where there was no water
to drink,
the place of your bitter argument with me."[c]

Pause in his presence

8 "Listen to me, my dear people.
For I'm warning you, and you'd better listen well!
For I hold something against you.
9 Don't ever be guilty of worshiping any other god but me.
10 I am your only God, the Living God!
Wasn't I the One who broke the strongholds over you
and raised you up out of bondage?

---

a 81:3 Or "on the day of the new moon and the day of the full moon."

b 81:6 Or "from holding the baskets," which alludes to the Hebrews carrying basket loads of burdens for their Egyptian masters.

c 81:7 The Hebrew includes the word *Meribah*, which means the place of strife and contention.

We'll destroy even the memory of her existence!"
5 They've made their pact, consulting and conspiring,
aligning together in their covenant against God!
6–8 All the sons of Ishmael, the desert sheiks and the nomadic tribes, Amalekites, Canaanites, Moabites,
and all the nations that surround us,
Philistines, Phoenicians, Gadarenes,[a] and Samaritans;
allied together they're ready to attack!

Pause in his presence

9 Do to them all what you did to the Midianites
who were defeated by Gideon.
Or what you did to Sisera and Jabin
when Deborah and Barak defeated them by the Kishon River.
10 Do to your enemies what you did at Endor
whose rotting corpses fertilized the land.
11–12 Repeat history, God! Make all their "noble ones"
die like Oreb, Zebah, and Zalmunna, who said in their pride,
"We will seize God's people along with all their pleasant lands!"
13 Just blow them away, God, like straw in the wind,
like a tumbleweed in the wilderness!

---

a 83:6–8 As translated from the Aramaic. The Greek is, "It includes the tents of Edom and Ishmael (Palestinians and those of southern Jordanians), Moab (Palestinians and those of central Jordanians) and Hagrites (Egyptians or possibly northern Jordanians), Gebal (Byblos and northern Lebanese), Ammon (Palestinians and northern Jordanians), and Amalek (Arabs of the Sinai Peninsula), Philistia (Gaza), and the inhabitants of Tyre (southern Lebanese). Even Assyria (Syrians and northern Iraqis) has become their ally as an arm (military might) for the sons of Lot." This comprises virtually every neighbor surrounding Israel.

14 Burn them up like a raging fire roaring down the
mountainside;
consume them all until only charred sticks remain!
15 Chase them away like before a mighty storm and terrifying
tempest!
16 O Lord, disgrace them until their faces fill with shame,
and make them acknowledge the glory of your name!
17 Make them utter failures in everything they do
until they perish in total disgrace and humiliation.
18 So that they will know that you, and you alone
are Yahweh, the only Most High God exalted over all the
earth!

84 Longing for God

For the Pure and Shining One
A prophetic song written by the sons of Korah
Set to the melody "For the Feast of Harvest"[a]

1 God of Heaven's Armies, you find so much beauty in your
people!
They're like lovely sanctuaries of your presence.[b]
2 So deep within me are these lovesick longings,
desires and daydreams of living in union with you.
When I'm near you my heart and my soul
will sing and worship with my joyful songs of you,
my true Source and Spring of life!
3 O Lord of Heaven's Armies, my King and my God,
even the sparrows and swallows are welcome to build a
nest
among your altars for the birds to raise their young.

---

a The Septuagint says, "For the wine vats."
b 84:1 The Hebrew word for lovely used here can also mean beloved. The translator has chosen to use both these concepts in this verse.

4 What pleasure fills those who live every day in your temple,
enjoying you as they worship in your presence!

Pause in his presence

5 How enriched are they who find their strength in the Lord;[a]
within their hearts are the highways of holiness![b]
6 Even when their path winds through the dark valley of tears,
they dig deep to find a pleasant pool *where others find only pain.*
He gives to them a brook of blessing
filled from the rain of an outpouring.
7 They grow stronger and stronger with every step forward
and the God of all gods will appear before them in Zion.
8 Hear my cry, O God of Heaven's Armies!
God of Jacob, listen to my loving prayer.

Pause in his presence

9 God, your wrap-around presence is our defense.
In your kindness look upon the faces of your anointed ones.[c]
10 For just one day of intimacy with you[d] is like
a thousand days of joy rolled into one!
I'd rather stand at the threshold in front of the Gate Beautiful,
ready to go in and worship my God,
than to live my life without you
in the most beautiful palace of the wicked.
11 For the Lord God is brighter than the brilliance of a sunrise!
Wrapping himself around me like a shield,
he is so generous with his gifts of grace and glory.

---

a 84:5 The Aramaic says, "How blessed is the Son of Man with you as his helper."

b 84:5 The Hebrew is literally, "roads are in their hearts." By implication it is the ways (roads) that lead us to God's holy presence.

c 84:9 Or "the face of your Anointed [Christ]."

d 84:10 Or "in your [temple] courts."

Those who walk along his paths with integrity
will never lack one thing they need for he provides it all!
12 O Lord of Heaven's Armies,
what euphoria fills those who forever trust in you!

85 Mercy and Truth

For the Pure and Shining One
A prophetic song composed by the sons of Korah

1 Lord, your love has poured out
so many amazing blessings on our land!
You've restored Israel's destiny from captivity.
2 You've forgiven our many sins and covered
every one of them in your love.

Pause in his presence

3 So now it's obvious that your blazing anger has ended and
the furious fire of wrath has been extinguished *by your mercy.*
4 So bring us back to loving you, God our Savior.
Restore our hearts so that we'll never again
feel your anger rise against us.
5 Will you forever hold a grudge?
Will your anger endure for all time?
6 Revive us again, O God! I know you will! Give us a fresh start!
Then all your people will taste your joy and gladness.
7 Pour out even more of your love on us!
Reveal more of your kindness and restore us back to you!
8 Now I'll listen carefully for your voice
and wait to hear whatever you say.
Let me hear your promise of peace—
the message every one of your godly lovers longs to hear.
Just don't let us in our ignorance turn back from following you.

9 For I know your power and presence shines on all your
lovers.
Your glory always hovers over all who bow low before you.
10 Your mercy and your truth have married each other.
Your righteousness and peace have kissed.
11 Flowers of your faithfulness are blooming on the earth.
Righteousness shines down from the sky.
12 Yes, the Lord keeps raining down blessing after blessing,
and prosperity will drench the land with a bountiful
harvest.
13 For deliverance and peace are his forerunners
preparing a path for his steps.

86 A Prayer of Faith

King David's prayer

1 Lord, bend down to listen to my prayer.
For I'm in deep trouble. I'm so broken and humbled,
and I desperately need your help.
2 Guard my life, for I'm your faithful friend, your loyal servant
for life.
I turn to you in faith, my God, my Hero; come and rescue
me!
3 Lord God, hear my constant cry for help;
show me your favor and bring me to your fountain of
grace!
4 Restore joy to your loving servant once again,
for all I am is yours, O God.
5 Lord, you are so good to me, so kind in every way[a]
and ready to forgive,
for your grace-fountain keeps overflowing,
drenching all your lovers who pray to you.
6 God, won't you pay attention to this urgent cry?

---

a 86:5 The Septuagint says, "You're my Provider."

Lord, bend down to listen to my prayer.
7 Whenever trouble strikes, I will keep crying out to you,
for I know your help is on the way.
8 God, there's just no one like you;
there's no other god as famous as you.
You outshine all others and your miracles make it easy to know you.
9 Lord Almighty, you are the One who created all the nations;
Look at them—they're all on their way!
Yes, the day will come when they all will worship you
and put your glory on display.
10 You are the one and only God!
What miracles! What wonders! What greatness belongs to you!
11 Teach me more about you, how you work and how you move,
so that I can walk onward in your truth
until everything within me brings honor to your name.
12 With all my heart and passion I will thank you, my God!
I will give glory to your name, always and forever!
13 You love me so much and you placed your greatness upon me.[a]
You rescued me from the deepest place of darkness,
and you have delivered me from a certain death.
14 God, look at how these arrogant ones have defied me.
Like a vicious band of violent men they have tried to kill me.
They wouldn't worry for moment that they were sinning against you!
15 But Lord, your nurturing love is tender and gentle.
You are slow to get angry, yet so swift to show your faithful love.

---

a 86:13 As translated from the Aramaic.

abandoned, pierced, with nothing to look forward to but
death.
6 They[a] have discarded me and thrown me down
into the deepest darkness as into a bottomless pit.
7 I feel your wrath and it's a heavy weight upon me,
drowning me beneath a sea of sorrow.

Pause in his presence

8 Why did you turn all my friends against me?
You've made me like a cursed man in their eyes.
No one wants to be with me now.
You've caught me in a trap with no way out.
9 Every day I beg for your help. Can't you see my tears?
My eyes are swollen with weeping.
My arms are wide, longing for mercy,[b]
but you're nowhere to be found.
10 How can those who are cut off from your care
even know that you are there?
How can I rise up to praise you if I'm dead and gone?

Pause in his presence

11 Who can give thanks for your love in the graveyard?
Who preaches your faithfulness in the place of destruction?
12 Does death's darkness declare your miracles?
How can anyone who's in the grave, where all is forgotten,
remember how you keep your promises?
13 Lord, you know my prayer before I even whisper it.[c]
At each and every sunrise you will
continue to hear my cry until you answer.
14 O Lord, why have you thrown my life away?

---

a 88:6 As translated from the Septuagint. The Hebrew reads, "You have discarded me."

b 88:9 As translated from the Septuagint. The Greek reads, "My hands are stretched out to you."

c 88:13 As translated from the Septuagint.

Will you keep turning the other way every time I call out
to you?
15 I've had to live in poverty and trouble all my life.[a]
Now I'm humiliated, broken, and helpless before your
terrors
and I can't take it anymore.
16 I'm so overwhelmed by your burning anger.
I've taken the worst you could give me
and I'm speechless before you.
17 I'm drowning beneath the waves of this sorrow,
cut off with no one to help.
18 All my loved ones and friends keep far away from me,
leaving me all alone with only darkness as my friend!

89 Will You Reject Us Forever?

Poems by Ethan the Ezrahite for instruction[b]

First poem—God's Promises to David

1 This forever-song I sing of the gentle love of God!
Young and old alike will hear about
your faithful, steadfast love—never failing!
2 Here's my chorus: "Your mercy grows through the ages.[c]
Your faithfulness is firm, rising up to the skies."
3 I heard the Lord say, "My covenant has been made
and I'm committed forever to my chosen one, David.
4 I have made my oath that there will be sons of David forever,
sons that are kings through every generation."

Pause in his presence

5–6 Can you hear it? Heaven is filled with your praises, O Lord!

---

a 88:15 As translated from the Septuagint. The Greek reads, "close to death all my life."

b Many scholars believe Ps. 89 contains four poems or stanzas. The translator has chosen to signify each poem with an inscription.

c 89:2 As translated from the Septuagint.

28 I will love him forever and always show him kindness.
My covenant with him will never be broken.
29 For I have decreed that he will always have an heir—
a dynasty that will release the days of heaven on earth.
30–32 But if his children turn from me and forsake my words,
refusing to walk in my truth, renouncing and violating my laws,
then I will surely punish them for their sins
with my stern discipline until they regret it!
33 But I will never, no never, lift my faithful love from off their lives.
My kindness will prevail and I will never disown them.
34–35 How could I revoke my covenant of love that I promised David?
For I have given him my word, my holy irrevocable word!
How could I lie to my loving servant David?
36–37 Sons of David will continue to reign on his throne,
and their kingdom will endure as long as the sun is in the sky.
This covenant will be an unbreakable promise that
I have established for all time!"

Pause in his presence

Third poem—Why Has Our King Been Defeated

38 Why have you rejected me, the one you anointed?
Why would you cast me away?
Why would you lose your temper with me?
39 You have torn up the contract you made with me, your servant.
You have stripped away my crown and thrown it to the ground.[a]

---

a 89:39 In place of the word *crown*, some translations render it "my dignity."

40 You have torn down all my walls of defense
and have made my every hiding place into ruins.
41 All the passersby attack and rob me while my neighbors
mock!
42 Instead of fighting for me, you took the side of my enemies,
even giving them strength to subdue me,
and then watched them celebrate their victory!
43 You are no longer helping me in battle.
You've forsaken me to the swords of those
who would strike me down.
44 You've made my regal splendor to decrease
and allowed my rule to be overthrown.
45 Because of you, I've become old before my time and
I'm publicly disgraced!

Pause in his presence

Fourth poem—"Save Me, God"

46 How long will you hide your love from me?
Have you left me for good?
How long will your anger continue to burn against me?
47 Remember, Lord, I am nothing but dust,
here today and so soon blown away.
Is this all you've created us for? For nothing but this?
48 Which one of us will live forever?
We are all mortal, terminal, for we will all one day die.
Which one of us would ever escape our appointment with
death
and dodge our own funeral?

Pause in his presence

49 So God, where is all this love and kindness you promised us?
What happened to your covenant with David?
50 Have you forgotten how your own servants are being
slandered?
Lord God, it seems like I'm carrying in my heart

so that we may accept your correction.[a]
13 Return to us again, O God!
How much longer will it take until you show us
your abundant compassion?
14 Let the sunrise of your love end our dark night.
Break through our clouded dawn again!
Only you can satisfy our hearts,
filling us with songs of joy to the end of our days.
15 We've been overwhelmed with grief;
come now and overwhelm us with gladness!
Replace our years of trouble with decades of delight!
16 Let us see your miracles again, and let the rising generation
see the glorious wonders you're famous for.
17 O Lord our God, let your sweet beauty rest upon us
and give us favor.
Come work with us, and then our works will endure
and give us success in all we do!

91 Safe and Secure

1 When you sit enthroned[b] under the shadow of Shaddai,[c]
you are hidden[d] in the strength of God Most High.
2 He's the hope that holds me, and the Stronghold to shelter me,
the only God for me, and my great Confidence.

---

a 90:12 As translated from the Septuagint.

b 91:1 Or "O, you who sits enthroned." The Hebrew word *yashab* is often associated with one seated as royalty. It is translated in Ezek. 27:8 as leaders or rulers.

c 91:1 *Shaddai* (*šadday*) is taken from a Hebrew root word with many expressive meanings. It can mean, "God of the Mountain, God the Destroyer of Enemies, God the Self-Sufficient One, God the Nurturer of Babies, God the Almighty."

d 91:1 Or "I endure through the night." See Job 39:28 where the same Hebrew word is used for an eagle passing the night on the high cliffs.

3 He will rescue you from every hidden trap of the enemy,[a]
and he will protect you from false accusation
and any deadly curse.[b]
4 His massive arms[c] are wrapped around you, protecting you.
You can run under his covering of majesty and hide.
His arms of faithfulness are a shield keeping you from harm.
5 You will never worry about an attack of demonic forces at night
nor have to fear a spirit of darkness coming against you.
6 Don't fear a thing!
Whether by night or by day, demonic danger will not trouble you,[d]
nor will the powers of evil launched against you.
7 Even in a time of disaster with thousands and thousands being killed,
You will remain unscathed and unharmed!
8 You will be a spectator as the wicked perish in judgment,
for they will be paid back for what they have done!
9–10 When we live our lives within the shadow of the God Most High,

---

a 91:3 Or "hunter."

b 91:3 As translated from the most ancient Hebrew manuscripts and the Septuagint. The Hebrew word can mean poisoned arrows.

c 91:4 Or "wings." Also found in the next sentence, "under his wings," which speaks not of God having wings, but his wings of the cherubim resting on the mercy seat. The implication is that you can always come to the mercy seat and rest without fear.

d 91:6 Verses 5–6 are seen by many Jewish scholars as a reference not merely to pestilence and natural dangers, but to the realm of spiritual darkness that would come against God's servants. These spirits are equated to"arrows that fly in daytime" or a "pestilence that walks" in the darkness. God's sheltered ones are kept from the harm that could come from natural sources or supernatural sources. What a wonderful place to hide and be secure!

our secret Hiding Place, we will always be shielded from harm!
How then could evil prevail against us, or disease infect us?
11 God sends angels with special orders to protect you wherever you go,
defending you from all harm.
12 If you walk into a trap, they'll be there for you
and keep you from stumbling!
13 You'll even walk unharmed among the fiercest powers of darkness,[a]
trampling every one of them beneath your feet!
14 For here is what the Lord has spoken to me:
"Because you have delighted in me as my great lover,
I will greatly protect you.
I will set you in a high place, safe and secure before my face.
15 I will answer your cry for help every time you pray,
and you will find and feel my presence
even in your time of pressure and trouble.
I will be your glorious Hero and give you a feast!
16 You will be satisfied with a full life and with all that I do for you.
For you will enjoy the fullness of my salvation!"

92 A Sunday Morning Song of Praise

A poetic praise song for the day of worship[b]

1 It's so enjoyable to come before you
with uncontainable praises spilling from our hearts!

---

a 91:13 The Hebrew includes the words for *lions*, *snakes*, and *dragons* (Heb. *basilisk*) as the three great symbols of satanic power.

b Ancient Jewish tradition holds that Adam composed this psalm on the first Sabbath of creation, and it was to be sung by the Levites on the Sabbath in the temple.

How we love to sing our praises over and over to you,
to the matchless God, high and exalted over all!
2 At each and every sunrise we will be thanking you
for your kindness and your love.
As the sun sets and all through the night,
we will keep proclaiming, "You are so faithful!"
3 Melodies of praise will fill the air as every musical
instrument,[a]
joined with every heart, overflows with worship.
4 No wonder I'm so glad; I can't keep it in!
Lord, I'm shouting with glee over all you've done,
for all you've done for me!
5 What mighty miracles and your power at work, just to name
a few!
Depths of purpose and layers of meaning
saturate everything you do.
6 Such amazing mysteries found within every miracle
that nearly everyone seems to miss.
Those with no discernment can never really discover
the deep and glorious secrets hidden in your ways!
7 It's true the wicked flourish, but only for a moment,
foolishly forgetting their destiny with death
that they will all one day be destroyed forevermore.
8 But you, O Lord, are exalted forever
in the highest place of endless glory,
9 While all your opponents, the workers of wickedness,
they will all perish, forever separated from you!
10 Your anointing has made me strong and mighty.
You've empowered my life for triumph[b]
by pouring fresh oil over me!

---

a 92:3 Or "a ten-stringed harp and lyre."

b 92:10 The Septuagint reads, "I will raise my horn high like a rhinoceros [Hebrew translated to *wild ox*], and in my old age I will still have plenty of oil [anointing]."

11 You've said that those lying in wait to pounce on me
would be defeated,
and now it's happened right in front of my eyes
and I've heard their cries of surrender!
12 Yes! Look how you've made all your lovers
to flourish like palm trees,
each one growing in victory, standing with strength! [a]
13 You've transplanted them into your heavenly courtyard
where they are thriving before you.
14 For in your presence they will still overflow and be anointed.
Even in their old age they will stay fresh,
bearing luscious fruit and abiding faithfully.
15 Listen to them! With pleasure they still proclaim:
"You're so good! You're my beautiful Strength!
You've never made a mistake with me!" [b]

93 The Majesty of God

A Friday song, composed by King David
after being resettled in the land [c]

1 Look! Yahweh now reigns as King!
He has covered himself with majesty and strength,
wearing them as his splendor-garments!
Regal power surrounds him as he sits securely on his
throne.
He's in charge of it all, the entire world,
and he knows what he's doing!

---

a 92:12 Or "growing high like a cedar in Lebanon." God makes us immortal and immovable.

b 92:15 Or "You are just and never unfair."

c This inscription is found in the Septuagint. Jews called this psalm "The Friday psalm." The Talmud indicates that this psalm was sung every Friday in the temple by the Levites.

2 Lord, you have reigned as King from the very beginning of time.
Eternity is your home.
3–4 Chaos once challenged you.
The raging waves lifted themselves over and over
high above the ocean's depths, letting out their mighty roar!
Yet at the sound of your voice they were all stilled by your might.
What a majestic King, filled with power!
5 Nothing could ever change your royal decrees;
they will last forever!
Holiness is the beauty that fills your house;[a]
you are the One who abides forevermore!

94 God of Vengeance

A Wednesday song composed by King David[b]

1 Lord God Almighty, you are the God
who takes vengeance on your enemies!
It's time for you to punish evil!
Let your rays of revelation-light shine from your people and
pierce the conscience of the wicked and punish them!
2 It's time to arise as Judge of all the earth;
arise to punish the proud with the penalty they deserve!
3 How much longer will you sit back and watch the wicked
triumph in their evil, boasting in all that is wrong?
4–5 Listen to them bragging among themselves,
gig in their own eyes, all because of the crimes
they've committed against your people!

---

a 93:5 Believers are now God's house, made holy by the blood of Jesus. See 1 Cor. 3:16 and Heb. 3:6.

b This inscription is taken from the Septuagint. The Mishnah states that this psalm was sung by the Levites on the fourth day of the week, each Wednesday, in the temple.

See how they're crushing those who love you, God,
cruelly oppressing those who belong to you.[a]
6 Heartlessly they murder the widows, the foreigners,
and even the orphaned children.
7 They say to themselves, "The Lord God doesn't see this.
Their God, the God of Jacob, he doesn't even care!"
8 But you'd better watch out, you stupid fools!
You'd better wise up! Why would you act like God doesn't exist?
Do you really think that God can't hear their cries?
9 God isn't hard of hearing; he'll hear all their cries!
God isn't blind! He who made the eye has superb vision
and he's watching all you do.
10 Won't the God who knows all things know what you've done?
The God who punishes nations will surely punish you!
11 The Lord has fully examined every thought of man
and found them all to be empty and futile.
12 Lord Yah, there's such a blessing that comes
when you teach us your Word and your ways.[b]
Even the sting of your correction can be sweet.
13 It rescues us from our days of trouble
until you are ready to punish the wicked.[c]
14 For the Lord will never walk away from his cherished ones,
nor would he forsake his chosen ones who belong to him.[d]
15 Whenever you pronounce judgments, they reveal righteousness.[e]

---

a 94:4–5 Or "[the people of] his inheritance." See also verse 14.

b 94:12 Or "from your Torah."

c 94:13 Or "until a pit is dug for the wicked."

d 94:14 Or "[the people of] his inheritance."

e 94:15 Or "justice will prevail."

All your lovers will be pleased.[a]
16 Lord, who will protect me from these wicked ones?
If you don't stand to defend me, who will? I have no one
but you!
17 I would have been killed so many times
if you had not been there for me.
18 When I screamed out, "Lord, I'm doomed!"
your fiery love was stirred and you raced to my rescue.
19 Whenever my busy thoughts were out of control,
the soothing comfort of your presence
calmed me down and overwhelmed me with delight.
20 It's obvious to all; you will have nothing to do
with corrupt rulers who pass laws that empower evil
and defeat what is right.
21 For they gang up against the lovers of righteousness
and condemn the innocent to death.
22–23 But I know that all their evil plans will boomerang back
onto them!
Every plot they hatch will simply seal their own doom!
For you, my God, you will destroy them,
giving them what they deserve.
For you are my true Tower of Strength,
my Safe Place, my Hideout, and my true Shelter.

95 It's Time to Sing

1 Come on, everyone! Let's sing for joy to the Lord!
Let's shout our loudest praises to our God who saved us!
2 Everyone come meet his face with a thankful heart!
Don't hold back your praises;
make him great by your shouts of joy!
3 For the Lord is the greatest of all!
King-God over all other gods!

---

a 94:15 The Hebrew reads, "and after it [judgment] are the pure in heart."

4 In one hand he holds the mysteries of the earth
and in the other he holds the highest mountain peaks!
5 He's the owner of every ocean,
the Engineer and Sculptor of earth itself!
6 Come and kneel before this Creator-God;
Come and bow before the mighty God, our majestic Maker!
7–9 For we are the lovers he cares for and he is the God we worship!
So drop everything else and listen to his voice!
For this is what he's saying:
"Today, when I speak,
don't even think about turning a deaf ear to me
like they did when they tested me at Meribah and Massah,[a]
the place where they argued with me, their Creator.
Your ancestors challenged me over and over with their complaining,
even though I had convinced them of my power and love.
They still doubted my care for them.
10 So for forty long years I was grieved and disgusted by them.
I described them as wicked wanderers
whose hearts would not follow my ways or keep my words!
11 So I made a vow in my anger and declared:
'They will never enter the resting place I've planned for them!'
So don't you ever be hard-hearted or stubborn like they were!"

96 King of the World

1 Go ahead—sing your new song to the Lord!
Let everyone in every language sing him a new song.[b]
2–3 Don't stop! Keep on singing! Make his name famous!

---

a 95:7–9 *Meribah* means strife, argument. *Massah* means testing.
b 96:1 Every new thing God does requires a new song to make it known.

Tell everyone every day how wonderful he is!
Give them the good news of our great Savior.
Take the message of his glory and miracles to every nation.
Tell them about all the amazing things he has done.
4 For the Lord's greatness is beyond description
and he deserves all the praise that comes to him.
He is our King-God and it's right to be in holy awe of him.
5 Other gods are absolutely worthless.[a]
For the Lord God is Creator God
who spread the splendor of the skies!
6 Breathtaking brilliance and awe-inspiring majesty
radiate from his shining presence.
His stunning beauty overwhelms all who come before him![b]
7 Surrender to the Lord Yahweh all you nations and peoples.
Surrender to him all your pride and strength.
8 Confess that Jehovah alone deserves all the glory and honor!
Bring an offering and come celebrate in his courts.
9 Come worship the Lord God wearing the splendor of holiness.
Let everyone wait in wonder as they tremble in awe before him.
10 Tell the nations plainly that Yahweh rules over all!
He is doing a great job, and nothing will disrupt him,
For he treats everyone fair and square.
11–12 Let the skies sing for joy! Let the earth join in the chorus.
Let oceans thunder and fields echo this ecstatic praise
until every swaying tree of every forest joins in,
lifting up their songs of joyous praise to him!
13 For here he comes, the Lord God,
and he's ready to judge the world.

---

a 96:5 The Septuagint reads "demons."
b 96:6 Or "strength and beauty are in his sanctuary."

He will do what's right and can be trusted
to always do what's fair!

97 God Rules Over All

A psalm of David when his kingdom was established[a]

1 Yahweh now reigns as King! Let everyone rejoice!
His rule extends everywhere, even to distant lands,
and the islands of the sea, let them all be glad!
2 Clouds both dark and mysterious now surround him.[b]
His throne of glory rests upon
a foundation of righteousness and justice.
3 All around him burns a blazing glory-fire consuming all his foes.
4 When his lightning strikes it lights up the world.
People are wide-eyed as they tremble and shake.
5 Mountains melt away like wax in a fire
when the Lord of all the earth draws near!
6 Heaven's messengers preach righteousness and
people everywhere see his glory in the sky!
7 Shame covers all who boast in other gods for they worship idols.
For all the supernatural powers once worshiped
the true and Living God!
8 But God's Zion-people are content
for they know and hear the truth.
The people of praise rejoice over all your judgments, O Lord!
9 For you are King-God, the Most High God over all the earth.
You are exalted above every supernatural power!
10 Listen, you lovers of God, hate evil,
for God can keep you from wrong

---

a This inscription is from the Septuagint.
b 97:2 See also Deut. 4:11 and 5:22.

and protect you from the power of wickedness.
11 For he sows seeds of light within his lovers,
and seeds of joy burst forth for the lovers of God!
12 So be glad and continue to give him thanks,
for God's holiness is seen in everything he does.

98 Sing a New Song

David's poetic praise [a]

1 Go ahead—sing your brand-new song to the Lord!
He is famous for his miracles and marvels,
for he is victorious through his mighty power and holy strength.
2 Everyone knows how God has saved us,
for he has displayed his justice throughout history.
3 He never forgets to show us his love and faithfulness.
How kind he has been to Israel!
All the nations know how he stands behind his people
and how he saves his own.
4 So go ahead everyone and shout out your praises with joy!
Break out of the box and let loose
with the most joyous sound of praise!
5 Sing your melody of praise to the Lord
and make music like never before! [b]
6 Blow those trumpets and shofars!
Shout with joyous triumph before King Yahweh!
7 Let the ocean's waves join in the chorus with their roaring praise
until everyone everywhere shouts out in unison:
"Glory to the Lord!"
8 Let the rivers and streams clap with applause

---

a The Septuagint has David as the author. The Hebrew says simply, "A psalm."
b 98:5 Or "accompanied by a harp and the sound of music."

as the mountains rise in a standing ovation
to join the mighty choir of exaltation!
9 Look! Here he comes! The Lord and Judge of all the earth!
He's coming to make things right and to do it fair and square.
And everyone will see that he does all things well!

99 God of Holiness

1 Yahweh is King over all! Everyone trembles in awe before him!
He rules enthroned between the wings of the cherubim.
So let the earth shake and quake in wonder before him!
2 For Yahweh is great and glorious in the midst of his Zion-people.
He is exalted above all!
3 Let everyone praise this breathtaking God, for he is holy!
4 A lover of justice is our mighty King; he is right in all his ways.
He insists on being fair to all,
promoting true justice and equity throughout Israel.
5 So everyone, exalt the Lord our God,
facedown before his glory-throne for he is great and holy!
6 *God has his praying priests*,
like Moses, Aaron, and Samuel, who all interceded,
asking God for help.
God heard their cries and came to their rescue.
7 He spoke to them from the pillar of clouds
and they followed his instructions,
doing everything he told them.
8 God, the great Forgiver, answered their prayers.
Yet he would punish them when they went astray.
9 Keep exalting the Lord our God,
facedown before his glory-throne for he is great and holy!

100 Praise God

A poetic song for thanksgiving

1 Lift up a great shout of joy to the Lord!
Go ahead and do it—everyone, everywhere!
2 As you serve him, be glad and worship him.
Sing your way into his presence with joy!
3 And realize what this really means—
we have the privilege of worshiping the Lord, our God.
For he is our Creator and now we belong to him!
We are the people of his pleasure.[a]
4 You can pass through his open gates with the password of praise.
Come right into his presence with thanksgiving.
Come bring your thank-offering to him
and affectionately bless his beautiful name!
5 For the Lord is always good and ready to receive you.
He's so loving that it will amaze you—
so kind that it will astound you!
And he is famous for his faithfulness toward all.
Everyone knows our God can be trusted,
for he keeps his promises to every generation!

101 Integrity

David's poetic praise

1 Lord, I will sing about your faithful love for me!
My song of praise will have your justice as its theme.
2 I'm trying my best to walk in the way of integrity,
especially in my own home.
But now I need your help!
I'm wondering, Lord, when will you appear?

---

a 100:3 Or "the sheep of his pasture."

and feel love for her every stone.
15 When you arise to intervene,
all the nations and kings will be stunned
and will fear your awesome name, trembling before your glory!
16 Yes, you will reveal yourself to Zion
and appear in the brightness of your glory
to restore her and give her children.
17 He responds to the prayer of the poor and broken
and will not despise the cry of the homeless.
18 Write all this down for the coming generation,
so re-created people[a] will read it and praise the Lord!
19 Tell them how Yah[b] looked down from his high and holy place,
gazing from his glory to survey the earth.
20 He listened to all the groaning of his people longing to be free
and set loose the sons of death to experience life.
21 Multitudes will stream to Jerusalem to
praise the Lord and declare his name in Zion!
22 Peoples from every land, their kings and kingdoms,
will gather together to worship the Lord!
23 But God has brought me to my knees, shortening my life.
24 So I cry out to you, my God, the Father of eternity,
please don't let me die!
I know my life is not yet finished!
25 With your hands you once formed the foundations of the earth
and handcrafted the heavens above.
26–27 They will all fade away one day like worn-out clothing

---

a 102:18 Or "those born anew [re-created]."

b 102:19 Taken from *Yah*weh. Yah is often used as the name of the God of Power.

ready to be discarded, but you'll still be here.
You will replace it all!
Your first creation will be changed,
but you alone will endure, the God of all eternity!
28 Generation after generation our descendants will live
securely,
for you are the One protecting us, keeping us for yourself.

103 Our Father's Love

King David's song of praise

1 With my whole heart, with my whole life,
and with my innermost being,
I bow in wonder and love before you, the Holy God!
2 Yahweh, you are my soul's celebration.
How could I ever forget the miracles of kindness
you've done for me?
3 You kissed my heart with forgiveness, in spite of all I've
done.[a]
You've healed me inside and out from every disease.
4 You've rescued me from hell[b] and saved my life.
You've crowned me with love and mercy.
5 You satisfy my every desire with good things.[c]
You've supercharged my life so that I soar again[d]
like a flying eagle in the sky!
6 You're a God who makes things right,

---

a 103:3 Starting from this verse and through the rest of the psalm, the writer shifts to the second person (you). The translator has chosen to leave the psalm in the first person to enhance the poetic nuance for the English reader.

b 103:4 Or "redeemed me from the pit," a term often used for Sheol or hell.

c 103:5 The Hebrew text is somewhat difficult to understand. It is literally "who satisfies with good ornaments."

d 103:5 Or "your youth [implying both strength and beauty] he restores."

giving justice to the defenseless.
7 You unveiled to Moses your plans
and showed Israel's sons what you could do.
8 Lord, you're so kind and tenderhearted
to those who don't deserve it[a]
and so very patient with people who fail you!
Your love is like a flooding river
overflowing its banks with kindness.[b]
9 You don't look at us only to find our faults,[c]
just so that you can hold a grudge against us.
10 You may discipline us for our many sins,
but never as much as we really deserve.
Nor do you get even with us for what we've done.
11 Higher than the highest heavens—
that's how high your tender mercy extends!
Greater than the grandeur of heaven above
is the greatness of your loyal love towering over all
who fear you and bow down before you!
12 Farther than from a sunrise to a sunset—
that's how far you've removed our guilt from us!
13 The same way a loving father feels toward his children—
that's but a sample of your tender feelings toward us,[d]
your beloved children, who live in awe of you!

---

a 103:8 Or "Lord, you're so compassionate and merciful." The Hebrew word for *compassion* is a homonym for "womb." The Lord carries his people like a mother carries a child in her womb.

b 103:8 See Ex. 34:6.

c 103:9 Or "You (he) will not always fight with us (like fighting with enemies)."

d 103:13 Or "like a father has deep compassion on his children." The Hebrew word for tender feelings is *raham*, which is a homonym and can also be translated "womb." Our Father carries you in his womb. What a beautiful word play that our Father has a mother's nurturing love for his children.

14 You know all about us inside and out.[a]
You are mindful that we're made from dust.
15 Our days are so few, and our momentary beauty[b]
so swiftly fades away!
16 Then all of a sudden we're gone,
like grass clippings blown away in a gust of wind,
taken away to our appointment with death,
leaving nothing to show that we were here.
17 But Lord, your endless love stretches
from one eternity to the other,
unbroken and unrelenting toward those who fear you
and those who bow facedown in awe before you!
Your faithfulness to keep every gracious promise you've made
passes from parents, to children, to grandchildren, and beyond.
18 You are faithful to all those who follow your ways
and keep your Word.
19 God's heavenly throne is eternal, secure, and strong,
and his sovereignty rules the entire universe!
20 So bless the Lord, all his messengers of power,
for you are his mighty heroes who listen intently
to the voice of his Word to do it!
21 Bless and praise the Lord, you mighty warriors,
ministers who serve him well and fulfill his desires!
22 I will bless and praise the Lord with my whole heart!

---

a 103:14 The Hebrew word *yatsar* is a homonym and can be translated "form," or "frame." God knows our frame. But *yatsar* also means "to be in distress," or "to be frustrated." This sentence could be translated, "You know all about our frustrations and distress." These thoughts combined would mean that God hasn't forgotten that he formed us from dust and we'll experience frustrations as human beings. God is sympathetic to our difficulties.

b 103:15 The Hebrew word translated *beauty* actually means "shining."

21 The mighty lions roar for their dinner,
but it's you, God, who feeds them all!
22 At sunrise they slink back to their dens
to crouch down in the shadows.
23 Then man goes out to his labor and toil,
working from dawn to dusk.
24 O Lord, what an amazing variety of all you have created!
Wild and wonderful is this world you have made,
while wisdom was there at your side!
This world is full of so many creatures, yet each belongs to
you!
25 And then there is the sea! So vast! So wide and deep—
swarming with countless forms of sea life, both small and
great!
26 Trading ships glide through the high seas,
And look! There are the massive whales
bounding upon the waves.
27 All the creatures wait expectantly for you
to give them their food as you determine.
28 You come near and they all gather around,
feasting from your open hands,
and each is satisfied from your abundant supply.
29 But if you were to withhold from them and turn away,
then they all would panic.
And when you choose to take away their breath,
each one dies and returns to the dust.
30 When you release your Spirit-Wind, life is created,
ready to replenish life upon the earth.
31 May God's glorious splendor endure forever!
May the Lord take joy and pleasure in all that he has made!
32 For the earth's Overseer has the power to make it tremble;
just a touch of his finger and volcanoes erupt
as the earth shakes and melts.
33 I will sing my song to the Lord as long as I live!

Every day I will sing my praises to God.
34 May you be pleased with every sweet thought I have about you,
for you are the source of my joy and gladness!
35 Now, let all the sinners be swept from the earth.
But I will keep on praising you, my Lord, with all that is within me.
My joyous, blissful shouts of "Hallelujah" are all because of you!

105 God's Wonderful Works [a]

1 Go ahead—and give God thanks
for all the glorious things he has done!
Go ahead and worship him!
Tell everyone about his wonders!
2 Let's sing his praises! Sing, and put all of his miracles to music!
3 Shine and make your joyful boast in him, you lovers of God.
Let's be happy and keep rejoicing no matter what.
4 Seek more of his strength! Seek more of him!
Let's always be seeking the light of his face!
5 Don't you ever forget his miracles and marvels.
Hold to your heart every judgment he has decreed.
6 For you are his servants, the true seed of Abraham,
and you are the chosen ones, Jacob's sons.
7 For he is the Lord our God,
and his wise authority [b] can be seen in all he does.
8–9 For though a thousand generations may pass away,
he is still true to his word.

---

a The first fifteen verses of this psalm were sung as the ark of glory was brought up to Jerusalem. See 2 Sam. 6 and 1 Chron. 13–16.
b 105:7 Or "judgments."

He has kept every promise[a] he made to Abraham and to
Isaac.
10 His promises have become an everlasting covenant to Jacob,
confirmed to Israel's tribes.
11 He said to them, "I will give you all the land of Canaan
as your inheritance."
12 They were only so very few in number
when God gave them that promise,
and they were all foreigners to that land.
13 They were wandering from one land to another
and from one kingdom to another.[b]
14 Yet God would not permit anyone to touch them,
punishing even kings who came against them.
15 He said to them, "Don't you dare lay a hand on my anointed
ones,
and don't do a thing to hurt my prophets!"
16 So God decreed a famine upon Canaan land,
cutting off their food supply.
17 But he had already sent a man ahead of his people to Egypt;
it was Joseph, who was sold as a slave.
18 His feet were bruised by strong shackles
and his soul was held by iron.
19 God's promise to Joseph purged his character
until it was time for his dreams to come true.
20 Eventually, the king of Egypt sent for him, setting him free
at last.
21 Then Joseph was put in charge of everything under the king;
he became the master of the palace
over all of the royal possessions.
22 Pharoah gave him authority over all the princes of the land,

---

a 105:8–9 Or "promise of the covenant [pact]."
b 105:13 Or "from a kingdom to another nation."

and Joseph became the teacher of wisdom to the king's
advisors.
23 Then Jacob, with all of Joseph's family,
came from Canaan to Egypt, and settled in Goshen.[a]
24 God made them very fruitful, and they multiplied incredibly
until they were greater in number than those who ruled
them.
25 God turned their hearts to hate his people
and to deal treacherously with his servants.
26 But he sent them his faithful servant, Moses, the deliverer,
and chose Aaron to accompany him.
27 Their command brought down signs and wonders,
working miracles in Egypt.
28 By God's direction, they spoke and released a plague
of thick darkness over the land.
29 God turned their rivers to blood, causing every fish to die.
30 And the judgment-plague of frogs came in enormous
numbers,
swarming everywhere, even into Pharaoh's bedroom!
31 God spoke and another plague was released—
massive swarms of flies, vast clouds of insects, covered the
land.
32 God rained down hail and flaming fire upon Egypt.
33 Their gardens and vines were all destroyed,
shattering trees into splinters throughout the territory.
34 God spoke, and devouring hordes of locusts swept over the
land,
35 Picking the ground clean of vegetation and crops.
36 Then God struck down their firstborn sons,
the pride and joy[b] of every Egyptian family.

---

a 105:23 Or "lived as a foreigner in the land of Ham [Egypt]." Ham was a son of Noah.

b 105:36 Or "the beginning of all their strength."

37 At last, God freed all the Hebrews from their slavery
and sent them away laden with the silver and gold of
Egypt.
And not even one was feeble[a] on their way out!
38 Egypt was relieved at their exodus, ready to see them go,
for the terror of the Lord of the Hebrews had fallen upon
them!
39 God spread out a cloud as shade as they moved ahead,
and a cloud of fire to light up their night.
40 Moses prayed and God brought them quail to eat.
He satisfied them with heaven's bread falling from the sky.
41 He broke open the boulder
and the waters poured out like a river in the desert.
42 For God could never forget
his holy promise to his servant, Abraham.
43 So God brought out his chosen ones with singing;
for with a joyful shout they were set free!
44 He gave them lands and nations, just like he promised.
Fruitful lands of crops they had never planted were now
theirs!
45 All this was done for them so that they would be faithful
to keep the ways of God, obeying his laws and following his
truths.
Hallelujah! Praise the Lord!

106 God is Good

1 Hallelujah! Praise the Lord!
Everyone, thank God, for he is good and easy to please!
Your tender love for us, Lord, continues on forever.
2 Who could ever fully describe your glorious miracles?
Yahweh, who could ever praise you enough?
3 The happiest one on earth is the one who keeps your Word

---

a 105:37 Or "not one of his tribes was a pauper." Or "not one stumbled."

and clings to righteousness every moment.
4 So remember me, Lord, as you take joy in your people.
And when you come to bring the blessings of salvation,
don't forget me!
5 Let me share in the wealth and beauty of all your lovers,
rejoice with your nation in all their joys,
and let me share in the glory you give to your chosen ones.
6 We have all sinned so much, just like our fathers.
"Guilty" is written over our lives.
7 Our fathers who were delivered from Egypt
didn't fully understand your wonders,
and they took you for granted.
Over and over you showed them such tender love and mercy!
Yet they were barely beyond the Red Sea
when they rebelled against you.
8 Nonetheless, you saved them more than once
so they would know how powerful you are,
showing them the honor of your name.
9 You roared over the waters of the Red Sea
making a dry path for your people to cross through.
10 You freed them from the strong power
of those that oppressed them
and rescued them from bondage.
11 Then the waters rushed over their enemies and drowned them all—
not one survived.
12 Seeing this, the people believed your words,
and they all broke out with songs of praise!
13 Yet how quickly they forgot your miracles of power.
They wouldn't wait for you to act when they were hungry,
14 But demanded you satisfy their cravings and give them food!
They tested you to the breaking point.
15 So you gave them what they wanted to eat,

but their souls starved away to nothing!
16 They became envious of Moses and Aaron, your holy ones.
17 You split open the earth and it swallowed up
Dathan and Abiram along with their followers.
18 Fire fell from heaven and burnt up all the band of rebels,
turning them to ashes.
19 They made an idol of a calf at Sinai
and bowed to worship their man-made statue.
20 They preferred the image of a grass-eating ox
to the presence of the glory-filled God.
21–22 They totally forgot it was you that saved them
by the wonders and awesome miracles you worked in
Egypt.
23 So you were fed up and decided to destroy them.
But Moses, your chosen leader,
stood in the gap between you and the people
and made intercession on their behalf
to turn away your wrath from killing them all.
24 Yet they still didn't believe your words
and they despised the land of delight you gave to them.
25 They grumbled and found fault with everything
and closed their hearts to your voice.
26 So you gave up and swore to them
that they would all die in the desert,
27 And you scattered their children to distant lands to die as
exiles.
28 Then our fathers joined the worshipers
of the false god named "Lord of the Pit."
They even ate the sacrifices offered to the dead!
29 All they did made you burn with anger.
It made you so angry that a plague broke out among them!

30 It continued until Phineas intervened and executed
the guilty for causing judgment to fall upon them.[a]
31 Because of this deed of righteousness,
Phineas will be remembered forever.
32 Your people also provoked you to wrath
at the stream called Strife.[b]
This is where Moses got into serious trouble!
33 Because the people were rebellious against you,
Moses exploded in anger and spoke to them out of his bitterness.
34 Neither did our fathers destroy the enemies in the land
as you had commanded them.
35 But they mingled themselves with their enemies
and learned to copy their works of darkness.
36 They began to serve their gods and bow before their idols.
All of this led them away from you
and brought about their downfall.
37 They even sacrificed their little children to the demon spirits,
38–39 Shedding the innocent blood of their sons and daughters.
These dark practices greatly defiled the land and their own souls,
through the murder and bloodshed of their own babies!
Their sins made them spiritual adulterers before you.
40 This is why you were furious.
As your anger burned hot against them,
you couldn't even stand to look
at your very own people any longer!
41 So you turned them over to the crushing hands of other nations

---

a 106:30 This is implicit information found in the story of Phineas (Num. 25:7–9).

b 106:32 The word used here is *Meribah*, the Hebrew word for strife (Num. 20:1–13).

15 So lift your hands and give thanks to God for his marvelous
kindness
and for his miracles of mercy for those he loves!
16 For he smashed through heavy prison doors and
shattered the steel bars that held us back, just to set us free!
17 Some of us were such fools, bringing on ourselves
sorrow and suffering all because of our sins.
18 Sick and feeble, unable to stand the sight of food,
we drew near to the gates of death.
19 Then we cried out, "Lord, help us! Rescue us!" And he did!
20 God spoke the words, "Be healed," and we were healed,
delivered from death's door!
21 So lift your hands and give thanks to God for his marvelous
kindness
and for his miracles of mercy for those he loves!
22 Bring your praise as an offering and your thanks as a
sacrifice
as you sing your story of miracles with a joyful song!
23 Some of us set sail upon the sea to faraway ports,
transporting our goods from ship to shore.
24 We were witnesses of God's power out in the ocean deep;
we saw breathtaking wonders upon the high seas.
25 For when God spoke he stirred up a storm,
lifting high the waves with hurricane winds.
26–27 Ships were tossed by swelling sea, rising to the sky,
then dropping down to the depths,
reeling like drunkards, spinning like tops,
everyone at their wits' end until even sailors despaired of
life,
cringing in terror.
28 Then we cried out, "Lord, help us! Rescue us!" And he did!
29 God stilled the storm, calmed the waves,
and he hushed the hurricane winds to only a whisper.
30 We were so relieved, so glad as he guided us

safely to harbor in a quiet haven.
31 So lift your hands and give thanks to God for his marvelous kindness
and for his miracles of mercy for those he loves!
32 Let's exalt him on high and lift up our praises in public;
let all the people and the leaders of the nation know
how great and wonderful is Yahweh, our God!
33 Whenever he chooses he can dry up a river
and turn the land into a desert.
34 Or he can take a fruitful land and make it into a saltwater swamp,
all because of the wickedness of those who dwell there.
35 But he also can turn a barren wilderness into an oasis with water!
He can make springs flow into desert lands,
36 And turn them into fertile valleys so that cities spring up,
and he gives it all to those who are hungry.
37 They can plant their fields and vineyards there
and reap a bumper crop and gather a fruitful harvest.
38 God will bless them and cause them to multiply and prosper.
39 But others will become poor,
humbled because of their oppression, tyranny, and sorrows.
40 For God pours contempt upon their arrogant abuse of power,
heaping scorn upon their princes,
and makes them wander among ruins.
41 But he raises up the poor and lowly with his favor,
giving them a safe place to live where no one can touch them!
God will grant them a large family and bless them!
42 The lovers of God will rejoice when they see this.
Good men are glad when the evil ones are silenced.
43 If you are truly wise, you'll learn from what I've told you!

It's time for you to consider these profound lessons
of God's great love and mercy!

108 A Prayer for God's Help

A poetic psalm by King David

1 My heart, O God, is quiet and confident all because of you.
Now I can sing my song with passionate praises!
2 Awake, O my soul, with the music of his splendor.
Arise my soul and sing his praises!
I will awaken the dawn with my worship,
greeting the daybreak with my songs *of light*!
3 Wherever I go I will thank you.
All the nations will hear my praise songs to you.
4 Your love is so extravagant, it reaches higher than the heavens!
Your faithfulness is so astonishing, it stretches to the skies!
5 Lord God, be exalted as you soar throughout the heavens.
May your shining glory be seen high above all the earth!
6 Come to your beloved ones and gently draw us out!
Answer our prayer for your saving help.
Come with your might and strength, *for we need you Lord*!
7–9 Then I heard the Lord speak in his holy splendor,
and from his sanctuary I heard the Lord promise:
"In my triumph I will be the One to measure out
the portion of my inheritance to my people,
and I will secure the land as I promised you.
Shechem, Succoth, Gilead, Manasseh;[a]

---

a 108:7–9 The Hebrew includes two geographical places in the text: Shechem and Succoth. Shechem is where Jacob (Israel) first bought title to the land, paying one hundred pieces of silver for the place where he camped. Succoth is another place where Jacob temporarily camped in the Land of Promise. These two places speak of God being the One who brought them in and portioned out the land for his people.

they are all still mine!" he says.
"Judah will continue to produce kings and lawgivers,
and Ephraim will produce great warriors.
Moab will become my lowly servant!
Edom will likewise serve my purposes!
I will lift up a shout of victory over the land of Philistia!
10 But who will bring my triumph into Edom's fortresses?"[a]
11 Lord, have you really rejected us, refusing to fight our battles?
12 Give us a Father's help when we face our enemies.
For to trust in any man is an empty hope.
13 With God's help we will prevail with might and power.
And with God's help we'll trample down our every foe!

109 God, It's Time for Vengeance

To the Pure and Shining One
A poetic song by King David

1 God of all my praise, don't stand silently by, aloof to my pain,
2 While the wicked slander me with their lies.
Even right in front of my face they lie through their teeth.
3 I've done nothing to them, but they still surrounds me
with their venomous words of hatred and vitriol.
4 Though I love them, they stand accusing me like Satan
for what I've never done.
I will pray until I become prayer itself.[b]
5 They continually repay me with evil when I show them good!
They give me hatred when I show them love!

---

a 108:10 *Edom* is a variant form of the word *Adam*.
b 109:4 In the face of accusation and slander, David says literally in Hebrew, "I am prayer!"

6–7 Show him how it feels! Let accusing liars be raised up
against him,
like Satan himself standing right next to him.
And let him be declared guilty by a wicked judge!
May even his prayers be seen as sinful!
8 Shorten his life and let another replace him!
9 Make his wife a widow and his children orphans!
10 Let them wander as beggars in the street,
like homeless vagabonds, evicted from their ruins!
11 Let the creditors seize his entire estate,
and strangers, like vultures, take all that's left!
12 Let no one be kind to him by showing pity to his fatherless
children!
13 May all his posterity die with him! Cut down his family tree!
14–15 And may all the sins of his ancestors be recorded,
remembered before you, forever!
Cut off even the memory of his family from the face of the
earth
16 Because he never once showed love or kindness to others,
but persecuted the poor, the brokenhearted, and afflicted
ones,
even putting them to death!
17 Since he enjoyed cursing them,
may all his curses now come raining back on him
until it all overwhelms him with misfortune!
Since he refused to bless others,
God, withhold every single blessing from him!
18 Bitterness, such vile vindictiveness, was upon everything he
did.
Cursing was his lifestyle.
19–20 So smother him now with his own curses as his just
reward.
This will be the Lord's punishment upon him and
all my lying accusers who speak evil against me.

21 But now, O Yahweh-God, make yourself real to me
like you promised me you would![a]
Because of your constant love and your heart-melting
kindness, come be my Hero and deliver me!
22 I'm so broken, needy and hurting.
My heart is pierced through and I'm so wounded.
23 I'm slipping down a dark slope, shaken to the core, and
helpless!
24 All my fasting has left me so weak I can hardly stand.
Now I'm shriveled up, nothing but skin and bones.
25 I'm the example of failure and shame to all who see me.
They just walk by me shaking their heads!
26 You have to help me, O Lord God!
My true Hero, come to my rescue and save me
for you are so loving and kind!
27 Then everyone will know that you have won my victory,
and they will all say to the Lord, "You have finished it!"
28 So let them curse me if they want,
but I know you will bless me!
All their efforts to destroy me will fail,
but I will succeed and be glad!
29 So let my satan-like accusers fail!
Make them look ridiculous if they try to come against me!
Clothe them with a robe of guilty shame from this day on!
30 But I will give my thanks to you over and over
and everyone will hear my lavish praises.
31 For you stand right next to the broken one
as their saving Hero to rescue them from all their accusers!

---

a 109:21 The Hebrew text states, "for your name's sake."

110 Messiah, King, and Priest [a]

King David's psalm

1 Yahweh said to my Lord, the Messiah:
"Sit with me as Enthroned Ruler [b]
while I subdue your every enemy.
They will bow low before you
as I make them a footstool for your feet!" [c]
2 Messiah, I know God himself will establish your kingdom
as you reign in Zion-glory.
For he says to you: "Rule in the midst of your enemies!"
3 Your people will be your love offerings
like living sacrifices spilled out before you!
In the day of your mighty power you will be exalted,
and in the brightness of your holy ones you will shine
as an army arising from the dawning rays of a new day,
anointed with the dew of your youth!
4 Yahweh has taken a solemn oath
and will never back away from it, saying:
"You are a priest for eternity, my King of righteousness!" [d]
5 The Lord stands in full authority [e] to shatter to pieces
the kings who stand against you

---

a This psalm is applied to Christ in the New Testament where it is quoted more often than any other Old Testament passage.

b 1:1 Or "at my right hand." The right hand is the position of authority and honor.

c 110:1 A footstool symbolizes what is subdued. It is taken from the root word "to subdue."

d 110:4 The Hebrew text includes the word *Melchizedek*, the name of a Canaanite king and priest over the Jebusite kingdom that later became Jerusalem. The name *Melchizedek* means, "my king of righteousness."

e 110:5 The Hebrew word used here for *Lord* is *Adonai*, or *Adonay*. It is the plural form of *Adhon*. Jesus is called Lord of lords, and we are the lords that he is Lord over. We are seated at his right hand (Benjamin) to rule with him.

on the day He displays his terrible wrath.
6 He will judge every rebellious nation,
filling their battlefield with corpses,
and will shatter the strongholds of ruling powers.
7 Yet he himself will drink from his inheritance
as from a flowing brook;
refreshed by love he will stand victorious!

111 Celebrate God's Greatness

1 Shout hallelujah to Yahweh!
May every one of his lovers hear my passionate praise to him,
even among the council of the holy ones!
2 For God's mighty miracles astound me!
His wonders are so delightfully mysterious
that they leave all who seek them astonished.
3 Everything he does is full of splendor and beauty!
Each miracle demonstrates his eternal perfection.
4 His unforgettable works of surpassing wonder
reveal his grace and tender mercy.
5 He satisfies all who love and trust him,
and he keeps every promise he makes.
6 He reveals mighty power and marvels to his people
by handing them nations as a gift!
7 All God accomplishes is flawless, faithful, and fair,
and his every word proves trustworthy and true.
8 They are steadfast forever and ever,
formed from truth and righteousness.
9 His forever-love paid a full ransom for his people
so that now we're free to come before Jehovah
to worship his holy and awesome name!
10 Where can wisdom be found? It is born in the fear of God.
Everyone who follows his ways

will never lack his living-understanding.
And the adoration of God will abide throughout eternity!

112 The Triumph of Faith

1 Shout in celebration of praise to the Lord!
Everyone who loves the Lord and delights in him
will cherish his words and be blessed beyond expectation!
2 Their descendants will be prosperous and influential.
Every generation of his godly lovers will experience his favor!
3 Great blessing and wealth fills their house *of the wise*,
for their integrity endures forever.
4 Even if darkness overtakes them,
sunrise-brilliance will come bursting through
because they are gracious to others, so tender and true.
5 Life is good for the one who is generous and charitable,
conducting affairs with honesty and truth.
6 Their circumstances will never shake them
and others will never forget their example.
7 They will not live in fear or dread of what may come,
for their hearts are firm, ever secure in their faith.
8 Steady and strong they will not be afraid,
but will calmly face their every foe
until they all go down in defeat.
9 Never stingy and always generous to those in need,
their lives of influence and honor will never be forgotten
for they were full of good deeds!
10 But the wicked take one look at a life lived like this
and they grit their teeth in anger, not understanding their bliss.
The wicked slink away speechless in the darkness that falls,
where hope dies, and all their dreams fade away to nothing,
to nothing at all!

113 God Is Kind

1 Hallelujah! Praise the Lord![a]
Go ahead—praise the Lord all you loving servants of God!
Keep it up! Praise him some more!
2 For the glorious name of the Lord is blessed forever and ever.
3 From sunrise brilliance to sunset beauty,
lift up his praise from dawn to dusk!
4 For he rules on high over the nations
with a glory that outshines even the heavens.
5 No one can be compared to God, enthroned on high!
6 He stoops down to look upon the sky and the earth.
7 He promotes the poor, picking them up from the dirt,
and rescues the needy from the garbage dump.
8 He turns paupers into princes and seats them
on their royal thrones of honor.
9 God's grace provides for the barren ones a joyful home with children
so that even childless couples find a family.
He makes them happy parents surrounded by their pride and joy.
That's the God we praise, so give it all to him!

114 A Song for Passover

1 Many years ago the Jewish people escaped Egypt's tyranny,
2 So that Israel, God's people of praise,[b]
would become his holy sanctuary,
his kingdom on the earth.

---

a 113:1 Ps. 113–114 were sung before the meal, during the Jewish family's celebration of Passover, while Ps. 115–118 were sung after the meal (see Mark 14:26).

b 114:2 Or *Judah*, which means praise.

3 The Red Sea waters saw them coming and ran the other
way!
Then later, the Jordan River too,
moved aside so that they could all pass through.
4 The land shuddered with fear.
Mountains and hills shook with dread.[a]
5 O Sea, what happened to you, to make you flee?
O Jordan, what was it that made you turn and run?
6 O mountains, what frightened you so?
And you hills, what made you shiver?
7 Tremble, O earth, for you are in the presence of the Lord,
the God of Jacob.
8 He splits open boulders and brings up bubbling water!
Gushing streams burst forth *when he is near*!

115 The One True God

1 God, glorify your name!
Yes, your name alone be glorified, not ours!
For you are the One who loves us passionately,
and you are faithful and true.
2 Why should the unbelievers mock us, saying,
"Where is this God of yours?"
3 But we know our God rules from the heavens
and he takes delight in all that he does.
4 The unbelievers worship what they make—
their wealth and their work.
5–8 They idolize what they own
and what they make with their hands,
but their things can't talk to them or answer their prayers.
Their possessions will never satisfy.

---

a 114:4 The literal Hebrew states, "mountains skipped like rams, the hills like lambs." This does not mean they skipped with joy, but shook with fear, as the context reveals.

Their futile faith in dead idols and dead works
can never bring life or meaning to their souls.
Blind men can only create blind things.
Those deaf to God can only make a deaf image.
Dead men can only create dead idols.
And everyone who trusts in these powerless, dead things
will be just like what they worship—powerless and dead![a]

9 So trust in the Lord, all his people.
For he is the only true Hero,
the wrap-around God who is our Shield!

10 You, his priests, trust in the Lord.
For he is the only true Hero,
God-wrapped-around-us as our Shield!

11 Yes, all his lovers who bow before him, trust in the Lord.
For he is our only true Hero,
God-wrapped-around-us as our Shield!

12 The Lord will never forget us in our need; he will bless us indeed!
He will bless the house of Israel;
he will bless the house of Aaron, his priest.

13 Yes! He will bless his lovers who bow before him,
no matter who they are.

14–15 God himself will fill you with more.
Blessings upon blessings will be heaped upon you
and upon your children from the Maker of heaven and earth,
the very God who made you!

16 The heavens belong to our God; they are his alone,

---

a 115:5–8 Referring to the idols, the literal Hebrew could be translated: "With mouths, but they cannot speak; with eyes, but they cannot see; with ears, but they cannot hear; with noses, but they cannot smell; with hands, but they cannot feel; with feet, but they cannot walk; they cannot talk. Those who make them will become like them, and everyone who trusts in them."

His faithfulness lasts forever and he will never fail you.
So go ahead, let it all out!
Praise Yah!
O Yah![a]

118 Glorious Thanksgiving

A praise-psalm[b]

1 Keep on giving your thanks to God, for he is so good!
His constant, tender love lasts forever!
2 Let all his princely people sing:
"His constant, tender love lasts forever!"
3 Let all his holy priests sing:
"His constant, tender love lasts forever!"
4 Let all his lovers who bow low before him sing:
"His constant, tender love lasts forever!"
5 Out of my deep anguish and pain I prayed,
and God, you helped me as a Father.
You came to my rescue and broke open the way
into a beautiful and broad place.
6 Now I know, Lord, that you are for me,
and I will never fear what man can do to me.
7 For you stand beside me as my Hero who rescues me.
I've seen with my own eyes the defeat of my enemies.
I've triumphed over them all!
8 Lord, it is so much better to trust in you to save me
than to put my confidence in someone else.
9 Yes, it is so much better to trust in the Lord to save me
than to put my confidence in celebrities.

---

a 117:2 The name *Yah* is not an abbreviated form of *Yahweh*; it is the name of God as he displays his power. *Yahweh* is found 6,830 times in the Hebrew text, and *Yah* is found 49 times.

b This is the psalm or "hymn" that Jesus likely sang after the Passover supper with his disciples, before making his way to Gethsemane and Calvary.

10 Once I was hemmed in and surrounded by those
who don't love you.
But by Yahweh's supernatural power I overcame them all!
11–12 Yes, they surrounded me,
like a swarm of killer bees swirling around me.
I was trapped like one trapped by a raging fire;
I was surrounded with no way out and at the point of
collapse.
But by Yahweh's supernatural power, I overcame them all!
13 They pushed me right up to the edge, and I was ready to
fall,
but you helped me to triumph, and together we overcame
them all.
14 Lord, you are my true strength and my glory-song,
my Champion, my Savior!
15 The joyful songs I now sing will be sung again
in the hearts and homes of all your lovers.
My loud shouts of victory will echo throughout the land.[a]
For Yahweh's right hand conquers valiantly!
16 The right hand of Yahweh exalts!
The right hand of Yahweh will never fail!
17 You will not let them kill me,
but I will live to tell the world what the Lord has done for
me.
18 Yes, the Lord punished me as I deserved,
but he'll never give me over to death.
19 Swing wide, you gates of righteousness, and let me pass
through,
and I will enter into your presence to worship only you!
20 I have found the gateway to God,
the pathway to his presence for all his lovers.
21 I will offer all my loving praise to you,

---

a 118:15 Or "in the tents of the righteous."

and I thank you so much for answering my prayer
and bringing me salvation!
22 The very stone the masons rejected as flawed
has turned out to be the most important capstone of the arch,[a]
holding up the very house of God.
23 The Lord himself is the One who has done this;
and it's so amazing, so marvelous to see!
24 This is the very day of the Lord that brings
gladness and joy, filling our hearts with glee!
25 O God, please come and save us again;
bring us your breakthrough-victory!
26 Blessed is this One who comes to us, the Sent-One of the Lord.
And from within the temple we cry: "We bless you!"
27–28 For the Lord our God has brought us his glory-light!
I offer him my life in joyous sacrifice.
Tied tightly to your altar I will bring you praise.
For you are the God of my life and I lift you high,
exalting you to the highest place.
29 So let's keep on giving our thanks to God, for he is so good!
His constant, tender love lasts forever!

---

a 118:22 The words "capstone of the arch" can also be translated "the head of the corner."

119 The Words of God [a]

The Way to Happiness

1 You're only truly happy when you walk in total integrity, [b]
walking in the light of God's Word!
2 What joy overwhelms everyone who keeps the ways of God,
those who seek him as their heart's passion!
3 They'll never do what's wrong
but will always choose the paths of the Lord.
4 God has prescribed the right way to live:
obeying his laws with all our hearts.
5 How I long for my life to bring you glory
as I follow each and every one of your holy precepts!
6 Then I'll never be ashamed,
for I take strength from all your commandments.
7 I will give my thanks to you from a heart of love and truth.
And every time I learn more of your righteous judgments,
8 I will be faithful to all that your Word reveals—
so don't ever give up on me!

True Joy

9 How can a young man stay pure?

---

a This psalm is an acrostic poem, a mathematical masterpiece. It consists of twenty-two stanzas of eight lines each. Each stanza begins with the same Hebrew letter at the beginning of every one of its eight lines, going in succession, by strophes, from *alef*—the first letter of the Hebrew alphabet, as the first letter of each line in the first strophe—to *taw*—the last letter of the Hebrew alphabet, as the first letter of each line in the last strophe. Like the eight lines of each stanza there are eight different Hebrew words, all synonyms, used to refer to the Word of God. Although many believe Ezra wrote Ps. 119, the acrostic poetic style is unique to King David within the book of Psalms, which points to his authorship of this psalm.

b 119:1 Or "perfection." The Hebrew reads "utterances."

Only by living in the Word of God and walking in its truth.
10 I have longed for you with the passion of my heart;
don't let me stray from your directions!
11 I consider your prophecies[a] to be my greatest treasure,
and I memorize them and write them on my heart
to keep me from committing sin's treason against you.
12 My wonderful God, you are to be praised above all;
teach me the power of your decrees!
13 I speak continually of your laws
as I recite out loud your counsel to me.
14 I find more joy in following what you tell me to do
than in chasing after all the wealth of the world!
15 I set my heart on your precepts
and pay close attention to all your ways.
16 My delight is found in all your laws,
and I won't forget to walk in your words.

The Abundant Life

17 Let me, your servant, walk in abundance of life
that I may always live to obey your truth.
18 Open my eyes to see the miracle-wonders hidden in your
Word!
19 My life on earth is so brief, so tutor me in the ways of your
wisdom.
20 I am continually consumed by these irresistible longings,
these cravings to obey your every commandment!
21 Your displeasure rests with those who are arrogant,
who think they know everything;
you rebuke the rebellious who refuse your laws.
22 Don't let them mock and scorn me for obeying you.
23 For even if the princes and my leaders choose to criticize
me,

---

a 119:11 As translated from the Septuagint.

I'll continue to serve you and walk in your plans for my life.
24 Your commandments are my counselors;
your Word is my light and delight!

Revived by the Word

25 Lord, I'm fading away. I'm discouraged and lying in the dust;
revive me by your Word, just like you promised you would!
26 I've poured out my life before you,
and you've always been there for me;
so now I ask: teach me more of your holy decrees.
27 Open up my understanding to the ways of your wisdom
and I will meditate deeply on your splendor and your wonders.
28 My life's strength melts away with grief and sadness;
come strengthen me and encourage me with your words.
29 Keep me far away from what is false;
give me grace to stay true to your laws.
30 I've chosen to obey your truth
and walk in the splendor-light of all that you teach me.
31 Lord, don't allow me to make a mess of my life,
for I cling to your commands and follow them as closely as I can.
32 I will run after you with delight in my heart,
for you will make me obedient to your instructions.

Understanding God's Ways

33 Give me revelation about the meaning of your ways
so I can enjoy the reward of following them fully!
34 Give me an understanding heart so that I can
passionately know and obey your truth.
35 Guide me into the paths that please you,
for I take delight in all that you say.
36 Cause my heart to bow before your words of wisdom
and not to the wealth of this world.

My True Treasure

65 Your extravagant kindness to me
makes me want to follow your words even more!
66 Teach me how to make good decisions,
and give me revelation-light for I believe in your commands.
67 Before I was humbled I used to always wander astray,
but now I see the wisdom of your words.
68 Everything you do is beautiful, flowing from your goodness;
teach me the power of your wonderful words!
69 Proud boasters make up lies about me
because I am passionate to follow all that you say.
70 Their hearts are dull and void of feelings,
but I find my true treasure in your truth.
71 The punishment you brought me through was the best thing
that could have happened to me, for it taught me your ways.
72 The words you speak to me are worth more
than all the riches and wealth in the whole world!

Growth Through the Word

73 Your very hands have held me and made me who I am;
give me more revelation-light so I may learn to please you more.
74 May all your lovers see how you treat me and be glad,
for your words are entwined within my heart!
75 Lord, I know that your judgments are always right.
Even when it's me you judge, you're still faithful and true.
76 Send your kind mercy-kiss to comfort me, your servant,
just like you promised you would!
77 Love me tenderly so I can go on,
for I delight in your life-giving truth.
78 Shame upon the proud liars! See how they oppress me,

all because of my passion for your precepts!
79 May all your lovers follow me
as I follow the path of your instruction.
80 Make me passionate and wholehearted to fulfill your every wish,
so that I'll never have to be ashamed of myself.

Deliver Me

81 I'm lovesick with yearnings for more of your salvation,
for my heart is entwined with your Word.
82 I'm consumed with longings for your promises,
so I ask, "When will they all come true?"
83 My soul feels dry and shriveled, useless and forgotten,
but I will never forget your living truth.
84 How much longer must I wait until you punish my persecutors?
For I am your loving servant.
85 Arrogant men who hate your truth and never obey your laws
have laid a trap for my life.
86 They don't know that everything you say is true,
so they harass me with their lies. Help me, Lord!
87 They've nearly destroyed my life, but I refuse to yield;
I still live according to your Word.
88 Revive me with your tender love and
spare my life by your kindness, and I'll continue to obey you!

Faith in the Word of God

89 Standing firm in the heavens and fastened to eternity
is the Word of God.
90 Your faithfulness flows from one generation to the next;
all that you created sits firmly in place to testify of you.
91 By your decree everything stands at attention,

Empower me to live every moment in the light of your
ways.
118 Lord, you reject those who reject your laws,
for they fool no one but themselves!
119 The wicked are thrown away, discarded and valueless.
That's why I will keep on loving all of your laws!
120 My body trembles in holy awe of you, leaving me
speechless;
for I'm frightened of your righteous judgments.

I Will Follow Your Ways

121 Don't leave me to the mercies of those who hate me,
for I live to do what is just and fair.
122 Let me hear your promise of blessing over my life,
breaking me free from the proud oppressors.
123 As a lovesick lover, I yearn for more of your salvation
and for your virtuous promises!
124 Let me feel your tender love for I am yours.
Give me more understanding of your wonderful ways.
125 I need more revelation from your Word
to know more about you, for I'm in love with you!
126 Lord, the time has come for you to break through,
for evil men keep breaking your laws!
127 Truly, your message of truth means more to me
than a vault filled with the purest gold.
128 Every word you speak, every truth revealed, is always right
and beautiful to me; for I hate what is phony or false.

I Long to Obey You

129 Your marvelous words are living miracles;
no wonder I long to obey everything you say.
130 Break open your Word within me until revelation-light
shines out!
Those with open hearts are given insight into your plans.

131 I open my mouth and inhale the Word of God
because I crave the revelation of your commands.
132 Turn your heart to me, Lord, and show me your grace
like you do to every one of your godly lovers.
133 Prepare before me a path filled with your promises,
and don't allow even one sin to have dominion over me.
134 Rescue me from the oppression of ungodly men
so that I can keep all your precepts.
135 Let your shining face shine brightly on me, your loving
servant!
Instruct me on what is right in your eyes.
136 When I witness the rebellious breaking your laws,
it makes me weep uncontrollably!

His Word is True

137 Lord, your judgments reveal your righteousness,
and your verdicts are always fair.
138 The motive behind your every word is pure,
and your teachings are remarkably faithful and true.
139 I've been consumed with a furious passion to do what's
right,
all because of the way my enemies disrespect your laws.
140 All your promises glow with fire;[a]
that's why I'm a lover of your Word.
141 Even though I'm considered insignificant and despised
by the world, I'll never abandon your ways.
142 Your righteousness has no end; it is everlasting,
and your rules are perfectly fair.
143 Even though my troubles overwhelm me with anguish,
I still delight and cherish every message you speak to me.
144 Give me more revelation so that I can live for you,
for nothing is more pure and eternal than your truth.

---

a 119:140 As translated from the LXX and implied in the Hebrew.

174 I wait for your deliverance, O Lord,
for your words thrill me like nothing else!
175 Invigorate my life so that I can praise you even more,
and may your truth be my strength!
176 I'll never forget what you've taught me, Lord,
but when I wander off and lose my way,
come after me, for I am your beloved!

120 God Helped Me

A song of the stairway[a]

1 I was desperate for you to help me in my struggles, and you did!
2 So come and deliver me now
from this treachery and false accusation.
3 O lying deceivers, don't you know what is your fate?
4 You will be pierced through with condemnation
and consumed with burning coals of fire!
5 Why am I doomed to live as an alien
scattered among these cruel savages?[b]
Am I destined to dwell in the darkened tents of desert nomads?[c]
6 For too long I've had to live among those who hate peace.

---

a Ps. 120–134 all begin with the words "A song to take you higher" or "A song of ascent" or "A song of the stairway." It is likely these fifteen songs were sung on the fifteen steps that would take the worshiper into the temple. On each step they would stop to worship and sing the corresponding psalm as they went up higher into the worship of God. Others believe they were the songs sung as David brought up the ark of glory to Jerusalem. They are also known as Songs of Degrees or Songs of Ascent. One Hebrew manuscript titles them, "Songs of the Homeward Marches."

b 120:5 The Hebrew text includes the word *Meshech*, which is a foreign land. The meaning of the word *Meshech* is to scatter, and may refer to ancient Persia.

c 120:5 The Hebrew text includes the word *Kedar*, who was one of Ishmael's

7 I speak words of peace while they speak words of war,
but they refuse to listen.

121 God Protects Us

A song of the stairway

1–2 I look up to the mountains and hills, longing for God's help.
But then I realize that our true help and protection
come only from the Lord,
our Creator who made the heavens and the earth.
3 He will guard and guide me, never letting me stumble or fall.
God is my Keeper; he will never forget or ignore me.
4 He will never slumber nor sleep;
he is the Guardian-God for his people, Israel.
5 Jehovah himself will watch over you;
he's always at your side to shelter you safely in his presence.
6 He's protecting you from all danger both day and night.
7 He will keep you from every form of evil or calamity
as he continually watches over you.
8 You will be guarded by God himself.
You will be safe when you leave your home
and safely you will return.
He will protect you now,
and he'll protect you forevermore!

122 Jerusalem

A song of the stairway by King David[a]

1 I was overjoyed when they said:
"Let's go up to the house of the Lord."

---

sons whose descendants became a wandering group of nomads. *Kedar* means a dark place. See Song 1:5.

a David wrote this song for the people to sing for the Feasts. It was sung when the worshipers entered the gates of the city, Jerusalem.

2 And now at last, we stand here, inside the very gates of
Jerusalem!
3 O Jerusalem, you were built as a city of praise
where God and man mingle together.[a]
4 This is where all the people of Israel are required
to come and worship Jehovah-God.
5 This is where the thrones of kings have been established
to rule in righteousness;
even King David ruled from here.
6 Pray and seek for Jerusalem's peace,
for all who love her will prosper!
7 O Jerusalem, may there be peace for those
who dwell inside your walls
and prosperity in your every palace.
8 I intercede for the sake of my family and friends
who dwell there, that they may all live in peace!
9 For the sake of your house, our God,
I will seek the welfare and prosperity of Jerusalem.

123 A Prayer for Mercy

A song of the stairway

1 O God-Enthroned in heaven, I worship and adore you!
2 The way I love you
is like the way a servant wants to please his master,
the way a maid waits for the orders of her mistress.
We look to you, our God, with passionate longing
to please you and discover more of your mercy and grace.
3–4 For we've had more than our fill of this scoffing and
scorn—
this mistreatment by the wealthy elite.

---

a 122:3 The Hebrew phrase "a city bound together" is taken from a root word that means joined, united, coupled. By inference in the context, it is the city where God dwells and man worships.

Lord, show us your mercy!
Lord, show us your grace!

124 Victory

A song of the stairway by King David

1 What if God had not been on our side? Let all Israel admit this!
2–3 What if God had not been there for us?
Our enemies, in their violent anger,
would have swallowed us up alive!
4–5 The nations, with their flood of rage, would have swept us away
and we would have drowned,
perished beneath their torrent of terror!
6 We can praise God over and over that he never left us!
God wouldn't allow the terror of our enemies to defeat us.
7 We are free from the hunter's trap;
their snare is broken and we have escaped!
8 For the same God who made everything,
our Creator and our mighty Maker,
he himself is our Helper and Defender!

125 God's Surrounding Presence

A song of the stairway

1 Those who trust in the Lord are as unshakeable, as unmovable,
as Mighty Mount Zion!
2 Just as the mountains surround Jerusalem,
so the Lord's *wrap-around* presence
surrounds his people, protecting them now and forever.
3 The wicked will not always rule over the godly,
provoking them to do what is evil.
4 God, let your goodness be given away to your good people,

to all your godly lovers!
5 But those who turn away from truth,
you will turn them away from you, to follow their crooked ways.
You will give them just what they deserve.
May Israel experience peace and prosperity!

126 Restored

A song of the stairway

1 It was like a dream come true
when you freed us from our bondage and brought us back to Zion!
2 We laughed and laughed, and overflowed with gladness!
We were left shouting for joy and singing your praise.
All the nations saw it and joined in, saying,
"The Lord has done great miracles for them!"
3 Yes, he did mighty miracles and we are overjoyed!
4 Now, Lord, do it again! Restore us to our former glory!
May streams of your refreshing flow over us
until our dry hearts are drenched again.
5 Those who sow their tears as seeds[a]
will reap a harvest with joyful shouts of glee.
6 They may weep as they go out carrying their seed to sow,
but they will return with joyful laughter and shouting with gladness
as they bring back armloads of blessing and a harvest overflowing!

---

a 126:5 Or "sow their seeds with tears." A sower weeps when he sows his precious seed while his children are hungry. This is a picture of sacrificing what little we have for the harvest to come.

127 God and His Gifts

A song of the stairway by King Solomon

1 If God's grace doesn't help the builders,
they will labor in vain to build a house.
If God's mercy doesn't protect the city,
all the sentries will circle it in vain!
2 It really is senseless to work so hard
from early morning till late at night,
toiling to make a living for fear of not having enough.
God can provide for his lovers, even while they sleep!
3 Children are God's love-gift; they are heaven's generous
reward.
4 Children born to a young couple will one day rise to protect
and provide for their parents.[a]
5 Happy will be the couple who has many of them!
A household full of children will not bring shame on your
name
but victory when you face your enemies,
for your kids will have influence and honor[b]
to prevail on your behalf!

128 The Blessings of the Lord

A song of the stairway

1 How joyous are those who love the Lord and bow low before
God,
Ready to obey him!

---

a 127:4 The Hebrew text refers to children as "arrows in the hands of a warrior." This means that children will be our future protection and provision. The more the merrier!

b 127:5 The Hebrew includes a reference to "speaking with your enemies at the gate." This is in the context of children being God's way of blessing parents in their old age.

2 Your reward will be prosperity, happiness, and well-being.
3 Your wife will bless your heart and home.
Your children will bring you joy as they gather around your table.
4 Yes, this is God's generous reward for those who love him.
5 May the Lord bless you out of his Zion-glory!
May you see the prosperity of Jerusalem
throughout your lifetime.
6 And may you be surrounded by your grandchildren.
Happiness to you! And happiness to Israel!

129 Persecuted But Not Defeated

A song of the stairway

1 Let all Israel admit it.
From our very beginning we have been persecuted by the nations.
2 And from our very beginning,
we have faced never-ending discrimination.
Nevertheless, our enemies have not defeated us. We're still here!
3 They have hurt us more than can be expressed,
ripping us to shreds, cutting deeply into our souls.
4 But no matter what, the Lord is good to us.
He is a righteous God who stood to defend us,
breaking the chains of the evil ones that bound us!
5 May all who hate the Jews
fall back in disgrace to a shameful defeat!
6 Let them be like grass planted in shallow soil
that soon withers with no sustenance.
7 Let them be like weeds ignored by the reaper
and worthless to the harvester.
8 Let no one who sees them say,

"May the blessings of Jehovah be upon your life.
May the Lord bless you."[a]

130 Out of the Depths

A song of the stairway

1 Lord, I cry out to you out of the depths of my despair!
2 Hear my voice, O God!
Answer this prayer and hear my plea for mercy.
3 Lord, if you measured us and marked us with our sins,
who would ever have their prayers answered?
4 But your forgiving love is what makes you so wonderful.
No wonder you are loved and worshiped!
5 This is why I wait upon you, expecting your breakthrough,
for your word brings me hope.
6 I long for you more than any watchman
would long for the morning light.
I will watch and wait for you, O God,
throughout the night.
7 O Israel, keep hoping, keep trusting,
and keep waiting on the Lord;
for he is tenderhearted, kind, and forgiving.
He has a thousand ways to set you free!
8 He himself will redeem you;
he will ransom you from the cruel slavery of your sins!

131 My Heart is Meek

A song of the stairway by King David

1 Lord, my heart is meek before you.
I don't consider myself better than others.
I'm content to not pursue matters that are over my head—
such as your complex mysteries and wonders—

---

a 129:8 In the Jewish culture, if you passed by one who was harvesting his crops, you would shout out: "The Lord bless you!"

that I'm not yet ready to understand.
2 I am humbled and quieted in your presence.
Like a contented child that rests on its mother's lap,[a]
I'm your resting child and my soul is content in you.
3 O people of God,[b] your time has come to quietly trust,
waiting upon the Lord now and forever.

132 David's Dynasty

A song of the stairway

1 Lord, please don't forget all the hardships
David had to pass through.
2 And how he promised you, Jacob's mighty God, saying,
3 "I will not cross the threshold of my own home
to sleep in my own bed.
4 I will not sleep or slumber,
nor even take time to close my eyes in rest,
5 Until I find a place for you to dwell, O mighty God of Jacob.
I devote myself to finding a resting place for you!"[c]
6 First we heard that the ark was at Bethlehem.[d]
Then we found it in the forest of Kiriath-Jearim.
7 Let's go into God's dwelling place
and bow down and worship before him.
8 Arise, O Lord, and enter your resting place,
both you and the ark of your glorious strength!

---

a 131:2 "Like a contented child" is literally "like a weaned child."

b 131:3 Or "O Israel."

c 132:5 Historically, this refers to David wanting to bring the ark of glory back to Jerusalem.

d 132:6 Although the Hebrew text does not have the words "ark" but simply "it," the translator supplies the word *ark* from its reference in verse 8. For the sake of understanding the text, the translator has substituted *Ephrathah* for *Bethlehem* (Ephrathah was the ancient name for Bethlehem) and *Jaar* for *Kiriath-Jearim*. (The fields of Jaar was a variant form for Kiriath-Jearim, which means, the city of forests.)

9 May your priests wear the robes of righteousness,
and let all your godly lovers sing for joy!
10 Don't forsake your anointed king now,
but honor your servant David!
11 For you gave your word and promised David
in an unbreakable oath that one of his sons
would be sitting on the throne to succeed him as king.
12 And you also promised that if David's sons
would be faithful to keep their promise to follow you,
obeying the words you spoke to them,
then David's dynasty would never end!
13 Lord, you have chosen Zion as your dwelling place,
for your pleasure is fulfilled in making it your home.
14 I hear you say, "I will make this place my eternal dwelling,
for I have loved and desired it as my very own!
15 I will make Zion prosper and
satisfy her poor with my provision.
16 I will cover my priests with salvation's power,
and all my godly lovers will shout for joy!
17 I will increase the anointing that was upon David,
and my glistening glory will rest upon my chosen ones.
18 But David's enemies will be covered with shame,
while on them I'll make holiness bloom!"[a]

133 Unity

A song to bring you higher by King David

1 How truly wonderful and delightful,
to see brothers and sisters living together in sweet unity!
2 It's as precious as the sacred scented oil
flowing from the head of the high priest, Aaron,

---

a 132:18 As translated from the Septuagint. The Hebrew reads, "His crown will sparkle and gleam."

dripping down upon his beard and running all the way down
to the hem of his priestly robes.[a]
3 This heavenly harmony can be compared to the dew
dripping down from the skies upon Mount Hermon,
refreshing the mountain slopes of Israel.
For from this realm of sweet harmony
God will release his eternal blessing, the promise of life forever!

134 The Night Watch

A song to bring you higher

1 All his loving priests who serve and sing,
come and sing your song of blessing to God.
Come and stand before him in the house of God
throughout the night watch,
2 Lifting up your hands in holy worship; come and bless the Lord!
3 May the Lord, whom you worship,
the mighty Maker of heaven and earth,
may he bless you from Zion's glory!

135 His Wonderful Works

A song to bring you higher

1 Shout hallelujah and praise the greatness of God!
All his godly lovers, praise him!
2 All you worshiping priests on duty in the temple,
3 Praise him, for he is beautiful!
Sing loving praises to his lovely name.
4 For Yahweh has chosen Israel for his own purpose,
and we're his special treasure.

---

a 133:2 Or "running down the collar of his robe."

5 Next to every other god the greatness of our God is
unequaled.
For our God is incomparable!
6 He does what he pleases with unlimited power and authority,
extending his greatness throughout the entire universe!
7 He forms the misty clouds and creates thunder and lightning,
bringing the wind and rain out of his heavenly storehouse.
8 He struck down the eldest child in each Egyptian home;
both men and beast perished that night.
9 He did great miracles—mighty signs and wonders
throughout
the land
before Pharaoh and all his subjects.
10 He conquered many nations and killed their mighty kings
11 Like Sihon, king of the Amorites; also Og, king of Bashan;
and kings from every kingdom in Canaan.
12 He gave their land to Israel as an inheritance for his people.
13 O Jehovah, your name endures forever!
Your fame is known in every generation.
14 For you will vindicate your persecuted people,
showing your tender love to all your servants.
15 The unbelieving nations worship what they make.
They worship their wealth and their work.
They idolize what they own and what they do.
16–18 Their possessions will never satisfy.
Their lifeless and futile works cannot bring life to them!
Their things can't talk to them or answer their prayers.
Blind men can only create blind things.
Those deaf to God can only make a deaf image.
Dead men can only create dead idols.
And everyone who trusts in these powerless, dead things
will be just like what they worship—powerless and dead! [a]

---

a 135:16–18 Referring to the idols, the Hebrew could be translated, "with

19 Praise Lord-Yahweh, all the families of Israel!
Praise Lord-Yahweh, you family of Aaron![a]
20 Let all the priests[b] bless Lord-Yahweh!
Let all His lovers[c] who bow low before him
praise the Lord-Yahweh!
21 So bless the Lord-Yahweh who lives in Jerusalem
and dwells in Zion's glory!
Hallelujah and praise the Lord!

136 His Saving Love

1 Let everyone thank God, for he is good, and he is easy to please!
His tender love for us continues on forever!
2 Give thanks to God, our King over all gods!
His tender love for us continues on forever!
3 Give thanks to the Lord over all lords!
His tender love for us continues on forever!
4 Give thanks to the only miracle working God!
His tender love for us continues on forever!
5 Give thanks to the Creator who made the heavens with wisdom![d]
His tender love for us continues on forever!
6 To him who formed dry ground, raising it up from the sea!
His tender love for us continues on forever!
7 Praise the One who created every heavenly light!
His tender love for us continues on forever!
8 He set the sun in the sky to rule over day!
His tender love for us continues on forever!

---

mouths, but they cannot speak; with eyes, but they cannot see; with ears, but they cannot hear."

a 135:19 The name Aaron means "light-bringer" or "light-bearer."
b 135:20 Or "All the family of Levi." Levi represents the holy priesthood.
c 135:20 Or "those who fear him."
d 136:5 See Ps. 104:24 and Prov. 8:27–31.

9 Praise him who set in place the moon and stars to rule over
the night!
His tender love for us continues on forever!
10 Give thanks to God, who struck down the firstborn in
Egypt!
His tender love for us continues on forever!
11 He brought his people out of Egypt with miracles!
His tender love for us continues on forever!
12 With his mighty power he brought them out!
His tender love for us continues on forever!
13 He split open the Red Sea for them!
His tender love for us continues on forever!
14 And led his people right through the middle!
His tender love for us continues on forever!
15 He vanquished Pharaoh's armies, drowning them all!
His tender love for us continues on forever!
16 He led his people through the wilderness!
His tender love for us continues on forever!
17 He's the One who smashed mighty kingdoms!
His tender love for us continues on forever!
18 He triumphed over powerful kings who stood in his way!
His tender love for us continues on forever!
19 He conquered Sihon, king of the Amorites!
His tender love for us continues on forever!
20 He conquered the giant named Og, king of Bashan![a]
His tender love for us continues on forever!
21 Then he gave away their lands as an inheritance!
His tender love for us continues on forever!
22 For he handed it all over to Israel, his beloved!
His tender love for us continues on forever!
23 He's the God who chose us when we were nothing!
His tender love for us continues on forever!

---

a 136:20 The name *Og* means giant.

24 He has rescued us from the power of our enemies!
His tender love for us continues on forever!
25 He provides food for hungry men and animals!
His tender love for us continues on forever!
26 Give thanks to the great God of the heavens!
His tender love for us continues on forever!

137 The Song of Our Captivity

1 Along the banks of Babylon's rivers
we sat as exiles mourning our captivity
and wept with great love for Zion.
2 *Our music and mirth were no longer heard, only sadness.*
We hung up our harps on the willow trees.
3 Our captors tormented us, saying: "Make music for us and
sing one of your happy Zion-songs!"
4 But how could we sing the song of the Lord
in this foreign wilderness?
5 May my hands never make music again
if I ever forget you, O Jerusalem;
6 May I never be able to sing again if I fail to honor Jerusalem
supremely!
7 And Lord, may you never forget
what the sons of Edom did to us, saying:
"Let's raze the city of Jerusalem and burn it to the
ground!" [a]
8 Listen, O Babylon, you evil destroyer!
The one who destroys you will be rewarded above all
others!
You will be repaid for what you've done to us.
9 Great honor will come to those who destroy you and your
future,

---

a 137:7 The Hebrew text reads, "strip her [Jerusalem] naked!'"

by smashing your infants against the rubble of your own
destruction.

138 The Divine Presence

by King David

1 I thank you, Lord, and with all the passion of my heart
I worship you in the presence of angels![a]
Heaven's mighty ones will hear my voice
as I sing my loving praise to you!
2 I bow down before your divine presence
and bring you my deepest worship
as I experience your tender love and your living truth.
For the promises of your Word and the fame of your name
have been magnified above all else!
3 At the very moment I called out to you, you answered me!
You strengthened me deep within my soul
and breathed fresh courage into me.
4 One day all the kings of the earth
will rise to give you thanks when they hear the living words
that I have heard you speak.
5 They too will sing of your wonderful ways
for your ineffable glory is so great!
6 For though you are lofty and exalted,
you stoop to embrace the lowly.
Yet you keep your distance from those filled with pride.
7 Through your mighty power I can walk through any
devastation
and you will keep me alive, reviving me.
Your power set me free from the hatred of my enemies.
8 You keep every promise you've ever made to me!
Since your love for me is so constant and endless,

---

a 138:1 Or "gods." The Hebrew *elohim* is literally, "mighty ones" and can refer to either angels or the gods of the heathen.

I ask you, Lord, to finish every good thing that you've
begun in me!

139 You Know All About Me

For the Pure and Shining One

King David's poetic song

1 Lord, you know everything there is to know about me.
2 You perceive every movement of my heart and soul,
and understand my every thought before it even enters my mind.
3–4 You are so intimately aware of me, Lord.
You read my heart like an open book
and you know all the words I'm about to speak
before I even start a sentence!
You know every step I will take before my journey even begins!
5 You've gone into my future to prepare the way,
and in kindness you follow behind me
to spare me from the harm of my past.[a]
With your hand of love upon my life,
you impart a blessing to me.
6 This is just too wonderful, deep, and incomprehensible!
Your understanding of me brings me wonder and strength.[b]
7 Where could I go from your Spirit?
Where could I run and hide from your face?
8 If I go up to heaven, you're there!
If I go down to the realm of the dead, you're there too!

---

a 139:5 Or "You hem me in (lit. "beseige me") before and behind." The implication is that God protects him from what may come in the future and what has happened in the past.

b 139:6 As translated from the Septuagint. The Hebrew reads, "too high to understand."

9 If I fly with wings into the shining dawn, you're there!
If I fly into the radiant sunset, you're there waiting![a]
10 Wherever I go, your hand will guide me;
your strength will empower me.
11 It's impossible to disappear from you
or to ask the darkness to hide me;
for your presence is everywhere bringing light into my night!
12 There is no such thing as darkness with you.
The night, to you, is as bright as the day;
there's no difference between the two.
13 You formed my innermost being, shaping my delicate inside
and my intricate outside,
and wove them all together in my mother's womb.[b]
14 I thank you, God, for making me so mysteriously complex!
Everything you do is marvelously breathtaking.
It simply amazes me to think about it!
How thoroughly you know me, Lord!
15 You even formed every bone in my body
when you created me in the secret place;[c]
carefully, skillfully shaping me[d] from nothing to something.
16 You saw who you created me to be before I became me![e]
Before I'd ever seen the light of day,
the number of days you planned for me

---

a 139:9 Implied in the Hebrew, which states, "the remote parts of the sea," or beyond the horizon to the west. The sea is west of Israel.

b 139:13 The Hebrew word for *knit*, or *wove* can also be translated "to cover" or "to defend." God places an eternal spirit inside the conceived child within the womb of a mother and covers that life, sends the child a guardian angel, and watches over every child.

c 139:15 The Hebrew text is literally, "the depths of the earth."

d 139:15 Or "embroidered me."

e 139:16 The Hebrew could be translated, "As an embryo."

were already recorded in your book.[a]
17–18 Every single moment you are thinking of me!
How precious and wonderful to consider
that you cherish me constantly in your every thought!
O God, your desires toward me are more
than the grains of sand on every shore!
When I awake each morning, you're still together with me.
19 O God, come and slay these bloodthirsty, murderous men!
For I cry out, "Depart from me, you wicked ones!"
20 See how they blaspheme your sacred name
and lift up themselves against you, but all in vain!
21 Lord, can't you see how I despise those who despise you?
For I grieve when I see them rise up against you.
22 I have nothing but complete hatred and disgust for them.
Your enemies shall be my enemies!
23 God, I invite your searching gaze into my heart.
Examine me through and through;
find out everything that may be hidden within me.
Put me to the test and sift through all my anxious cares.
24 See if there is any path of pain I'm walking on,
and lead me back to your glorious, everlasting ways—
the path that brings me back to you.

140 A Prayer for Protection

For the Pure and Shining One
King David's poetic song

1 Lord, protect me from this evil one!
Rescue me from these violent schemes!
2 He concocts his secret strategy to divide and harm others,
stirring up trouble one against another.

---

a 139:16 See Ps. 69:28.

3 They are known for their sharp rhetoric
of poisonous, hateful words.

Pause in his presence

4 Keep me safe, Lord, out of reach from these wicked and violent men,
and guard me, God, for they have plotted an evil scheme
to ruin me and bring me down.
5 They are proud and insolent; they've set an ambush for me in secret.
They are determined to snare me in their net like captured prey.

Pause in his presence

6–7 O Lord, you are my God and my saving strength!
My Hero-God, you wrap yourself around me to protect me.
For I'm surrounded by your presence in my day of battle.
Lord Yahweh, hear my cry.
May my voice move your heart to show me mercy.
8 Don't let the wicked triumph over me,
but bring down their every strategy to subdue me
or they will become even more arrogant!

Pause in his presence

9 Those who surround me are nothing but proud troublemakers.
May they drink the poison of their own poisonous words.
10–11 May their slanderous lives never prosper!
Let evil itself hunt them down and pursue them relentlessly
until they are thrown into fiery pits
from which they will never get out!
Let burning coals of hellfire fall upon their heads!
12 For I know, Lord, that you will be the Hero
of all those they persecute,
and you will secure justice for the poor.
13 Your godly lovers will thank you no matter what happens.

For they choose and cherish your presence
above everything else!

141 An Evening Prayer

King David's poetic song

1 Please, Lord, come close and come quickly to help me!
Listen to my prayer as I call out to you!
2 Let my prayer be as the evening sacrifice
that burns like fragrant incense, rising as my offering to you
as I lift up my hands in surrendered worship!
3 God give me grace to guard my lips[a]
from speaking what is wrong.
4 Guide me away from temptation and doing evil.
Save me from sinful habits and from keeping company
with those who are experts in evil.
Help me not to share in their sin in any way!
5 When one of your godly lovers corrects me
or one of your faithful ones rebukes me,
I will accept it like an honor I cannot refuse.
It will be as healing medicine that I swallow
without an offended heart.
For even if they are mistaken I will continue to pray.[b]
6 When the leaders and judges are condemned,
falling upon the rocks of justice,[c]
then they'll know my words to them were true!
7 So like an earthquake splits open the earth,
so the world of hell will open its mouth

---

a 141:3 The Septuagint reads, "set a fortress door before my lips."

b 141:5 This is one of most difficult verses to translate, with scholars divided over the meaning of the Hebrew text. Another translation could be, "Don't let the oil of the wicked anoint my head, for I pray continually against their wickedness."

c 141:6 See 2 Chron. 25:12.

to swallow their scattered bones.
8 But you are my Lord and my God; I only have eyes for you!
I hide myself in you, so don't leave me defenseless.
9 Protect me! Keep me from the traps of wickedness they set for me.
10 Let them all stumble into their own traps
while I escape without a scratch!

142 My Only Hope

King David's poetic song of instruction
A prayer when he was confined in a cave

1 God, I'm crying out to you!
I lift up my voice boldly to beg for your mercy!
2 I spill out my heart to you and tell you all my troubles.
3 For when I was desperate, overwhelmed, and about to give up,
you were the only One there to help.
You gave me a way of escape
from the hidden traps of my enemies.
4 I look to my left and right to see if there is anyone who will help,
but there's no one who takes notice of me.
I have no hope of escape, and no one cares whether I live or die.
5 So I cried out to you, Lord, my only Hiding Place.
You're all I have, my only hope in this life,
my last chance for help.
6 Please listen to my heart's cry,
for I am so low and in desperate need of you!
Rescue me from all those who persecute me,
for I am no match for them.
7 Bring me out of this dungeon so I can declare your praise!
And all your godly lovers will celebrate
all the wonderful things you've done for me!

143 My Humble Prayer

King David's poetic song when he was chased by Absalom[a]

1 Lord, you must hear my prayer,
for you are faithful to your promises.
Answer my cry, O righteous God!
2 Don't bring me into your courtroom for judgment,
for there is no one who is righteous before you!
3 My enemies have chased and caught me
and crushed my life into dust.
Now I'm living in the darkness of death's shadow.
4 My inner being is in depression
and my heart is heavy, dazed with despair.
5 I remember the glorious miracles of days gone by,
and I often think of all the wonders of old.
6 Now I'm reaching out to you, thirsting for you
like the dry, cracked ground thirsts for rain.

Pause in his presence

7 Lord, come quickly and answer me,
for my depression deepens and I'm about to give up.
Don't leave me now or I'll die!
8 Let the dawning day bring me revelation
of your tender, unfailing love.
Give me light for my path and teach me, for I trust in you!
9 Save me from all my enemies for I hide myself in you.
10 I just want to obey all you ask of me;
so teach me, Lord, for you are my God.
Your gracious Spirit is all I need; so lead me on good paths
that are pleasing to you, my one and only God!
11 Lord, if you rescue me, it will bring you more glory,
for you are true to your promises.
Bring me out of these troubles!

---

a As translated from the Septuagint.

12 Since I am your loving servant, destroy all those
who are trying to harm me.
And because you are so loving and kind to me,
silence all of my enemies!

144 Rescue Me

King David's poetic song as he stood before Goliath[a]

1 There is only one strong, safe, and secure place for me;
it's in God alone and I love him!
He's the One who gives me strength and skill for the battle.
2 He's my Shelter of love and my Fortress of faith,
who wraps himself around me as a secure shield.
I hide myself in this One who subdues enemies before me!
3 Lord, what is it about us that you would even notice us?
Why do you even bother with us?
4 For man is nothing but a faint whisper, a mere breath.
We spend our days like nothing more than a passing
shadow.
5 Step down from heaven, Lord, and come down!
Make the mountains melt at your touch.
6 Loose your fiery lightning flashes and scatter your enemies.
Overthrow them with your terrifying judgments.
7 Reach down from your heavens
and rescue me from this hell,
and deliver me from these dark powers.
8 They speak nothing but lies; their words are pure deceit.
Nothing they say can ever be trusted.
9 My God, I will sing you a brand-new song!
The harp inside my heart will make music to you!
10 I will sing of you, the One who gives victory to kings—

---

a As translated from the Septuagint. Put yourself in David's place as he faced a giant named Goliath. Imagine how he felt as you read through this psalm.

the One who rescues David, your loving servant
from the fatal sword.
11 Deliver me and save me from these dark powers
who speak nothing but lies.
Their words are pure deceit
and you can't trust anything they say.
12 Deliver us! Then our homes will be happy.
Our sons will grow up as strong, sturdy men
and our daughters with graceful beauty,
royally fashioned as for a palace.
13–14 Our barns will be filled to the brim,
overflowing with the fruits of our harvest.
Our fields will be full of sheep and cattle,
too many to count,
and our livestock will not miscarry their young.
Our enemies will not invade our land,
and there'll be no breach in our walls.
15 What bliss we experience when these blessings fall!
The people who love and serve our God will be happy
indeed!

145 God's Greatness

King David's poetic song of praise

1 My heart explodes with praise to you!
Now and forever my heart bows in worship to you,
my King and my God!
2 Every day I will lift up my praise to your name
with praises that will last throughout eternity.
3 Lord, you are great and worthy of the highest praise!
For there is no end to the discovery
of the greatness that surrounds you.
4 Generation after generation will declare more of your
greatness
and declare more of your glory.

5 Your magnificent splendor and the miracles of your majesty
are my constant meditation.
6 Your awe-inspiring acts of power have everyone talking!
I'm telling people everywhere about your excellent
greatness!
7 Our hearts bubble over as we celebrate the fame
of your marvelous beauty, *bringing bliss to our hearts*.
We shout with ecstatic joy over your breakthrough for us.
8 You're so kind and tenderhearted to those who don't deserve
it
and so very patient with people who fail you.
Your love is like a flooding river overflowing its banks with
kindness.
9 God, everyone sees your goodness,
for your tender love is blended into everything you do.
10 Everything you have made will praise you, fulfilling its
purpose.
And all your godly lovers will be found bowing before you!
11 They will tell the world of the lavish splendor of your
kingdom
and preach about your limitless power.
12 They will demonstrate for all to see your miracles of might
and reveal the glorious majesty of your kingdom.
13 You are the Lord that reigns over your never-ending
kingdom through all the ages of time and eternity!
You are faithful to fulfill every promise you've made.
You manifest yourself as Kindness in all you do! [a]
14 Weak and feeble ones you will sustain.
Those bent over with burdens of shame you will lift up.
15 You have captured our attention

---

a 145:13 The last two lines of this verse are only found in one reliable Hebrew manuscript and in the Septuagint. It could also be translated, "all your works are very holy."

and the eyes of all look to you.
You give what they hunger for at just the right time!
16 When you open your generous hand, it's full of blessings,
satisfying the longings of every living thing.
17 You are fair and righteous in everything you do,
and your love is wrapped into all your works.
18 You draw near to those who call out to you,
listening ever closely, especially when their hearts are true.
19 Every one of your godly lovers receives
even more than what they ask for.
For you hear what their hearts really long for
and you bring them your saving strength!
20 God, you watch carefully over all your lovers like a
bodyguard,
but you will destroy the ungodly.
21 I will praise you, Lord!
Let everyone everywhere join me in praising
the beautiful Lord of holiness from now through eternity!

146 Our True Help

A poetic psalm by Haggai and Zechariah[a]

1 Hallelujah! Praise the Lord!
My innermost being will praise you, Lord!
2 I will spend my life praising you and
singing high praises to you, my God, every day of my life!
3–4 We can never look to men for help;
no matter who they are they can't save us,
for even our great leaders fail and fall!
They too are just mortals who will one day die.

---

a As translated from the Septuagint. Ps. 146–150 are called "Hallelujah Psalms" because they all begin in Hebrew with the words "Hallelujah, praise the Lord."

At death the spirits of all depart and their bodies return to dust.
In the day of their death all their projects and plans are over.
5 But those who hope in the Lord will be happy and pleased!
Our help comes from the God of Jacob!
6 You keep all your promises.
You are the Creator of heaven's glory,
earth's grandeur, and ocean's greatness.
7 The oppressed get justice with you.
The hungry are satisfied with you.
Prisoners find their freedom with you.
8 You open the eyes of the blind
and you fully restore those bent over with shame.
You love those who love and honor you.
9 You watch over strangers and immigrants
and support the fatherless and widows.
But you subvert the plans of the ungodly.
10 Lord, you will reign forever!
Zion's God will rule throughout time and eternity!
Hallelujah! Praise the Lord!

147 Our Amazing God

1 Hallelujah! Praise the Lord!
How beautiful it is when we sing our praises to the beautiful God;
for praise makes you lovely before him
and brings him great delight!
2 The Lord builds up Jerusalem;
he gathers up the outcasts and brings them home!
3 He heals the wounds of every shattered heart.
4 He sets all his stars in place, calling them all by their names.
5 How great is our God!
There's absolutely nothing his power cannot accomplish

and he has infinite understanding of everything.
6 God supports and strengthens the humble,
but the ungodly will be brought down to the dust.
7 Sing out with songs of thanksgiving to the Lord!
Let's sing our praises with melodies overflowing!
8 He fills the sky with clouds, sending showers to water the earth
so that the grass springs up on the mountain fields
and the earth produces food for man.[a]
9 All the birds and beasts who cry with hunger to him
are fed from his hands.
10 His people don't find security in strong horses,
for horsepower is nothing to him.
Man power is even less impressive!
11 The Lord shows favor to those who fear him,
to his godly lovers who wait for his tender embrace.
12 Jerusalem, praise the Lord! Zion, worship your God!
13 For he has strengthened the authority of your gates.
He even blesses you with more children.
14 He's the One who brings peace to your borders,[b]
feeding you the most excellent of fare.
15 He sends out his orders throughout the world;
his words run as swift messengers bringing them to pass.
16 He blankets the earth with glistening snow,
painting the landscape with frost.
17 Sleet and hail fall from the sky
causing waters to freeze before winter's icy blast.
18 Then he speaks his word and it all melts away;
as the warm spring winds blow, the streams begin to flow.
19 In the same way, he speaks to his people and to Israel,
bringing them his life-giving words.

---

a 147:8 As translated from the Septuagint.
b 147:14 Or "He makes peace your borders" (LXX).

20 He has dealt with Israel differently than with any other
people,
for they have received his laws.
Hallelujah! Praise the Lord!

148 The Cosmic Chorus of Praise

1 Hallelujah! Praise the Lord! Let the skies be filled with praise
and the highest heavens with the shouts of glory!
2 Go ahead—praise him, all you his messengers!
Praise him some more, all you heavenly hosts!
3 Keep it up—sun and moon!
Don't stop now, all you twinkling stars of light!
4 Take it up even higher—up to the highest heavens
until the cosmic chorus thunders his praise![a]
5 Let the entire universe erupt with praise to God.
From nothing to something he spoke and created it all.
6 He established the cosmos to last forever,
and he stands behind his commands
so his orders will never be revoked.
7 Let the earth join in with this parade of praise!
You mighty creatures of the ocean's depths,
echo in exaltation!
8 Lightning, hail, snow, and clouds,
and the stormy winds that fulfill his word.
9 Bring your melody, O mountains and hills;
trees of the forest and field, harmonize your praise!
10–12 Praise him all beasts and birds, mice and men,
kings, queens, princes, and princesses,
young men and maidens, children and babes,
old and young alike, everyone everywhere!
13 Let them all join in with this orchestra of praise.

---

a 148:4 Poetic implication in the text. The literal Hebrew reads, "the waters above the sky."

For the name of the Lord is the only name we raise!
His stunning splendor ascends higher than the heavens.
14 He anoints his people with strength and authority,
showing his great favor to all his godly lovers,
even to his princely people, Israel,
who are so close to his heart.
Hallelujah! Praise the Lord!

149 Triumphant Praise

1 Hallelujah! Praise the Lord!
It's time to sing to God a brand-new song[a]
so that all his holy people will then hear how wonderful he is!
2 May Israel be enthused with joy all because of him,
and may the sons of Zion pour out
their joyful praises to their King.
3 Break forth with dancing!
Make music and sing God's praises with the rhythm of drums!
4 For he enjoys his faithful lovers.
He adorns the humble with his beauty
and he loves to give them the victory.
5 His godly lovers triumph in the glory of God,
and their joyful praises will rise even while others sleep.
6 God's high and holy praises fill their mouths,
for their shouted praises are their weapons of war!
7 These warring weapons will bring vengeance
on every opposing force and every resistant power—
8 To bind kings with chains and rulers with iron shackles.
9 Praise-filled warriors will enforce
the judgment-doom decreed against their enemies.

---

a 149:1 Or "a spontaneous song."

This is the glorious honor he gives to all his godly lovers.
Hallelujah! Praise the Lord!

150 The Hallelujah Chorus

1 Hallelujah! Praise the Lord! Praise God in his holy sanctuary!
Praise him in his stronghold in the sky!
2 Praise him for his miracles of might!
Praise him for his magnificent greatness!
3 Praise him with the trumpets blasting!
Praise him with piano and guitar!
4–5 Praise him with drums and dancing!
Praise him with the loud, resounding clash of cymbals!
Praise him with every instrument you can find!
6 Let everyone everywhere join in the crescendo
of ecstatic praise to Yahweh!
Hallelujah! Praise the Lord! Translator's Introduction to Proverbs

Proverbs

Introduction

AT A GLANCE

Author: Mostly Solomon, King of Israel, but other various contributors, too.

Audience: Originally Israel, but these words of wisdom are for everyone—they are written to you.

Date: Preexile (Chapters 10–29) and Postexile (Chapters 1–9, 30–31), the tenth to fifth centuries BC.

Type of Literature: Poetry and wisdom literature.

Major Themes: the fear of the Lord; God's transcendence and immanence; Godly wisdom and human foolishness; the righteous and wicked wealth and poverty; men and women; husbands and wives; Jesus and wisdom.

Outline:

Collection I: 1:1–9:18 — Introduction to Wisdom
Collection II: 10:1–22:16 — Sayings of Solomon, Part 1
Collection III: 22:17–24:22 — Sayings of the Wise
Collection IV: 24:23–34 — More Sayings of the Wise
Collection V: 25:1–29:27 — Sayings of Solomon, Part 2
Collection VI: 30:1–31:31 — Sayings of Agur and Lemuel

ABOUT PROVERBS

The Bible is a book of poetry, not simply starched, stiff doctrines, devoid of passion. The Bible, including Proverbs, is full of poetic beauty and subtle nuances ripe with meaning. The ancient wisdom of God fills its pages!

Proverbs is a book of wisdom from above tucked inside of metaphors, symbols, and poetic imagery. God could properly be described as the divine Poet and master Artisan who crafted the cosmos to portray his glory and has given us his written Word to reveal his wisdom. Inspired from eternity, the sixty-six books of our Bible convey the full counsel and wisdom of God. Do you need wisdom? God has a verse for that!

Five books of divine poetry show us the reality of knowing God through experience, not just through history or doctrines. Job points us to the end of our self-life to discover the greatest revelation of the Lord, which is his tender love and wisdom. Psalms reveals the new life we enter into with God, expressed through praise and prayer. Next is Proverbs, where we enroll in the divine seminary of wisdom and revelation to learn the ways of God. Ecclesiastes teaches us to set our hearts not on the things of this life but on those values that endure eternally. And finally in Song of Songs, the sweetest lyrics ever composed lead us into divine romance where we are immersed in Jesus' love for his bride.

The nature of Hebrew poetry is quite different from that of English poetry. There is a pleasure found in Hebrew poetry that transcends rhyme and meter. The Hebrew verses come in a poetic package, a form of meaning that imparts an understanding that is deeper than mere logic. True revelation unfolds an encounter—an experience of knowing God as he is revealed through the mysterious vocabulary of riddle, proverb, and parable.

For example, the Hebrew word for proverb, *mashal*, has two meanings. The first is "parable, byword, metaphor, a pithy saying that expresses wisdom." But the second meaning is overlooked by many. The homonym *mashal* can also mean "to rule, to take dominion," or "to reign with power."

What you have before you now is a dynamic translation of the ancient book of Proverbs. These powerful words will bring you revelation from the throne room—the wisdom you need to guide your steps and direct your life. What you learn from these verses will change your life and launch you into your destiny.

BOOK PROFILE

Purpose

Within this divinely anointed compilation of Proverbs, there is a deep well of wisdom to reign in life and to succeed in our destiny. The wisdom that God has designed for us to receive will cause us to excel—to rise up as rulers-to-be on earth for his glory. The kingdom of God is brought into the earth as we implement the godly wisdom of Proverbs.

Although the Proverbs can be interpreted in their most literal and practical sense, the wisdom contained herein is not unlocked by a casual surface reading. The Spirit of revelation has breathed upon every verse to embed a deeper meaning of practical insight to guide our steps into the life God meant for us to live.

Author & Audience

You're about to read the greatest book of wisdom ever written, mostly penned by the wisest man to ever live. God gave his servant Solomon this wisdom to pass along to us, his servants, who continue the ministry of Jesus, the embodiment of wisdom, until he returns in full glory. While it is believed Solomon penned most of these words of wisdom, it is believed others had a hand, too, including advisers to King Hezekiah and the unknown men Agur and Lemuel—who could be pseudonyms for Solomon himself. Regardless, the one who edited the final version of Proverbs brought together the wisest teachings from the the wisest person to ever live to write a book containing some of the deepest revelation in the Bible. When Solomon pens a proverb, there is more than meets the eye!

Who are these proverbs written to? This compilation of

wisdom's words is written to you! Throughout the book we find words like "Listen, my sons. Listen, my daughters." The book of Proverbs is written to us as sons and daughters of the living God. The teaching we receive is not from a distant god who tells us we'd better live right or else. These are personal words of love and tenderness from our wise Father, the Father of eternity, who speaks right into our hearts with healing, radiant words. Receive deeply the words of the kind Father of heaven as though he were speaking directly to you.

Major Themes

The kind of Hebrew wisdom found in the Proverbs is about the art of successful living. The universal appeal of these wise insights is that they touch on universal problems and issues that affect human behavior in us all. Several major themes are present in these godly wisdom sayings of God's servant Solomon:

Lady Wisdom, Revelation-Knowledge, Living-Understanding. Throughout Proverbs wisdom is personified with the metaphor of Lady Wisdom, who dispenses revelation-knowledge and living-understanding. Lady Wisdom is a figure of speech for God and His divine wisdom, who invites us to receive the best way to live, the excellent and noble way of life found. She is personified as a guide (6:22), a beloved sister or bride (7:4), and a hostess (9:1–6) who generously invites people to "come and dine at my table and drink of my wine."In Proverbs, wisdom is inseparable from knowledge and understanding, which is not received independent of God's revelation. We are invited to "come to the one Who has living-understanding" (9:10) in order to receive what Lady Wisdom has to offer. For God promises that revelation-knowledge will flow to the one who hungers her gift of understanding (14:6).

The Fear of the Lord. From the beginning in 1:7, Proverbs makes it clear that a person gains "the essence of wisdom" and crosses "the threshold of true knowledge" only when we fear the Lord—or, as The Passion Translation translates it, we live "in complete awe and adoration of God." This theme of living in a way that our entire being worships and adores God is a constant theme throughout Proverbs.

God's Transcendence and Immanence. Proverbs teaches that God is both the Author of (transcendent) and Actor within (immanent) our human story. First, God is above and outside the world: As Creator "He broke open the hidden fountains of the deep, bringing secret springs to the surface" (3:20); "God sees everything you do and his eyes are wide open as he observes every single habit you have" (5:21); He is sovereign and steers "a king's heart for his purposes as it is for him to direct the course of a stream" (21:1).

Second, God is also apart of and involved with the world: "The rich and the poor have one thing in common: The Lord God created each one" (22:2); "The Lord champions the widow's cause" (15:25) and He "will rise to plead [the poor's] case" (22:23).

So Proverbs teaches God is all-powerful and transcendent, while also taking part in our human story as our defender and protector!

The Wise and Fool, Righteous and Wicked. Solomon believes there are basically two different kinds of people in the world: the wise righteous and wicked fools. The wise person possesses God's revelation-knowledge and living-understanding. Therefore, he is prudent, shrewd, insightful, and does what is right because he is righteous, a God-lover. This lover of God in turn is just, peaceful, upright, blameless, good, trustworthy, and kind.

The wicked fool is a completely different person. He is greedy, violent, deceitful, cruel, and speaks perversely—it's no wonder "The Lord detests the lifestyle of the wicked!" (15:9). As a foolish person, he is described as being gullible, an idiot, self-sufficient, a mocker, lazy, senseless, and rejects revelation-knowledge and living-understanding.

Many of Solomon's wise sayings relate to these two different kinds of people, teaching us how to avoid being a wicked fool and instead live as God intends us to live as his wise, righteous lovers!

Wealth and Poverty. Like many of Solomon's wise sayings, you cannot take one thought on wealth and poverty and apply it to every situation. Instead, Solomon teaches us seven major things about having wealth and being poor, and how wisdom and foolishness affect them both: the righteous are blessed with wealth by God himself; foolishness leads to poverty; fools who have wealth will soon lose it; poverty results from injustice and oppression; the wealthy are called to be generous with their wealth; gaining wisdom is far better than gaining wealth; and the value of wealth is limited.[a]

Jesus and the Church. As with the rest of the Old Testament, we are called to read Proverbs in light of Jesus and his ministry. Throughout the gospels Jesus associates himself with wisdom. For instance, in Matthew 11:18–19 Jesus claims his actions represent Lady Wisdom herself. Where he is identified with Lady Wisdom in the New Testament, it is a powerful way of saying that Jesus is the full, entire embodiment of Wisdom. In many ways Colossians 1:15–17 mirrors Proverbs 8. Likewise, the great preface to John's gospel resonates with this same chapter when Jesus is associated with the Word, another personification of Wisdom.

The great reformer Martin Luther said, "The Scriptures must be understood in favor of Christ, not against him. For that reason they must either refer to him or must not be held to be true Scriptures." Luther understood that Jesus stood at

---

a Tremper Longman III, *Proverbs*. (Grand Rapids: Baker Academic, 2006), 573–574.

the center of Scripture; he was found throughout Scripture, not just in the New Testament. So as you read these important words of wisdom, consider how they point to the One who perfectly embodied and is our Wisdom.

Proverbs

WISDOM FROM ABOVE

The Prologue

1 Here are kingdom revelations, words to live by,
and words of wisdom given to empower you to reign in life,[a]
written as proverbs by Israel's King Solomon,[b] David's son.
2 Within these sayings will be found the revelation of wisdom[c]
and the impartation of spiritual understanding.
Use them as keys to unlock the treasures of true knowledge.
3 Those who cling to these words will receive discipline

---

a 1:1 As stated in the introduction, the Hebrew word for "proverbs" means more than just a wise saying. It can also mean "to rule, to reign in power, to take dominion."

b 1:1 The name Solomon means "peaceable." There is a greater one than Solomon who gives peace to all of his followers. His name is Jesus. Solomon was the seed of David; we are the seed of Jesus Christ. Solomon had an encounter with God after asking for a discerning heart (1 Kings 3:5–14). This pleased God, so he gave Solomon wisdom, riches, and power. God is ready to impart these same things today to those who ask Him. See James 1:5–8.

c 1:2 There are six Hebrew words translated "wisdom" in the book of Proverbs. Some of them require an entire phrase in English to convey its meaning. The word used here is *chokmah*, and it is used in Proverbs forty-two times. Forty-two is the number of months Jesus ministered and the number of generations from Abraham to Christ listed in Matt. 1.

to demonstrate wisdom in every relationship,[a]
and to choose what is right and just and fair.
4 These proverbs will give you great skill
to teach the immature and make them wise,
to give youth the understanding of their design and destiny.
5 For the wise, these proverbs will make you even wiser,
and for those with discernment,
you will be able to acquire brilliant strategies for leadership.
6 These kingdom revelations will break open your understanding
to unveil the deeper meaning of parables,
poetic riddles, and epigrams,
and to unravel the words and enigmas of the wise.
7 How then does a man gain the essence of wisdom?
We cross the threshold of true knowledge
when we live in obedient devotion to God.[b]
Stubborn know-it-alls[c] will never stop to do this,
for they scorn true wisdom and knowledge.

The Wisdom of a Father

8 Pay close attention, my child, to your father's wise words

---

a 1:3 The Hebrew word translated "wisdom" here also means "righteousness."

b 1:7 Many translations render this "the fear of the Lord." This is much more than the English concept of fear. It also implies submission, awe, worship, and reverence. The Hebrew word used here is found fourteen times in Proverbs. The number fourteen represents spiritual perfection. The number fourteen is mentioned three times in the genealogy of Jesus (Matt. 1:1–17). It is also the number for Passover. You will pass from darkness to wisdom's light by the *fear* of the Lord.

c 1:7 Or "foolish ones." There are three Hebrew words translated "fool" in Proverbs and another six that are related to a fool or foolish acts. A fool is described in Proverbs as one who hates true wisdom and correction, with no desire to acquire revelation knowledge.

and never forget your mother's instructions.[a]
9 For their insight will bring you success,
adorning you with grace-filled thoughts
and giving you reins to guide your decisions.[b]
10 When peer pressure compels you to go with the crowd
and sinners invite you to join in,
you must simply say, "No!"
11 When the gang says,
"We're going to steal and kill and get away with it.
12 We'll take down the rich and rob them.
We'll swallow them up alive
and take what we want from whomever we want.
13 Then we'll take their treasures and fill our homes with loot.
14 So come on and join us.
Take your chance with us.
We'll divide up all we get—
we'll each end up with big bags of cash!"
15 My son, refuse to go with them and stay far away from them.
16 For crime is their way of life and bloodshed their specialty.
17 To be aware of their snare is the best way of escape.
18 They'll resort to murder to steal their victim's assets,
but eventually it will be their own lives that are ambushed.
19 In their ungodly disrespect for God
they bring destruction on their own lives.

---

a 1:8 Many expositors see this as the words of David to Solomon, yet we all must give heed to this. The words of our father (God) and our mother (the church, the freewoman) will bring us wisdom. See Gal. 4:21–31.

b 1:9 The Hebrew text here is literally translated "adornment for your head, chains for your neck." Our head is a metaphor for our thoughts, our neck a symbol for willing obedience that guides our decisions, in contrast to being stiff-necked or proud. See Phil. 2:5.

Wisdom's Warning

20 Wisdom's praises are sung in the streets
and celebrated far and wide.
21 Yet wisdom's song is not always heard in the halls of higher learning.
But in the hustle and bustle of everyday life
its lyrics can always be heard above the din of the crowd.[a]
You will hear wisdom's warning as she preaches courageously
to those who stop to listen:
22 "Foolish ones, how much longer will you cling to your deception?[b]
How much longer will you mock wisdom,
cynical scorners who fight the facts?
23 Come back to your senses and be restored to reality.
Don't even think about refusing my rebuke!
Don't you know that I'm ready
to pour out my spirit of wisdom upon you
and bring to you the revelation of my words
that will make your heart wise?
24 I've called to you over and over
still you refuse to come to me.
I've pleaded with you again and again,
yet you've turned a deaf ear to my voice.
25 Because you have laughed at my counsel
and have insisted on continuing in your stubbornness,
26 I will laugh when your calamity comes
and will turn away from you at the time of your disaster.
Make a joke of my advice, will you?

---

a 1:21 Literally translated, this verse reads, "Wisdom sings out in the streets and speaks her voice in the squares, crying out at the head of noisy crowds and at the entrance of the city gates." This is a parabolic statement of wisdom being heard everywhere and in every place.

b 1:22 Or "Childish ones, how long will you love your childishness?"

Then I'll make a joke out of you!
27 When the storm clouds of terror gather over your head,
when dread and distress consume you
and your catastrophe comes like a hurricane,
28 You will cry out to me, but I won't answer.
Then it will be too late to expect my help.
When desperation drives you to search for me,
I will be nowhere to be found.
29 Because you have turned up your nose at me
and closed your eyes to the facts
and refused to worship me in awe—[a]
30 Because you scoffed at my wise counsel
and laughed at my correction—
31 Now you will eat the bitter fruit of your own ways.
You've made your own bed; now lie in it!
So how do you like that?
32 Like an idiot you've turned away from me
and chosen destruction instead.
Your self-satisfied smugness[b] will kill you.
33 But the one who always listens to me
will live undisturbed in a heavenly peace.
Free from fear, confident and courageous,
you will rest unafraid and sheltered from the storms of life.

Searching for Wisdom

2 My child, will you treasure my wisdom?
Then, and only then, will you acquire it.
And only if you accept my advice
and hide it within will you succeed.

---

a 1:29 The Hebrew word used here can be translated "fear, dread, awe, and worship." Nearly every translation uses the word *fear* or *reverence* while ignoring the other aspects of the Aramaic word, *dekhlatha*. The New Testament is clear that there is no fear in love. See 1 John 4:18.

b 1:32 Or "your abundant prosperity."

2 So train your heart to listen when I speak
and open your spirit wide to expand your discernment—
then pass it on to your sons and daughters.[a]
3 Yes, cry out for comprehension and intercede for insight.
4 For if you keep seeking it like a man would seek for sterling silver,
searching in hidden places for cherished treasure,
5 Then you will discover the fear of the Lord
and find the true knowledge of God.
6 Wisdom is a gift from a generous God,
and every word he speaks is full of revelation
and becomes a fountain of understanding within you.[b]
7–8 For the Lord has a hidden storehouse of wisdom
made accessible to his godly lovers.[c]
He becomes your personal bodyguard as you follow his ways,
protecting and guarding you as you choose what is right.
9 Then you will discover all that is just, proper, and fair,
and be empowered to make the right decisions
as you walk into your destiny.
10 When wisdom wins your heart and revelation breaks in,
true pleasure enters your soul.
11 If you choose to follow good counsel,
divine design will watch over you
and understanding will protect you
from making poor choices.
12 It will rescue you from evil in disguise
and from those who speak duplicities.
13 For they have left the highway of holiness
and walk in the ways of darkness.

---

a 2:2 As translated from the Septuagint.
b 2:6 The Septuagint adds, "found in his presence."
c 2:7–8 Or "the righteous."

14 They take pleasure when evil prospers
and thoroughly enjoy a lifestyle of sin.
15 But they're walking on a path to nowhere,
wandering away into deeper deception.

Wisdom, the Way of the Pure

16 Only wisdom can save you from the flattery
of the promiscuous woman—
she's such a smooth-talking seductress!
17 She left her husband and has forgotten her wedding vows.[a]
18 You'll find her house on the road to hell,
19 And all the men who go through her doors
will never come back to the place they were—
they will find nothing but desolation and despair.
20 Follow those who follow wisdom and stay on the right path.
21 For all my godly lovers will enjoy life to the fullest
and will inherit their destinies.[b]
22 But the treacherous ones who love darkness
will not only lose all they could have had—
they will lose even their own souls!

---

a 2:17 Clearly, this is a warning to those who would commit adultery, but there is a deeper meaning within this text. Proverbs tells us of two women: the adulteress and the virtuous woman of Prov. 31. Both women speak a parable of two systems in the church. One is religious and alluring, tempting the young anointed ones to come to her "bed" of compromise (Mark 7:13). The other is the holy bride, virtuous and pure, keeping her first love ("wedding vows") for Christ alone. Her "house" is the house of the Lord. One system brings shame and despair; the other brings favor, honor, and glory. It is wisdom that protects us from one and unites us to the other. See Jer. 50–52 and Rev. 17–18.

b 2:21 Literally, "shall dwell in the land."

The Rewards of Wisdom

3 1–2 My child, if you truly want a long and satisfying life,
never forget the things that I've taught you.
follow closely every truth that I've given you.
Then you will have a full, rewarding life.
3 Hold on to loyal love and don't let go,
and be faithful to all that you've been taught.
Let your life be shaped by integrity,[a]
with truth written upon your heart.
4 That's how you will find favor and understanding
with both God and men—
you will gain the reputation of living life well.

Wisdom's Guidance

5 Trust in the Lord completely,
and do not rely on your own opinions.
With all your heart rely on him to guide you,
and he will lead you in every decision you make.
6 Become intimate with him in whatever you do,
and he will lead you wherever you go.[b]
Don't think for a moment that you know it all,[c]
7 For wisdom comes when you adore him with undivided devotion
and avoid everything that's wrong—
8 For then you will find the healing refreshment
your body and spirit long for.[d]
9 Glorify God with all your wealth,

---

a 3:3 Or "tie them around your neck." The neck is a symbol of our will and conscience.

b 3:6 Or "He will cut a straight path before you."

c 3:6 We should always be willing to listen to correction and instruction.

d 3:8 Literally, "healing to your navel and moistening to your bones." The blood supply for a baby in the womb comes through the navel. New cells are made in the marrow of our bones. As the navel and bones picture the

honoring him with your very best,[a]
with every increase that comes to you.
10 Then every dimension of your life will overflow with
blessings
from an uncontainable source of inner joy!

Wisdom's Correction

11 My child, when the Lord God speaks to you,
never take his words lightly,
and never be upset when he corrects you.
12 For the Father's discipline comes only
from his passionate love and pleasure for you.
Even when it seems like his correction is harsh,
it's still better than any father on earth gives to his child.
13 Those who find true wisdom obtain the tools for
understanding,
the proper way to live,[b]
for they will have a fountain of blessing pouring into their
lives.
To gain the riches of wisdom is far greater
than gaining the wealth of the world.
14 As wisdom increases, a great treasure is imparted,
greater than many bars of refined gold.
15 It is a more valuable commodity than gold and gemstones,[c]
for there is nothing you desire that could compare to her!
16 Wisdom extends to you long life in one hand

---

life flow of our bodies, so the navel and bones are a picture of our inner being. See John 7:37–39.

a 3:9 Or "the firstfruits."

b 3:13 The Hebrew-Aramaic text here implies that wisdom gives the ability to take raw facts and draw right conclusions and meaning from them.

c 3:15 The Hebrew word translated as "gemstones" here can also refer to rubies, coral, or pearls.

and wealth and promotion[a] in the other.
Out of her mouth flows righteousness,
and her words release both law and mercy.[b]
17 The ways of wisdom are sweet,
always drawing you into the place of wholeness.[c]
18 Seeking for her brings the discovery of untold blessings,
for she is the healing tree of life to those who taste her fruits.[d]

Wisdom's Blueprints

19 The Lord laid the earth's foundations with wisdom's blueprints.
By his living-understanding all the universe came into being.[e]
20 By his divine revelation he broke open
the hidden fountains of the deep,
bringing secret springs to the surface
as the mist of the night dripped down from heaven.[f]

Wisdom, Our Hiding Place

21 My child, never drift off course from these two goals for your life:

---

a 3:16 Or "honor."

b 3:16 The Septuagint adds this last sentence, which is not found in the Hebrew.

c 3:17 The Hebrew word translated as "wholeness" here can also mean "peace" or "prosperity."

d 3:18 Verses 17 and 18 are recited in contemporary Torah services as the Torah scroll is returned to the ark, where it is kept.

e 3:19 When compared with Col. 1:16, we can see that Wisdom is used as a title in Proverbs for the Living Wisdom, Jesus Christ. See also 1 Cor. 1:30.

f 3:20 The dew is a metaphor of the Holy Spirit, who comes from the heavens and drenches us with God's presence. See Gen. 27:28, Deut. 32:2, Ps. 133:3, and Judg. 6:37–40.

To walk in wisdom and to discover discernment.[a]
Don't ever forget how they empower you.
22 For they strengthen you inside and out
and inspire you to do what's right;[b]
you will be energized and refreshed by the healing they bring.
23 They give you living hope to guide you,
and not one of life's tests will cause you to stumble.
24 You will sleep like a baby, safe and sound—
your rest will be sweet and secure.
25 You will not be subject to terror, for it will not terrify you.
Nor will the disrespectful be able to push you aside,[c]
26Because God is your confidence in times of crisis,
keeping your heart at rest in every situation.[d]

Wisdom in Relationships

27 Why would you withhold payment on your debt[e]
when you have the ability to pay? Just do it![f]
28 When your friend comes to ask you for a favor,
why would you say, "Perhaps tomorrow,"
when you have the money right there in your pocket?
Help him today!
29 Why would you hold a grudge[g] in your heart

---

a 3:21 Like many Hebrew words, there are various possible translations. The word translated as "discernment" here can also mean "discretion, counsel, meditation, and purpose."

b 3:22 Or "adorn your neck." The neck is a picture of our will and conscience.

c 3:25 As translated from the Septuagint.

d 3:26 Or "keeping your foot from being caught."

e 3:27 The LXX is "Why would withhold from the poor (those who need it)."

f 3:27 The Hebrew text here literally means "Do not withhold *wealth* from its owners." See Rom. 13:7.

g 3:29 Or "plot evil."

toward your neighbor who lives right next door?
30 And why would you quarrel with those
who have done nothing wrong to you?
Is that a chip on your shoulder?[a]
31 Don't act like those bullies or learn their ways.
32 Every violent thug is despised by the Lord,
but every tender lover finds friendship with God
and will hear his intimate secrets.[b]
33 The wicked walk under God's constant curse,
but godly lovers walk under a stream of his blessing,
for they seek to do what is right.
34 If you walk with the mockers you will learn to mock,
but God's grace and favor flow to the meek.[c]
35 Stubborn fools fill their lives with disgrace,
but glory and honor rest upon the wise.

A Father's Instruction

4 Listen to my correction, my sons,
for I speak to you as your father.[d]
Let discernment enter your heart
and you will grow wise with the understanding I impart.
2 My revelation truth[e] is a gift to you,
so remain faithful to my instruction.
3 For I, too, was once the delight of my father[f]
and cherished by my mother, their beloved child.[g]

---

a 3:30 See Rom. 12:18.

b 3:32 See Ps. 25:14.

c 3:34 See James 4:6 and 1 Peter 5:5.

d 4:1 Read and study this entire chapter as though it were Jesus Christ speaking to you. He is the everlasting Father and we are called his sons. See Isa. 9:6–7 and Rev. 21:6–7.

e 4:2 Literally, "Torah."

f 4:3 See Matt. 17:5 and John 3:35.

g 4:3 Or "unique." See Luke 1–2.

4 Then my father taught me, saying:
"Never forget my words.
If you do everything that I teach you, you will reign in life." [a]
5 So make wisdom your quest—
search for the revelation of life's meaning.
Don't let what I say go in one ear and out the other.
6 Stick with wisdom and she will stick to you,
protecting you throughout your days.
She will rescue all those who passionately listen to her voice. [b]
7 Wisdom is the most valuable commodity—so buy it!
Revelation knowledge is what you need—so invest in it!
8 Wisdom will exalt you when you exalt her truth. [c]
She will lead you to honor and favor
when you live your life by her insights.
9 You will be adorned with beauty and grace, [d]
and wisdom's glory will wrap itself around you, [e]
making you victorious in the race.

Two Pathways

10 My sons, if you will take the time to stop and listen to me
and embrace what I say,
you will live a long and happy life

---

a 4:4 The lessons of wisdom are meant to be passed on from parents to children.

b 4:6 It is not enough to acquire wisdom; we must love her and listen wholeheartedly to her instruction.

c 4:8 The Septuagint says, "Build a fort for wisdom and she will lift you high."

d 4:9 Literally, "She will place a garland of grace on your head and a crown of beauty upon you." A garland and a crown are metaphors for what is awarded a victor in a race. See 1 Cor. 9:24.

e 4:9 Or "wisdom's laurel of glory shielding you."

full of understanding in every way.
11 I have taken you by the hand in wisdom's ways,
pointing you to the path of integrity.
12 Your progress will have no limits when you come along with me,
and you will never stumble as you walk along the way.
13 So receive my correction[a] no matter how hard it is to swallow,
for wisdom will snap you back into place—
her words will be invigorating life to you.
14 Do not detour into darkness or even set foot on that path.
15 Stay away from it; don't even go there!
16 For troublemakers are restless if they are not involved in evil.
They are not satisfied until they have brought someone harm.
17 They feed on darkness and drink
until they're drunk on the wine of wickedness.[b]
18 But the lovers of God walk on the highway of light,[c]
and their way shines brighter and brighter
until they bring forth the perfect day.
19 But the wicked walk in thick darkness,
like those who travel in fog
and yet don't have a clue why they keep stumbling!

Healing Words

20 Listen carefully, my dear child, to everything that I teach you,
and pay attention to all that I have to say.

---

a 4:13 Wisdom will correct us and adjust our hearts to discipline. We must embrace the corrections of wisdom in order to mature spiritually.

b 4:17 Or "violence."

c 4:18 Or "the glow of sunlight."

21 Fill your thoughts with my words
until they penetrate deep into your spirit.[a]
22 Then, as you unwrap my words,[b]
they will impart true life and radiant health
into the very core of your being.
23 So above all, guard the affections of your heart,[c]
for they affect all that you are.
Pay attention to the welfare of your innermost being,
for from there flows the wellspring of life.
24 Avoid dishonest speech and pretentious words.
Be free from using perverse words no matter what!

Watch Where You're Going

25 Set your gaze on the path before you.
With fixed purpose, looking straight ahead,
ignore life's distractions.[d]
26 Watch where you're going!
Stick to the path of truth,
and the road will be safe and smooth before you.
27 Don't allow yourself to be sidetracked for even a moment,
or take the detour that leads to darkness.

Avoid Promiscuity

5 Listen to me, my son,
for I know what I'm talking about.
Listen carefully to my advice
2 So that wisdom and discernment will enter your heart,

---

a 4:21 See Col. 3:16.

b 4:22 Or "discover my words."

c 4:23 The Hebrew word, *levav*, is the most common word for heart. It includes our thoughts, our will, our discernment, and our affections.

d 4:25 Implied in the text. See also Heb. 12:1–2.

and then the words you speak will express what you've
learned.
3 Remember this:
The lips of a seductress seem sweet like honey,
and her smooth words are like music in your ears.[a]
4 But I promise you this:
In the end all you'll be left with is a bitter conscience.[b]
For the sting of your sin will pierce your soul like a sword.
5 She will ruin your life, drag you down to death,
and lead you straight to hell.[c]
6 She has prevented many from considering the paths of life.
Yes, she will take you with her where you don't want to go,
sliding down a slippery road
and not even realizing where the two of you will end up!
7 Listen to me, young men,
and don't forget this one thing I'm telling you—
run away from her as fast as you can!
8 Don't even go near the door of her house
unless you want to fall into her seduction.
9 In disgrace you will relinquish your honor to another,
and all your remaining years will be squandered—
given over to the cruel one.[d]

---

a 5:3 Some Jewish expositors view this "promiscuous woman" as a metaphor for heresy. She seduces, deceives, and drags to hell. For the believer, the promiscuous woman can be a picture of the false anointing of the religious spirit that attempts to seduce us, weaken our message, and rob the anointing of God from our ministries. Of course, there is also a clear and dire warning for all to stay sexually pure or face the consequences.

b 5:4 Or "bitter as wormwood." See Rev. 8:10–11.

c 5:5 Or "Sheol." This is the Aramaic and Hebrew word for the place of the dead. The Greeks call it Hades. Sheol is not eternal; it will be destroyed. See Hos. 13:14 and Rev. 20:4.

d 5:9 This would be the Devil, who torments the conscience as the result of this sin.

10 Why would you let strangers take away your strength[a]
while the labors of your house go to someone else?
11 For when you grow old you will groan in anguish and
shame[b]
as sexually transmitted diseases consume your body.[c]
12 And then finally you'll admit that you were wrong and say,
"If only I had listened to wisdom's voice
and not stubbornly demanded my own way,
because my heart hated to be told what to do!
13 Why didn't I take seriously the warning of my wise
counselors?
Why was I so stupid to think that I could get away with it?
14 Now I'm totally disgraced and my life is ruined!
I'm paying the price—
for the people of the congregation are now my judges."[d]

Sex Reserved for Marriage

15 My son, share your love with your wife alone.
Drink from her well of pleasure and from no other.
16 Why would you have sex with a stranger,
or with anyone other than her?
17 Reserve this pleasure for you and her alone and not with
another.[e]

---

a 5:10 Or "wealth." This could also refer to spiritual strength and wealth.

b 5:11 The Hebrew word translated as "groan" here is also used for the roar of a lion or the ocean's roar.

c 5:11 Implied in the context of the topic of sexual promiscuity. The Hebrew word her means "diseases."

d 5:14 See John 8:1–11.

e 5:17 Because of the sudden change in the Hebrew text to the masculine gender ("stranger" or "another"), there is an inference that men having sex with men is forbidden, as well as sex with a woman who is not your wife.

18 Your sex life will be blessed[a]
as you take joy and pleasure in the wife of your youth.
19 Let her breasts be your satisfaction,[b]
and let her embrace[c] intoxicate you at all times.
Be continually delighted and ravished with her love!
20 My son, why would you be exhilarated by an adulteress—
by embracing a woman[d] who is not yours?
21 For God sees everything you do and his eyes are wide open
as he observes every single habit you have.
22 Beware that your sins don't overtake you
and the scars of your own conscience
become the ropes that tie you up.
23 Those who choose wickedness die for lack of self-control,
for their foolish ways lead them astray,
carrying them away as hostages—
kidnapped captives robbed of destiny.

Words of Wisdom

6 My son, if you cosign a loan for an acquaintance
and guarantee his debt,
you'll be sorry that you ever did it!
2 You'll be trapped by your promise
and legally bound by the agreement.
So listen carefully to my advice—
3 Quickly get out of it if you possibly can!
Swallow your pride, get over your embarrassment

---

a 5:18 The Hebrew phrase used here includes the word *fountain*, which is an obvious metaphor for the sex act. The root word for *fountain* can also refer to the eyes. It may be a poetic subtlety that the eyes should only be on your wife, not on the nakedness of another. See verse 19.

b 5:19 The Hebrew includes a picturesque metaphor of the wife being like a "friendly deer and a favored filly."

c 5:19 The Septuagint reads, "Let her share conversation with you."

d 5:20 Or "breasts."

spilling the blood of the innocent,
18 Plotting evil in your heart toward another,
gloating over doing what's plainly wrong,
19 Spouting lies in false testimony,
and stirring up strife *between friends*.[a]
These are entirely despicable to God!
20 My son, obey your father's godly instruction
and follow your mother's life-giving teaching.[b]
21 Fill your heart with their advice
and let your life be shaped by what they've taught you.[c]
22 Their wisdom will guide you wherever you go
and keep you from bringing harm to yourself.
Their instruction will whisper to you at every sunrise
and direct you through a brand new day.
23 For truth[d] is a bright beam of light
shining into every area of your life,
instructing and correcting you to discover the ways to godly living.

Truth or Consequences

24–25 Truth will protect you from immorality
and from the promiscuity of another man's wife.
Your heart won't be enticed by her flatteries[e]
or lust over her beauty—
nor will her suggestive ways conquer you.
26 Prostitutes reduce a man to poverty,[f]
and the adulteress steals your soul—

---

a 6:19 The Aramaic is "deception among brothers."
b 6:20 For the New Testament believer, our mother is the church, who nurtures us and feeds us life-giving words. See Gal. 4:21–31.
c 6:21 Or "bind their words on your heart and tie them around your neck."
d 6:23 Or "Torah."
e 6:24–25, Or "Don't let her captivate you with her fluttering eyelids."
f 6:26 Or "beg for a loaf of bread."

she may even cost you your life![a]

27 For how can a man light his pants on fire and not be burned?

28 Can he walk over hot coals of fire[b] and not blister his feet?

29 What makes you think that you can sleep with another man's wife
and not get caught?
Do you really think you'll get away with it?
Don't you know it will ruin your life?

30 You can almost excuse a thief if he steals to feed his own family.

31 But if he's caught, he still has to pay back what he stole sevenfold;
his punishment and fine will cost him greatly.

32 Don't be so stupid as to think
you can get away with your adultery.
It will destroy your life,[c] and you'll pay the price
for the rest of your days.

33 You'll discover what humiliation, shame,
and disgrace are all about,
for no one will ever let you forget what you've done.

34 A husband's jealousy makes a man furious;
he won't spare you when he comes to take revenge.

35 Try all you want to talk your way out of it—
offer him a bribe and see if you can manipulate him
with your money.
Nothing will turn him aside
when he comes to you with vengeance in his eyes!

---

a 6:26 The Hebrew phrase here is literally translated, "She hunts for your precious soul."

b 6:28 A picture of the lusts of the flesh.

c 6:32 Or "The destroyer of his soul will do this."

Wisdom, Your True Love

7 Stick close to my instruction, my son,
and follow all my advice.
2 If you do what I say you will live well.
Guard your life with my revelation-truth,
for my teaching is as precious as your eyesight.[a]
3 Treasure my instructions, and cherish them within your heart.[b]
4 Say to wisdom, "I love you."
And to understanding, "You're my sweetheart."
5 "May the two of you protect me, and may we never be apart!"
For they will keep you from the adulteress
with her smooth words meant to seduce your heart.
6 Looking out the window of my house one day
7 I noticed among the mindless crowd
a simple, naïve young man who was about to go astray.
8 There he was, walking down the street.
Then he turned the corner,
going on his way as he hurried on to the house of the harlot—
the woman he had planned to meet.
9 There he was in the twilight as darkness fell,
convinced no one was watching
as he entered the black shadows of hell.[c]
10 That's when their rendezvous began.
A woman of the night appeared,
dressed to kill the strength of any man.
She was decked out as a harlot, pursuing her amorous plan.

---

a 7:2 Or "like you would the pupil of your eye," Literally, "the little man of the eye," which is a figure of speech for your most prized possession.

b 7:3 Or "Write them upon the tablets of your heart."

c 7:9 Implied from verse 27.

11 Her voice was seductive, rebellious, and boisterous
as she wandered far from what's right.
12 Her type can be found soliciting on street corners
on just about any night.[a]
13 So she wrapped her arms around the senseless young man
and held him tight—
she enticed him with kisses which seemed so right.
Then, with insolence, she whispered in his ear,
14 "Come with me. It'll be all right.
I've got everything we need for a feast.
I'll cook you a wonderful dinner.[b]
So here I am—I'm all yours!
15 You're the very one I've looked for,
the one I knew I wanted from the moment I saw you.
That's why I've come out here tonight,

---

a 7:12 This parable not only warns against the obvious evils of adultery and immorality, but also serves as a warning to the anointed young men in ministry not to be seduced by the religious system. Wisdom looks from the window (revelation and insight—Ezek. 8) of her house (the true church of Jesus) and sees a young man (not fully mature—1 John 2:12–14) who has placed himself in the path of sin. This made him vulnerable to the seduction of the "harlot" system of a works-based religion that enticed him into her bed (partnership, covering, and ordination with her and her system—Rev. 17–18) covered with Egyptian linens (Egypt is a picture of the world system that holds people in bondage). She is loud and stubborn (the old self-life never dealt with) and will not remain in her house (the true church of Jesus). She lives in the darkness of compromise and her ways are the ways of death. She doesn't remain faithful to her husband (the Bridegroom-God). The two women of Proverbs are the harlot mentioned here and the virtuous woman found in chapter 31, who speak of two systems of worship. One is true and virtuous; the other is false and seductive.

b 7:14 Or "offered peace offerings and paid my vows [in the Temple]." This is a way of saying, "I have lots of meat left over from the sacrifices I've offered, enough for a great meal."

so I could meet a man just like you.[a]
16 I've spread my canopy bed with coverings,
lovely multicolored Egyptian linens spread
and ready for you to lie down on.
17 I've sprinkled the sheets with intoxicating perfume
made from myrrh, aloes, and sweet cinnamon.[b]
18 Come, let's get comfortable and take pleasure in each other
and make love all night!
19 There's no one home, for my husband's away on business.
20 He left home loaded with money to spend,
so don't worry.
He won't be back until another month ends."[c]
21–22 He was swayed by her sophistication,
enticed by her longing embrace.
She led him down the wayward path right into sin and
disgrace.
So quickly he went astray with no clue
where he was truly headed,
taken like a dumb ox alongside of the butcher.
She was like a venomous snake coiled to strike,
so she set her fangs into him![d]

---

a 7:15 Compared to Song 3:1–4, this seems to be a parodic reversal of the Shulamite who goes out into the city to seek a man, and when she finds him, embraces him. This account of the harlot seems to be the converse of the theme of Song of Songs.

b 7:17 Although these spices are found in the sacred anointing oil, the adulteress (religious system) has only a false anointing, with no true power.

c 7:20 Or "He left with a bag of money and won't be back until the new moon."

d 7:21–22 This last sentence is arguably a difficult verse to translate with many variant options. The Aramaic is "taken like a dog to captivity." The Hebrew can be translated "bounding like a stag to a trap." Other ancient Jewish commentaries refer to this portion as "rushing like a venomous snake to discipline the foolish one," meaning that with the swiftness of a snake striking its prey, a fool lunges into his own destruction.

23 He 's like a man about to be executed with an arrow
right through his heart—
like a bird that flies into the net,
unaware of what's about to happen.
24 So listen to me, you young men.
You'd better take my words seriously!
25 Control your sexual urges and guard your hearts from lust.
Don't let your passions get out of hand
and don't lock your eyes onto a beautiful woman.
Why would you want to even get close
to temptation and seduction,
to have an affair with her?
26 She has pierced the souls of multitudes of men—
many mighty ones have fallen
and have been brought down by her.[a]
27 If you're looking for the road to hell,
just go looking for her house!

Wisdom Calling

8 1–3 Can't you hear the voice of wisdom?[b]
From the top of the mountains of influence
she speaks into the gateways of the glorious city.[c]
At the place where pathways merge,

---

a 7:26 The Aramaic is even more descriptive: "She has slain a multitude of mighty ones; they've all been killed by her."

b 8:1–3 Wisdom is personified throughout the book of Proverbs. Lady Wisdom is a figure of speech for God himself, who invites us to receive the best way to live, the excellent and noble way of life found in Jesus Christ. Jesus is wisdom personified, for he was anointed with the Spirit of wisdom. See 1 Cor. 1:30, Col. 2:3, and Isa. 11:1–2.

c 8:1–3 As translated from the Aramaic. The church is also a gateway, the house of God, the portal to heaven, that Jesus calls a "city set on a hill." Christ is the head of the church, where the wisdom of God is revealed. See 1 Cor. 1 and Eph. 3:10–12.

at the entrance of every portal,
there she stands, ready to impart understanding,
shouting aloud to all who enter,
preaching her sermon to those who will listen.[a]
4 "I'm calling to you, sons of Adam,
yes, and to you daughters as well.
5 Listen to me and you will be prudent and wise.
For even the foolish and feeble can receive an understanding heart
that will change their inner being.
6 The meaning of my words will release within you revelation
for you to reign in life.[b]
My lyrics will empower you to live by what is right.
7 For everything I say is unquestionably true,
and I refuse to endure the lies of lawlessness—
my words will never lead you astray.
8 All the declarations of my mouth can be trusted;
they contain no twisted logic or perversion of the truth.
9 All my words are clear and straightforward to everyone
who possesses spiritual understanding.
If you have an open mind, you will receive revelation-knowledge.
10 My wise correction is more valuable than silver or gold.
The finest gold is nothing compared to the revelation-knowledge
I can impart.

---

a 8:1–3 In chapter 7 it was the harlot calling out to the simple; here it is Lady Wisdom. True wisdom is easy to find—we only have to listen to her voice. Though it comes from above, it is found on street level. Creation and conscience are two voices that speak to our hearts. To discover wisdom we don't need a brilliant intellect but a tender, attentive heart.

b 8:6 The Hebrew word is literally translated as "princely" or "noble" things. The implication is that these words of wisdom are for ruling and reigning in life.

11 Wisdom is so priceless that it exceeds the value of any jewel.[a]
Nothing you could wish for can equal her.
12 For I am wisdom, and I am shrewd and intelligent.
I have at my disposal living-understanding
to devise a plan for your life.[b]
13 Wisdom pours into you
when you begin to hate every form of evil in your life,
for that's what worship and fearing God is all about.
Then you will discover
that your pompous pride and perverse speech
are the very ways of wickedness that I hate!

The Power of Wisdom

14 "You will find true success when you find me,
for I have insight into wise plans that are designed just for you!
I hold in my hands living-understanding, courage, and strength.
They're all ready and waiting for you.
15 I empower kings to reign[c] and rulers to make laws that are just.
16 I empower princes to rise and take dominion,
and generous ones to govern the earth.[d]
17 I will show my love to those who passionately love me.[e]

---

a 8:11 Literally, "corals" or "pearls."

b 8:12 Or "to discover clever inventions."

c 8:15 We have been made kings and priestly rulers by the grace of redemption.

d 8:16 As translated from many Hebrew manuscripts and the Septuagint. Other Hebrew manuscripts have, "and all nobles who govern justly." The word *nobles* can also be translated "generous ones."

e 8:17 Wisdom is not found by the halfhearted. One must love wisdom to gain it. A superficial desire will only yield a superficial knowledge.

For they will search and search continually until they find
me.
18 Unending wealth and glory
come to those who discover where I dwell.
The riches of righteousness and a long, satisfying life
will be given to them.[a]
19 What I impart has greater worth than gold and treasure.
and the increase I bring benefits more than a windfall of
income.
20 I lead you into the ways of righteousness,
to discover the paths of true justice.
21 Those who love me gain great wealth[b] and a glorious
inheritance,
and I will fill their lives with treasures.

Wisdom in the Beginning

22 "In the beginning I was there,
for God possessed me[c] even before he created the universe.
23 From eternity past I was set in place,
before the world began.
I was anointed from the beginning.[d]

---

a 8:18 Or "riches and righteousness." The phrase "a long, satisfying life" is from the Aramaic.

b 8:21 The Aramaic is "I will leave great hope as an inheritance to my friends."

c 8:22 The Aramaic and the Septuagint read, "The Lord created me at the beginning." The Hebrew verb translated here as "possessed" has two basic meanings. One is "acquired"; the other is "created." Poetically, it is a statement that the existence of Wisdom (Christ) was not independent of God at creation but was manifested and possessed by God as he created all things. Otherwise, it would sound like God was without wisdom before he created it.

d 8:23 The Hebrew word translated "anointed" here literally means "poured out" and is often used to describe the anointing oil poured out over a king.

24 Before the oceans depths were poured out,
and before there were any glorious fountains
overflowing with water,[a]
I was there, dancing![b]
25 Even before one mountain had been sculpted
or one hill raised up,
I was already there, dancing!
26 When he created the earth, the fields,
even the first atom of dust,
I was already there.
27 When he hung the tapestry of the heavens
and stretched out the horizon of the earth,
28 When the clouds and skies were set in place
and the subterranean fountains began to flow strong,
I was already there.
29 When he set in place the pillars of the earth
and spoke the decrees of the seas,
commanding the waves
so that they wouldn't overstep their boundaries,
30 I was there, close to the Creator's side[c] as his master artist.[d]
Daily he was filled with delight in me
as I playfully rejoiced before him.[e]
31 I laughed and played,

---

a 8:24 The Hebrew uses the word *kabad*, which means "glory," in describing the fountains. It could also be translated "fountains of glory" or "glorious fountains."

b 8:24 Many translation have "I was born (or brought forth)." The Hebrew word for "born" is taken from a word that means "to kick and twirl" or "to dance."

c 8:30 See John 1:1.

d 8:30 Or "architect."

e 8:30 The Hebrew word translated here as "rejoicing" can also be translated as "joyfully playing" or "laughing."

so happy with what he had made,
while finding my delight in the children of men.[a]

Wisdom Worth Waiting For

32 "So listen, my sons and daughters to everything I tell you,
for nothing will bring you more joy than following my
ways.
33 Listen to my counsel,
for my instruction will enlighten you.
You'll be wise not to ignore it.
34 If you wait at wisdom's doorway,[b]
longing to hear a word for every day,
joy will break forth within you as you listen for what I'll say.
35 For the fountain of life pours into you every time that you
find me,
and this is the secret of growing in the delight
and the favor of the Lord.
36 But those who stumble and miss me will be sorry they did!
For ignoring what I have to say will bring harm to your
own soul.
Those who hate me are simply flirting with death!"[c]

---

a 8:31 What a beautiful picture we find here of Wisdom (Christ), who finds his fulfillment in us. See also Ps. 8:4–9 and 16:3, and Eph. 2:10 and 19–22.

b 8:34 Or "guard the door of my entrances."

c 8:36 To hate wisdom is not only a sign of stupidity, it is a mark of depravity.

Wisdom's Feast

9 Wisdom[a] has built herself a palace[b]
upon seven pillars to keep it secure.[c]
2 She has made ready a banquet feast
and the sacrifice has been killed.[d]
She has mingled her wine, and the table's all set.[e]
3 She has sent out her maidens,
crying out from the high place,
inviting everyone to come
and eat until they're full.
4 "Whoever wants to know me and receive my wisdom,
5 Come and dine at my table and drink of my wine.
6 Lay aside your simple thoughts and leave your paths behind.
Agree with my ways, live in my truth,
and righteousness you will find."
7 If you try to correct an arrogant cynic,

---

a 9:1 Lady Wisdom is a poetic personification representing Christ, the Wisdom of God (1 Cor. 1:30). This is a classic form of a synecdoche. The Hebrew word *Chokmah* ("wisdom") can also mean "sacred sense." It is the understanding and insight given only by God.

b 9:1 There is a fascinating word play in the Hebrew text. The verb meaning "to build" and the word translated "son" come from the same root. "Build" is *banah* and "son" is *ben*. The house Wisdom is building is a son. You and I are sons of God who are being built into a spiritual house. There is also a verb in the Hebrew for "hewn" (as in stones). We are living stones raised up to be God's temple. See Ps. 127:1, Heb. 3:5–6, and Matt. 7:24–27 and 16:18.

c 9:1 The seven pillars of wisdom (plural, "wisdoms") point us to the seven days of creation, the seven spirits of God, and the seven components of heavenly wisdom given in James 3:17–18.

d 9:2 As translated from the Aramaic. The sacrifice points us to Calvary. Wisdom's pillar is a cross. The Hebrew phrase here literally means "She has prepared her meat."

e 9:2 Wisdom's feast will teach us the ways of God. We feed our hearts on revelation truth that transforms us; then we implement with wise strategies the understanding we have learned at the feasting table.

expect an angry insult in return.
And if you try to confront an evil man,
don't be surprised if all you get is a slap in the face!
8 So don't even bother to correct a mocker,
for he'll only hate you for it.
But go ahead and correct the wise;
they'll love you even more.[a]
9 Teach a wise man what is right
and he'll grow even wiser.
Instruct the lovers of God
and they'll learn even more.
10 The starting point for acquiring wisdom
is to be consumed with awe as you worship Jehovah God.
To receive the revelation of the Holy One,[b]
you must come to the one who has living-understanding.
11 Wisdom will extend your life,
making every year more fruitful than the one before.
12 So it is to your advantage to be wise.
But to ignore the counsel of wisdom
is to invite trouble into your life.[c]

A Spirit Named Foolish

13 There is a spirit named Foolish,
who is boisterous and brash;
she's seductive and restless.
14 And there she sits at the gateway to the high places,

---

a 9:8 See Ps. 141:5.

b 9:10 Literally, "holy ones."

c 9:12 The Aramaic adds here: "The liar feeds on the wind and chases fantasies, for he has forsaken what is true to travel in a barren wilderness; forgetting the right paths, he leaves his own vineyard to walk with thirst and gather nothing." The Septuagint adds here: "If you forsake folly you will reign forever. Seek discretion and your understanding will bring you knowledge."

on her throne overlooking the city.
15 She preaches to all who walk by her
who are clueless as to what is happening:[a]
16 "Come home with me."
She invites those who are easily led astray, saying,
17 "Illicit sex is the best sex of all.
Our secret affair will be sweeter than all others."[b]
18 Little do they know when they answer her call
that she dwells among the spirits of the dead,
and all her guests soon become citizens of hell![c]

10 The wisdom of Solomon:[d]
When wisdom comes to a son,
joy comes to a father.
When a son turns from wisdom,
a mother grieves.
2 Gaining wealth through dishonesty[e] is no gain at all.
But honesty brings you a lasting happiness.[f]

---

a 9:15 Or "who are walking straight ahead on their path."

b 9:17 The Hebrew phrase here literally means "Stolen waters are sweet, and bread eaten in secret is pleasant." This is an obvious metaphor of finding sexual pleasure with someone other than your spouse and trying to get away with it. Finding pleasure in your relationship with your spouse is like drinking from a pure, clean fountain. But stolen water from someone else's fountain is yielding to foolishness. Adultery is always sin.

c 9:18 Older Aramaic and Septuagint manuscripts add a verse here not found in the Hebrew: "But turn away, linger not in the place or even look at her. Don't drink from a strange fountain. Abstain and drink not from an alien fountain, so that you will enjoy a long life."

d 10:1 The title of this section starting with Prov. 10 indicates a different form. Solomon's four hundred sayings of wisdom fill this section, going through 22:16. This compilation is an assorted collection of proverbs that is not easily outlined but is profound in its scope.

e 10:2 Or "the treasures of wickedness."

f 10:2 Or "Righteousness (honesty) delivers you from death."

3 The Lord satisfies the longings of all his lovers,[a]
but he withholds from the wicked what their souls crave.[b]
4 Slackers will know what it means to be poor,
while the hard worker becomes wealthy.
5 Know the importance of the season you're in
and a wise son you will be.
But what a waste when an incompetent son
sleeps through his day of opportunity![c]
6 The lover of God is enriched beyond belief,
but the evil man only curses his luck.[d]
7 The reputation of the righteous
becomes a sweet memorial to him,
while the wicked life only leaves a rotten stench.[e]
8 The heart of the wise will easily accept instruction.
But those who do all the talking
are too busy to listen and learn.
They'll just keep stumbling ahead
into the mess they created.
9 The one who walks in integrity[f]
will experience a fearless confidence in life,
but the one who is devious
will eventually be exposed.
10 The troublemaker always has a clever plan
and won't look you in the eye,

---

a 10:3 Or "satisfies the souls of the righteous."

b 10:3 The Aramaic is, "the property of the evil he demolishes."

c 10:5 Or "To gather in the summer is to be a wise son, but to sleep through the harvest is a disgrace."

d 10:6 The Hebrew is ambiguous and is literally translated "The mouth of the wicked covers violence."

e 10:7 Some Hebrew manuscripts and the Aramaic read, "The name of the wicked will be extinguished."

f 10:9 Or "innocence." The Aramaic is "He who walks in perfection walks in hope."

but the one who speaks correction honestly
can be trusted to make peace.[a]
11 The teachings of the lovers of God are like
living truth flowing from the fountain of life,
but the words of the wicked
hide an ulterior motive.[b]
12 Hatred keeps old quarrels alive,[c]
but love draws a veil over every insult[d]
and finds a way to make sin disappear.
13 Words of wisdom flow from the one with true discernment.
But to the heartless, words of wisdom
become like rods beating their backside.
14 Wise men don't divulge all that they know,[e]
but chattering fools blurt out words
that bring them to the brink of ruin.
15 A rich man's wealth becomes like a citadel of strength,[f]
but the poverty of the poor leaves their security in
shambles.
16 The lovers of God earn their wages for a life of
righteousness,
but the wages of the wicked are squandered on a life of
sin.[g]
17 If you readily receive correction,
you are walking on the path to life.
But if you reject rebuke,

---

a 10:10 As translated from the Septuagint. The Hebrew is "The babbling fool comes to ruin."
b 10:11 Or "hide violence."
c 10:12 The Aramaic is "Hatred stirs up judgment."
d 10:12 Love will cover up offenses against us, but never our own offenses.
e 10:14 Or "Those who are wise store up knowledge (like treasure)."
f 10:15 Or "his fortified city."
g 10:16 Or "their harvest of wickedness."

you're guaranteed to go astray.[a]
18 The one who hides his hatred while pretending to be your friend
is nothing but a liar.
But the one who slanders you behind your back
proves that he's a fool, never to be trusted.
19 If you keep talking, it won't be long
before you're saying something really wrong.
Prove you're wise from the very start—
just bite your tongue and be strong!
20 The teachings of the godly ones are like pure silver,
bringing words of redemption to others,[b]
but the heart of the wicked is corrupt.
21 The lovers of God feed many with their teachings,[c]
but the foolish ones starve themselves
for lack of an understanding heart.
22 True enrichment comes from the blessing of the Lord,
with rest and contentment[d] in knowing
that it all comes from him.
23 The fool finds his fun in doing wrong,[e]
but the wise delight in having discernment.
24 The lawless are haunted by their fears
and what they dread will come upon them,[f]
but the longings of the lovers of God will all be fulfilled.
25 The wicked are blown away by every stormy wind.

---

a 10:17 The Aramaic is even more blunt: "Reject rebuke and you're a moron!"

b 10:20 Or "The tongue of the just is like choice silver." Silver is a metaphor for redemption.

c 10:21 The Aramaic is "The lips of the righteous multiply mercy."

d 10:22 Or "with no labor or sorrow attached."

e 10:23 The word translated "fool" means "moron" in the Aramaic.

f 10:24 This speaks of the consequences of sin. There is a Judge who sees all that we do and will call us to account one day.

But when a catastrophe comes,
the lovers of God have a secure anchor.
26 To trust a lazy person to get a job done
will be as irritating as smoke in your eyes—
as enjoyable as a toothache!
27 Living in the worship and awe of God
will bring you many years of contented living.
So how could the wicked ever expect to have a long, happy life?
28 Lovers of God have a joyful feast of gladness,
but the ungodly see their hopes vanish right before their eyes.
29 The beautiful ways of God are a safe resting place[a]
for those who have integrity.
But to those who work wickedness
the ways of God spell doom.
30 God's lover can never be greatly shaken.
But the wicked will never inherit
the covenant blessings.[b]
31 The teachings of the righteous are loaded with wisdom,
but the words of the evil are crooked and perverse.
32 Words that bring delight pour from the lips of the godly,
but the words of the wicked are duplicitous.

Living in Righteousness

11 To set high standards for someone else,[c]
and then not live up to them yourself,
is something that God truly hates.
but it pleases him when we apply the right standards

---

a 10:29 The Aramaic is "The way of Jehovah is power to the perfect."
b 10:30 Or "land." This is metaphor for all of the covenantal blessings.
c 11:1 The Hebrew phrase here literally means "scales of deception [false balances]."

of measurement.[a]

2 When you act with presumption,
convinced that you're right,
don't be surprised if you fall flat on your face!
But walking in humility helps you to make wise decisions.

3 Integrity will lead you to success and happiness,
but treachery will destroy your dreams.

4 When Judgment Day comes,
all the wealth of the world won't help you one bit.
So you'd better be rich in righteousness,
for that's the only thing that can save you in death.

5 Those with good character walk on a smooth path,
with no detour or deviation.
But the wicked keep falling because of their own
wickedness.

6 Integrity will keep a good man from falling.
But the unbeliever is trapped,
held captive to his sinful desires.

7 When an evil man dies, all hope is lost,
for his misplaced confidence goes in the coffin
and gets buried along with him.

8 Lovers of God are snatched away from trouble,
and the wicked show up in their place.[b]

9 The teachings of hypocrites can destroy you,
but revelation knowledge will rescue the righteous.[c]

10 The blessing that rests on the righteous
releases strength and favor to the entire city,[d]

---

a 11:1 The Hebrew phrase here literally means "a perfect stone." Stones were used as the legitimate weights of balance. Jesus is the perfect Stone. See Rev. 2:17.

b 11:8 Haman is a classic example of this principle. See Est. 7:10; 9:24–25.

c 11:9 Or "The righteous will be strengthened."

d 11:10 As translated from the Aramaic and the Septuagint.

but shouts of joy will be heard when the wicked one dies.
11 The blessing of favor resting upon the righteous
influences a city to lift it higher,[a]
but wicked leaders tear it apart by their words.
12 To quarrel with a neighbor is senseless.[b]
Bite your tongue; be wise and keep quiet!
13 You can't trust a gossiper with a secret;
they'll just go blab it all.
Put your confidence instead in a trusted friend,
for he will be faithful to keep it in confidence.
14 People lose their way without wise leadership,
but a nation succeeds and stands in victory
when it has many good counselors to guide it.
15 The evil man will do harm when confronted by a righteous man,
because he hates those who await good news.[c]
16 A gracious, generous woman
will be honored with a splendid[d] reputation,
but the woman who hates the truth
lives surrounded with disgrace[e] and by men
who are cutthroats, only greedy for money.[f]
17 A man of kindness attracts favor,

---

a 11:11 Jesus describes the church as a city. See Matt. 5:14.

b 11:12 Or "To disparage your neighbor is being heartless."

c 11:15 As translated from the Aramaic and the Septuagint. There is a vast difference between this and the Hebrew text, which reads, "You'll be ruined if you cosign for a stranger, and a hater of handshakes will be safe."

d 11:16, Or "glorious."

e 11:16 As translated from the older Aramaic and Septuagint texts, but is not included in newer Hebrew manuscripts. There is an additional line added by the Aramaic and the Septuagint: "The lazy will lack, but the diligent support themselves financially."

f 11:16 The Septuagint is "the diligent obtain wealth."

while a cruel man attracts nothing but trouble.[a]
18 Evil people may get a short-term gain,[b]
but to sow seeds of righteousness
will bring a true and lasting reward.
19 A son of righteousness[c] experiences the abundant life,
but the one who pursues evil hurries to his own death.
20 The Lord can't stand the stubborn heart bent toward evil,
but he treasures those whose ways are pure.[d]
21 Assault your neighbor and you will certainly be punished,[e]
but God will rescue the children of the godly.
22 A beautiful woman who abandons good morals
is like a fine gold ring dangling from a pig's snout.
23 True lovers of God are filled with longings
for what is pleasing and good,
but the wicked can only expect doom.
24 Generosity brings prosperity,
but withholding from charity brings poverty.
25 Those who live to bless others[f]
will have blessings heaped upon them,
and the one who pours out his life to pour out blessings
will be saturated with favor.
26 People will curse the businessman with no ethics,

---

a 11:17 The Hebrew text indicates this trouble could be physical, related to one's health.

b 11:18 Or "wages of deception."

c 11:19 As translated from one Hebrew manuscript, the Aramaic, and the Septuagint. Most Hebrew manuscripts have "The one who pursues righteousness."

d 11:20 Or "wholehearted."

e 11:21 As translated from the Aramaic and the Targum (Hebrew-Aramaic commentary).

f 11:25 The Hebrew phrase here literally means "the soul of blessing will grow fat."

but the one with a social conscience receives praise from all.[a]

27 Living your life seeking what is good for others brings untold favor,
but those who wish evil for others will find it coming back on them.

28 Keep trusting in your riches and down you'll go!
But the lovers of God rise up like flowers in the spring.

29 The fool who brings trouble to his own family
will be cut out of the will,
and the family servant will do better than he.

30 But a life lived loving God bears lasting fruit,
for the one who is truly wise wins souls.[b]

31 If the righteous are barely saved,
what's in store for all the wicked?[c]

It's Right to Live for God

12 To learn the truth you must long to be teachable,[d]
or you can despise correction and remain ignorant.

2 If your heart is right, favor flows from the Lord,
but a devious heart invites His condemnation.

3 You can't expect success by doing what's wrong.
But the lives of his lovers are deeply rooted and firmly planted.

4 The integrity and strength of a virtuous wife[e]

---

a 11:26 The Hebrew phrase here literally means "The one who withholds produce will be cursed, but blessing will be on the head of the one who sells it."

b 11:30 As translated from the Hebrew. The Aramaic and the Septuagint read, "The souls of violent ones will be removed."

c 11:31 As translated from the Septuagint. See also 1 Peter 4:18.

d 12:1 There are times when even the wise need correction, but they will appreciate its value.

e 12:4 There is an amazing Hebrew word used here. It is more commonly

transforms her husband into an honored king.[a]
but the wife who disgraces her husband
weakens the strength of his identity.[b]
5 The lovers of God are filled with good ideas
that are noble and pure,
but the schemes of the sinner
are crammed with nothing but lies.
6 The wicked use their words to ambush and accuse,[c]
but the lovers of God speak to defend and protect.
7 The wicked are taken out, gone for good,
but the godly families shall live on.
8 Everyone admires a man of principles,
but the one with a corrupt heart is despised.
9 Just be who you are and work hard for a living,
for that's better than pretending to be important
and starving to death.
10 A good man takes care of the needs of his pets,
while even the kindest acts of a wicked man are still cruel.
11 Work hard at your job and you'll have what you need.
Following a get-rich-quick scheme is nothing but a fantasy.
12 The cravings of the wicked are only for what is evil,[d]

---

used to describe warriors, champions, and mighty ones. Many translations read, "an excellent wife." But the meaning of the Hebrew word *chayil* is better translated "an army that is wealthy, strong, mighty, powerful, with substance, valiant, virtuous, or worthy."

a 12:4 Or "An excellent wife is the crown of her husband." By implication, her dignity makes him a king.

b 12:4 Or "She is like cancer in his bones." Bones are a metaphor for inner strength, our inner being or identity.

c 12:6 Or "lie in wait for blood." This is a figure of speech for accusation.

d 12:12 As translated from the Septuagint. The Hebrew is "Thieves crave the loot of other thieves."

but righteousness is the core motivation for
the lovers of God,
and it keeps them content and flourishing.[a]

Wisdom Means Being Teachable

13 The wicked will get trapped by their words
of gossip, slander, and lies.[b]
But for the righteous, honesty is its own defense.
14 For there is great satisfaction in speaking the truth,
and hard work brings blessings back to you.
15 A fool is in love with his own opinion,
but wisdom means being teachable.

Learning to Speak Wisely

16 If you shrug off an insult and refuse to take offense,
you demonstrate discretion indeed.[c]
But the fool has a short fuse
and will immediately let you know when he's offended.
17 Truthfulness marks the righteous,
but the habitual liar can never be trusted.
18 Reckless words are like the thrusts of a sword,
cutting remarks meant to stab and to hurt.
But the words of the wise soothe and heal.
19 Truthful words will stand the test of time,
but one day every lie will be seen for what it is.
20 Deception fills the hearts of those who plot harm,
but those who plan for peace[d] are filled with joy.
21 Calamity is not allowed to overwhelm the righteous,

---

a 12:12 The meaning of the Hebrew text of verse 12 is uncertain.

b 12:13 The Hebrew is simply, "sinful words," which imply gossip, slander and lies.

c 12:16 Or "A shrewd man conceals his shame."

d 12:20 Or "counselors of peace."

but there's nothing but trouble waiting for the wicked.
22 Live in the truth and keep your promises,
and the Lord will keep delighting in you,
but he detests a liar.
23 Those who possess wisdom don't feel the need
to impress others with what they know,
but foolish ones make sure their ignorance is on display.
24 If you want to reign in life,[a]
don't sit on your hands.
Instead work hard at doing what's right,
for the slacker will end up working to make someone else succeed.
25 Anxious fear brings depression,
but a life-giving word of encouragement
can do wonders to restore joy to the heart.[b]
26 Lovers of God give good advice to their friends,[c]
but the counsel of the wicked will lead them astray.
27 A passive person won't even complete a project,[d]
but a passionate person makes good use
of his time, wealth, and energy.

---

a 12:24 The Hebrew word for "reign" (*mashal*) is the title of the book—Proverbs. See introduction and the footnote on 1:1.

b 12:25 This insightful proverb can also be translated "Stop worrying! Think instead of what brings you gladness." Our focus must never be on what we can't change but on the everlasting joy we have in Christ. Sometimes we have to find the life-giving word of encouragement rising up in our own hearts. This is the secret of finding perpetual encouragement by the Word that lives in us.

c 12:26 As translated from older Aramaic manuscripts. The Hebrew is uncertain.

d 12:27 Implied in the text, paraphrased from an uncertain Hebrew phrase. An alternate translation would be "A lazy person won't get to roast the game he caught, but the wealth of a diligent person is precious."

28 Abundant life is discovered by walking in righteousness,
but holding on to your anger leads to death.[a]

Living Wisely

13 A wise son or daughter desires a father's discipline,
but the know-it-all never listens to correction.
2 The words of the wise are kind and easy to swallow,
but the unbeliever just wants to pick a fight and argue.
3 Guard your words and you'll guard your life,
but if you don't control your tongue,
it will ruin everything.
4 The slacker wants it all and ends up with nothing,
but the hard worker ends up with all that he longed for.
5 Lovers of God hate what is phony and false,
but the wicked are full of shame and behave shamefully.[b]
6 Righteousness is like a shield of protection
guarding those who keep their integrity,
but sin is the downfall of the wicked.
7 One pretends to be rich but is poor.
Another pretends to be poor but is quite rich.[c]
8 The self-assurance of the rich is their money,[d]
but people don't kidnap and extort the poor!
9 The virtues of God's lovers shine brightly in the darkness,
but the flickering lamp of the ungodly will be extinguished.
10 Wisdom opens your heart to receive wise counsel,
but pride closes your ears to advice
and gives birth to only quarrels and strife.

---

a 12:28 As translated from the Septuagint and the Aramaic. The Hebrew is uncertain.

b 13:5 The Hebrew word used here literally means "to cause a stink" or "to emit an odor." This is a figure of speech for what is shameful.

c 13:7 It is never godly to be a phony. It's always better to be who you are and avoid pretense.

d 13:8 The Aramaic is "The salvation of the soul is a man's true wealth."

11 Wealth quickly gained is quickly wasted—[a]
easy come, easy go!
But if you gradually gain wealth,
you will watch it grow.
12 When hope's dream seems to drag on and on,
the delay can be depressing.
But when at last your dream comes true,
life's sweetness will satisfy your soul.[b]
13 Despise the Word, will you?
Then you'll pay the price and it won't be pretty!
But the one who honors the Father's holy instructions
will be rewarded.
14 When the lovers of God teach you truth,
a fountain of life opens up within you,
and their wise instruction will deliver you from the ways of death.
15 Everyone admires a wise, sensible person,
but the treacherous walk on the path of ruin.[c]
16 Everything a wise and shrewd man does
comes from a source of revelation-knowledge,[d]
but the behavior of a fool puts foolishness on parade![e]
17 An undependable messenger causes a lot of trouble,
but the trustworthy and wise messengers
release healing wherever they go.[f]
18 Poverty and disgrace come to the one

---

a 13:11 Or "Wealth gained by fraud will dwindle."

b 13:12 Or "It is a tree of life."

c 13:15 As translated from the Aramaic and the Septuagint. The Hebrew is uncertain.

d 13:16 Or "A wise person thinks ahead."

e 13:16 The implication is that the fool is unable to finish anything he begins.

f 13:17 God's sons and daughters are peacemakers, healers, and faithful deliverers for others.

who refuses to hear criticism.[a]
But the one who is easy to correct is on the path of honor.
19 When God fulfills your longings,
sweetness fills your soul.
But the wicked refuse to turn from darkness
to see their desires come to pass.[b]
20 If you want to grow in wisdom,
then spend time with the wise.
Walk with the wicked
and you'll eventually become just like them.
21 Calamity chases the sin-chaser,
but prosperity pursues the God-lover.
22 The benevolent man leaves an inheritance
that endures to his children's children,
but the wealth of the wicked is treasured up for the righteous.
23 The lovers of God will live a long life and get to enjoy their wealth,
but the ungodly will suddenly perish.[c]
24 If you withhold correction and punishment[d] from your children,
you demonstrate a lack of true love.
So prove your love and be prompt to punish them.[e]

---

a 13:18 As translated from the Hebrew. The Septuagint is "Instruction removes poverty and disgrace."

b 13:19 Implied by the Hebrew parallelism of the text.

c 13:23 As translated from the Septuagint. The Hebrew is "In the fallow ground of the poor there is abundance of food, but injustice sweeps it away." The Aramaic is "Those who don't find the way of life destroy many years of wealth and some are utterly destroyed." There is a vast difference in the three translations. The translator has chosen to follow the Septuagint.

d 13:24 Or "sparing the rod." Corporal punishment was common in pre-modern societies.

e 13:24 Or "The one who spares the rod hates his child."

25 The lovers of God will have more than enough,
but the wicked will always lack what they crave.

The House of Wisdom

14 Every wise woman encourages and builds up her family,
but a foolish woman over time will tear it down by her own actions.
2 Lovers of truth follow the right path
because of their wonderment and worship of God.
But the devious display their disdain for him.
3 The words of a proud fool will all come back to haunt him.
But the words of the wise
will become a shield of protection around them.
4 The only clean stable is an empty stable.
So if you want the work of an ox and enjoy an abundant harvest,
you'll have a mess or two to clean up!
5 An honest witness will never lie,
but a deceitful witness lies with every breath.
6 The intellectually arrogant seek for wisdom,
but they never seem to discover
what they claim they're looking for.
For revelation-knowledge flows to the one
who hungers for understanding.
7 The words of the wise are like weapons of knowledge.[a]
If you need wise counsel, stay away from the fool.
8 For the wisdom of the wise will keep life on the right track,
while the fool only deceives himself
and refuses to face reality.
9 Fools mock the need for repentance,[b]

---

a 14:7 As translated from the Aramaic.

b 14:9 Or "Fools mock guilt (or guilt offering)." The Septuagint is "The house of the transgressor owes purification."

while the favor of God rests upon all his lovers.
10 Don't expect anyone else to fully understand
both the bitterness and the joys
of all you experience in your life.
11 The household of the wicked is soon torn apart,
while the family of the righteous flourishes.
12 You can rationalize it all you want
and justify the path of error you have chosen,
but you'll find out in the end that you took the road to destruction.
13 Superficial laughter can hide a heavy heart,
but when the laughter ends, the pain resurfaces.
14 Those who turn from the truth get what they deserve,
but a good person receives a sweet reward.[a]
15 A gullible person will believe anything,
but a sensible person will confirm the facts.
16 A wise person is careful in all things and turns quickly from evil,
while the impetuous fool moves ahead with overconfidence.
17 An impulsive person has a short fuse and can ruin everything,
but the wise show self-control.[b]
18 The naïve demonstrate a lack of wisdom,
but the lovers of wisdom are crowned with revelation-knowledge.
19 Evil ones will pay tribute to good people
and eventually come to be servants of the godly.[c]

---

a 14:14 As translated from Hebrew manuscripts. The Aramaic is "A good man will be filled from the awe of his soul."

b 14:17 As translated from the Aramaic. The Hebrew is "And a crafty schemer is hated." The Greek Septuagint is "A sensible man bears up under many things."

c 14:19 The Hebrew phrase literally means "They will come [or bow] at

20 The poor are disliked even by their neighbors,
but everyone wants to get close to the wealthy.
21 It's a sin to despise one who is less fortunate than you,[a]
but when you are kind to the poor,
you will prosper and be blessed.
22 Haven't you noticed how evil schemers always wander astray?
But kindness and truth come to those
who make plans to be pure in all their ways.[b]
23 If you work hard at what you do,
great abundance will come to you.
But merely talking about getting rich
while living to only pursue your pleasures[c]
brings you face-to-face with poverty.[d]
24 The true net worth of the wise[e] is the wealth that wisdom imparts.
But the way of life for the fool is his foolishness.[f]
25 Speak the truth and you'll save souls,
but in the spreading of lies treachery thrives.
26 Confidence and strength flood the hearts
of the lovers of God who live in awe of him,
and their devotion provides their children

---

the gates of the righteous."

a 14:21 Implied in the Hebrew parallelism. The Hebrew phrase here literally means "your neighbor."

b 14:22 Both the Aramaic and the Septuagint insert a verse here that is not found in the Hebrew: "The followers of evil don't understand mercy and faith, but you'll find kindness and faith with those who do good."

c 14:23 As translated from the Septuagint.

d 14:23 There is an additional verse found here in the Aramaic that is missing from the Hebrew text: "The Lord Jehovah heals every sickness, but evil speaking makes you sick [harms you]."

e 14:24 Or "the crown of the wise."

f 14:24 The Aramaic word translated here as "foolishness" can also mean "insanity."

with a place of shelter and security.[a]

27 To worship God in wonder and awe
opens a fountain of life within you,
empowering you to escape death's domain.[b]

28 A king glories in the number of his loyal followers,
but a dwindling population spells ruin for any leader.

29 When your heart overflows with understanding
you'll be very slow to get angry.
But if you have a quick temper,
your impatience will be quickly seen by all.

30 A tender, tranquil heart will make you healthy,[c]
but jealousy can make you sick.

31 Insult your Creator, will you?
That's exactly what you do
every time that you oppress the powerless![d]
Showing kindness to the poor is equal to honoring your Maker.

32 The wicked are crushed by every calamity,
but the lovers of God find a strong hope
even in the time of death.[e]

33 Wisdom soothes the heart of the one with living-understanding,
but the heart of the fool just stockpiles stupidity.

34 A nation is exalted by the righteousness of its people,
but sin heaps disgrace upon the land.

---

a 14:26 To live as a passionate lover of God will bring benefit even to your children.

b 14:27 Or "empowering you to turn from the deadly snares."

c 14:30 Or "A heart of healing is the life of the flesh."

d 14:31 Or "slander the poor." Every human being is made in God's image, including the poor.

e 14:32 Our strong hope is that our lives will continue in the presence of God in the resurrection glory. Both the Septuagint and the Aramaic read quite differently: "But the one who trusts in his integrity is righteous."

35 A wise and faithful servant receives promotion from the king,
but the one who acts disgracefully
gets to taste the anger of the king.[a]

Wisdom Far Better than Wickedness

15 Respond gently when you are confronted
and you'll defuse the rage of another.
Responding with sharp, cutting words[b] will only make it worse.
Don't you know that being angry
can ruin the testimony of even the wisest of men?[c]
2 When wisdom speaks, understanding becomes attractive.
But the words of the fool make their ignorance look laughable.[d]
3 The eyes of the Lord are everywhere[e]
and he takes note of everything that happens.
He watches over his lovers,
and he also sees the wickedness of the wicked.
4 When you speak healing words,
you offer others fruit from the tree of life.
But unhealthy, negative words do nothing but crush their hopes.[f]
5 You're stupid to mock the instruction of a father,
but welcoming correction will make you brilliant.[g]

---

a 14:35 As translated from the Hebrew. The Septuagint reads, "And by his good behavior shame is removed."
b 15:1 Or "painful words."
c 15:1 This is found only in the Septuagint.
d 15:2 The Aramaic reads, "The mouths of fools vomit a curse."
e 15:3 The eyes of the Lord can also be a metaphor of His prophets.
f 15:4 Or "Perverse words are the crushing of the spirit."
g 15:5 The Septuagint adds a verse that is not found in the Hebrew: "In

6 There is power in the house of the righteous,[a]
but the house of the wicked is filled with trouble,
no matter how much money they have.
7 When wisdom speaks, revelation-knowledge is released,[b]
but finding true wisdom in the word of a fool is futile.
8 It is despicable to the Lord
when people use the worship of the Almighty
as a cloak for their sin,[c]
but every prayer of his godly lovers is pleasing to his heart.
9 The Lord detests the lifestyle of the wicked,
but he loves those who pursue purity.[d]
10 Severe punishment awaits the one
who turns away from the truth,
and those who rebel against correction will die.
11 Even hell itself holds no secrets from the Lord God,
for all is exposed before his eyes,
and so much more the heart of every human being.
12 The know-it-all never esteems the one who tries to correct him.
He refuses to seek good advice from the wise.[e]

Living an Ascended Life

13 A cheerful heart puts a smile on your face,

---

great righteousness there is great strength. But the ungodly will one day perish from the earth."

a 15:6 As translated from the Septuagint and the Aramaic. The Hebrew changes the concept of power to prosperity. Both concepts are valid.

b 15:7 Or "is scattered like seed."

c 15:8 Or "the sacrifice of the wicked"; that is, worshipping God with a wicked heart, only to hide sin. Our yielded heart must be the sacrifice we offer to God.

d 15:9 The Aramaic reads, "He shows mercy to the one who practices righteousness."

e 15:12 Another way to say this is "The one who hates authority has no love for being taught."

but a broken heart leads to depression.
14 Lovers of God[a] hunger after truth,
but those without understanding
feast on foolishness and don't even realize it.
15 Everything seems to go wrong
when you feel weak and depressed.
But when you choose to be cheerful,
every day will bring you more and more joy and fullness.[b]
16 It's much better to live simply,
surrounded in holy awe and worship of God,
than to have great wealth with a home full of trouble.
17 It's much better to have a kind, loving family, even with little,
than to have great wealth
with nothing but hatred and strife all around you.[c]
18 A touchy, hot-tempered man picks a fight,
but the calm, patient man knows how to silence strife.
19 Nothing seems to work right[d] for the lazy man,
but life seems smooth and easy when your heart is virtuous.
20 When a son learns wisdom,
a father's heart is glad.
But the man who shames[e] his mother is a foolish son.
21 The senseless fool treats life like a joke,
but the one with living-understanding makes good choices.
22 Your plans will fall apart right in front of you
if you fail to get good advice.

---

a 15:14 Or "the upright" (Aramaic).
b 15:15 The Septuagint reads quite differently: "And the good (heart) is always calm."
c 15:17 Or "Better to have a meal of vegetables surrounded with love and grace than a fattened ox where there is hatred."
d 15:19 Or "The way is blocked with thorns."
e 15:20 Or "despises."

But if you first seek out multiple counselors,
you'll watch your plans succeed.
23 Everyone enjoys giving great advice.
But how delightful it is to say the right thing at the right time!
24 The life path of the prudent lifts them progressively heavenward,
delivering them from the death spiral
that keeps tugging them downward.
25 The Lord champions the widow's cause,[a]
but watch him as he smashes down the houses of the haughty!
26 The Lord detests wicked ways of thinking,[b]
but he enjoys lovely and delightful words.
27 The one who puts earning money above his family
will have trouble at home,
but those who refuse to exploit others
will live *in peace*.
28 Lovers of God think before they speak,
but the careless blurt out wicked words meant to cause harm.
29 The Lord doesn't respond to the wicked,
but he's moved to answer the prayers of his godly lovers.
30 Eyes that focus on what is beautiful[c] bring joy to the heart,
and hearing a good report
refreshes and strengthens the inner being.[d]
31 Accepting constructive criticism
opens your heart to the path of life,

---

a 15:25 Or "The Lord maintains the boundaries of the widow."

b 15:26 Or "the thoughts of the wicked."

c 15:30 As translated from the Septuagint. The Hebrew is "The light of the eyes brings joy."

d 15:30 The Hebrew here literally means "makes fat your bones." Bones picture our inner being.

making you right at home among the wise.
32 Refusing constructive criticism shows
you have no interest in improving your life,
for revelation-insight only comes as you accept correction
and the wisdom that it brings.
33 The source of revelation-knowledge is found
as you fall down in surrender before the Lord.
Don't expect to see Shekinah glory[a]
until the Lord sees your sincere humility.

Wisdom Exalts God

16 Go ahead and make all the plans you want,
but it's the Lord who will ultimately direct your steps.[b]
2 We are all in love with our own opinions,
convinced they're correct.
But the Lord is in the midst of us,[c]
testing and probing our every motive.
3 Before you do anything,
put your trust totally in God and not in yourself.[d]
Then every plan you make will succeed.
4 The Lord works everything together to accomplish his purpose.[e]
Even the wicked are included in his plans—
he sets them aside for the day of disaster.

---

a 15:33 Or "Before honor is humility." The Hebrew uses the word *kabod*, which is translated as "glory" 156 times in the Old Testament..
b 16:1 As translated from the Septuagint. The Hebrew and Aramaic read, "The Lord gives the right reply."
c 16:2 Or "in the midst of spirits."
d 16:3 Or "Commit your business to God."
e 16:4 Or "for its answer."

5 Exalting yourself is disgusting to the Lord,
for pride attracts his punishment—
and you can count on that!
6 You can avoid evil through surrendered worship
and the fear of God,
for the power of his faithful love
removes sin's guilt and grip over you.
7 When the Lord is pleased with the decisions you've made,
he activates grace to turn enemies into friends.
8 It is better to have little with a heart that loves justice
than to be rich and not have God on your side.
9 Within your heart you can make plans for your future,
but the Lord chooses the steps you take to get there.

Living like a King

10 A king speaks the revelation of truth,
so he must be extraordinarily careful in the decrees that he makes.
11 The Lord expects you to be fair in every business deal,
for he is the one who sets the standards for righteousness.[a]
12 Kings and leaders despise wrongdoing,
for the true authority to rule and reign
is built on a foundation of righteousness.
13 Kings and leaders love to hear godly counsel,
and they love those who tell them the truth.
14 The anger of a king releases the messenger of death,[b]
but a wise person will know how to pacify his wrath.
15 Life-giving light streams from the presence of a king,[c]
and his favor is showered upon those who please him.

---

a 16:11 Or "Honesty with scales and balances is the way of the Lord, for all the stones in the bag are established by Him."

b 16:14 See 1 Kings 2:25, 29–34, 46.

c 16:15 The Septuagint reads, "The king's son is in the light of life."

16 Everyone wants gold, but wisdom's worth[a] is far greater.
Silver is sought after,
but a heart of understanding yields a greater return.
17 Repenting from evil places you on the highway of holiness.
Protect purity and you protect your life.[b]
18 Your boast becomes a prophecy of a future failure.
The higher you lift up yourself in pride,[c]
the harder you'll fall in disgrace.
19 It's better to be meek and lowly and live among the poor
than to live high and mighty among the rich and famous.
20 One skilled in business discovers prosperity,
but the one who trusts in God is blessed beyond belief!

Walking with Wisdom

21 The one with a wise heart is called "discerning,"
and speaking sweetly to others
makes your teaching even more convincing.
22 Wisdom is a deep well of understanding
opened up within you as a fountain of life for others,
but it's senseless to try to instruct a fool.
23 Winsome words pour from a heart of wisdom,
adding value to all you teach.
24 Nothing is more appealing
than speaking beautiful, life-giving words.
For they release sweetness to our souls
and inner healing to our spirits.[d]

---

a 16:16 The Septuagint is, "nests of wisdom."

b 16:17 There are two proverbs inserted here in the Septuagint that are not found in the Hebrew or Aramaic: "Receive instruction and you'll be prosperous; he who listens to correction shall be made wise." "He who guards his ways preserves his own soul; he who loves his life will watch his words."

c 16:18 Or "overconfidence."

d 16:24 Or "healing to the bones." Bones become a metaphor of our inner

25 Before every person there is a path
that seems like the right one to take,
but it leads them straight to hell![a]
26 Life motivation comes from the deep longings of the heart,
and the passion to see them fulfilled urges you onward.[b]
27 A wicked scoundrel wants to dig up dirt on others,
only to spread slander and shred their reputation.
28 A twisted person spreads rumors;
a whispering gossip ruins good friendships.
29 A vicious criminal can be persuasive,
enticing others to join him as partners in crime,
but he leads them all down a despicable path.
30 It's easy to tell when a wicked man
is hatching some crooked scheme—
it's written all over his face.
His looks betray him as he gives birth to his sin.
31 Old age with wisdom will crown you with dignity and
honor,
for it takes a lifetime of righteousness to acquire it.[c]
32 Do you want to be a mighty warrior?
It's better to be known as one who is patient and slow to
anger.[d]
Do you want to conquer a city?
Rule over your temper before you attempt to rule a city.

---

being.

a 16:25 As translated from the Septuagint. The Hebrew is "the ways of death."

b 16:26 The meaning of the Hebrew in this verse is uncertain.

c 16:31 Or "Gray hair is a crown of splendor." In the Hebrew culture the old were honored above all, especially if they acquired wisdom. See Lev. 19:32.

d 16:32 The Septuagint is, "It's better to be forgiving than strong."

33 We may toss the coin and roll the dice,
but God's will is greater than luck.[a]

Wisdom's Virtues

17 A simple, humble life with peace and quiet
is far better than an opulent lifestyle with nothing
but quarrels and strife at home.
2 A wise, intelligent servant will be honored above a shameful son.
He'll even end up having a portion left to him in his master's will.
3 In the same way that gold and silver are refined by fire,
the Lord purifies your heart by the tests and trials of life.
4 Those eager to embrace evil listen to slander,
for a liar loves to listen to lies.
5 Mock the poor, will you?
You insult your Creator every time you do!
If you make fun of others' misfortune,
you'd better watch out—your punishment is on its way.
6 Grandparents have the crowning glory of life:
Grandchildren!
And it's only proper for children to take pride in their parents.[b]
7 It is not proper for a leader to lie and deceive,
and don't expect excellent words to be spoken by a fool.[c]
8 Wise instruction is like a costly gem.

---

a 16:33 Or "Into the center the lot is cast and from Jehovah is all its judgment." The casting of lots was a common form of divination in the premodern societies.

b 17:6 Or "fathers." There is an additional verse inserted here that is found in the Septuagint: "A whole world of riches belongs to the faithful, but the unfaithful don't get even a cent."

c 17:7 Two absurd things are to find a fool in leadership and to have a leader in foolishness.

It turns the impossible into success.[a]
9 Love overlooks the mistakes of others,
but dwelling on the failures of others devastates friendships.
10 One word of correction breaks open a teachable heart,
but a fool can be corrected a hundred times
and still not know what hit him.
11 Rebellion thrives in an evil man,
so a messenger of vengeance[b] will be sent to punish him.[c]
12 It's safer to meet a grizzly bear robbed of her cubs
than to confront a reckless fool.
13 The one who returns evil for good
can expect to be treated the same way for the rest of his life.[d]
14 Don't be one who is quick to quarrel,
for an argument is hard to stop,
and you never know how it will end,
so don't even start down that road![e]
15 There is nothing God hates more
than condemning the one who is innocent
and acquitting the one who is guilty.
16 Why pay tuition to educate a fool?
For he has no intention of acquiring true wisdom.
17 A dear friend will love you no matter what,
and a family sticks together through all kinds of trouble.
18 It's stupid to run up bills you'll never be able to pay
or to cosign for the loan of your friend.
Save yourself the trouble and don't do either one.

---

a 17:8 "Instruction" is taken from the Aramaic and the Septuagint. The Hebrew reads, "bribe."

b 17:11 Or "merciless angels."

c 17:11 This could mean an evil spirit, or calamities and sorrows.

d 17:13 Or "Evil will haunt his house."

e 17:14 The Aramaic for this verse reads, "To shed blood provokes the judgment of a ruler."

19 If you love to argue,
then you must be in love with sin.
For the one who loves to boast[a] is only asking for trouble.
20 The one with a perverse heart never has anything good to say,[b]
and the chronic liar tumbles into constant trouble.
21 Parents of a numskull will have many sorrows,
for there's nothing about his lifestyle that will make them proud.
22 A joyful, cheerful heart brings healing to both body and soul.
But the one whose heart is crushed
struggles with sickness and depression.
23 When you take a secret bribe,
your actions reveal your true character,
for you pervert the ways of justice.
24 Even the face of a wise man shows his intelligence.
But the wandering eyes of a fool will look for wisdom everywhere
except right in front of his nose.
25 A father grieves over the foolishness of his child,
and bitter sorrow fills his mother.
26 It's horrible to persecute a holy lover of God
or to strike an honorable man for his integrity!
27 Can you bridle your tongue when your heart is under pressure?
That's how you show that you are wise.
An understanding heart keeps you cool, calm, and collected,
no matter what you're facing.

---

a 17:19 Or "He who builds a high gate." The gate becomes a picture of the mouth. This is a figure of speech for proud boasting.
b 17:20 Or "can expect calamity."

28 When even a fool bites his tongue [a]
he's considered wise.
So shut your mouth when you are provoked—
it will make you look smart.

Wisdom Gives Life

18 An unfriendly person isolates himself
and seems to care only about his own issues.
For his contempt of sound judgment makes him a recluse. [b]
2 Senseless people find no pleasure in acquiring true wisdom,
for all they want to do is impress you with what they know.
3 An ungodly man is always cloaked with disgrace,
as dishonor and shame are his companions.
4 Words of wisdom [c] are like a fresh, flowing brook—
like deep waters that spring forth from within,
bubbling up inside the one with understanding.
5 It is atrocious when judges show favor to the guilty
and deprive the innocent of justice.
6 A senseless man jumps headfirst into an argument;
he's just asking for a beating for his reckless words. [d]
7 A fool has a big mouth that only gets him into trouble,
and he'll pay the price for what he says.
8 The words of a gossip merely reveal the wounds of his own
soul, [e]
and his slander penetrates into the innermost being.

---

a 17:28 The Septuagint is "when an unthinking man asks a question."

b 18:1 There are alternate possible translations of this verse in the Hebrew-Aramaic; for example, "An idle man meditates on his lusts and mocks wise instruction."

c 18:4 Or "words that touch the heart."

d 18:6 The Aramaic is "His rash words call for death."

e 18:8 Scholars are somewhat uncertain about an exact translation of this phrase. The Aramaic is "The words of a lazy man lead him to fear and evil."

9 The one who is too lazy to look for work
is the same one who wastes his life away.
10 The character of God is a tower of strength,[a]
for the lovers of God delight to run into his heart
and be exalted on high.
11 The rich, in their conceit, imagine that their wealth
is enough to protect them.
It becomes their confidence in a day of trouble.[b]
12 A man's heart is the proudest when his downfall is nearest,
for he won't see glory until the Lord sees humility.
13 Listen before you speak,
for to speak before you've heard the facts will bring
humiliation.
14 The will to live sustains you when you're sick,[c]
but depression crushes courage and leaves you unable to
cope.
15 The spiritually hungry are always ready to learn more,
for their hearts are eager to discover new truths.
16 Would you like to meet a very important person?
Take a generous gift.
It will do wonders to gain entrance into his presence.
17 There are two sides to every story.
The first one to speak sounds true until you hear the other
side
and they set the record straight.[d]
18 A coin toss[e] resolves a dispute

---

a 18:10 The Hebrew word *migdal*, translated as "tower of strength," is a homonym that can also be translated "bed of flowers."

b 18:11 The Aramaic is "The wealth of the rich is a strong city, and its glory casts a broad shadow."

c 18:14 The Septuagint is "A wise servant can calm a man's anger."

d 18:17 The text implies that a legal testimony in a courtroom may seem to be correct until cross-examination begins.

e 18:18 The Hebrew is "casting lots."

and can put an argument to rest
between formidable opponents.
19 It is easier to conquer a strong city
than to win back a friend whom you've offended.
Their walls go up, making it nearly impossible to win them back.[a]
20 Sharing words of wisdom is satisfying to your inner being.
It encourages you to know
that you've changed someone else's life.[b]
21 Your words are so powerful
that they will kill or give life,
and the talkative person will reap the consequences.
22 When a man finds a wife,
he has found a treasure!
For she is the gift of God to bring him joy and pleasure.
But the one who divorces a good woman
loses what is good from his house.[c]
To choose an adulteress is both stupid and ungodly.[d]
23 The poor plead for help from the rich,
but all they get in return is a harsh response.
24 Some friendships don't last for long,[e]
but there is one loving friend who is joined to your heart[f]
closer than any other!

---

a 18:19 Or "A brother supported by a brother is like a high, strong city. They hold each other up like the bars of a fortress."

b 18:20 Or "A man's belly is filled with the fruits of his mouth, and by the harvest of his lips he will be satisfied."

c 18:22 The reference to divorce is not found in the Hebrew text but is included in both the Aramaic and the Septuagint.

d 18:22 This is not included in the Hebrew or Aramaic, but is found in the Septuagint.

e 18:24 Or "A man with too many friends may be broken to pieces."

f 18:24 The Hebrew word used here can be translated "joined together," "stick close," "to cleave," "to pursue," or "to overtake."

Wisdom Exalted

19 It's better to be honest, even if it leads to poverty,
than to live as a dishonest fool.
2 The best way to live is with revelation-knowledge,
for without it, you'll grow impatient and run right into
error.[a]
3 There are some people who ruin their own lives
and then blame it all on God.
4 Being wealthy means having lots of "friends,"
but the poor can't keep the ones they have.
5 Perjury won't go unpunished,
and liars will get all that they deserve.
6 Everyone wants to be close to the rich and famous,
but a generous person has all the friends he wants!
7 When a man is poor, even his family has no use for him.
How much more will his "friends" avoid him—
for though he begs for help, they won't respond.[b]
8 Do yourself a favor and love wisdom.
Learn all you can,
then watch your life flourish and prosper!
9 Tell lies and you're going to get caught,
and the habitual liar is doomed.
10 It doesn't seem right when you see a fool
living in the lap of luxury
or a prideful servant ruling over princes.
11 A wise person demonstrates patience,
for mercy[c] means holding your tongue.
When you are insulted,

---

a 19:2 Or "sin."

b 19:7 The Aramaic and the Septuagint add a sentence not found in the Hebrew: "The one who is malicious with his words is not to be trusted."

c 19:11 The word translated "mercy" ("merciful") here is found only in the Septuagint.

be quick to forgive and forget it,
for you are virtuous when you overlook an offense.
12 The rage of a king is like the roar of a lion,
but his sweet favor is like a gentle, refreshing rain.
13 A rebellious son breaks a father's heart,
and a nagging wife can drive you crazy!
14 You can inherit houses and land from your parents,
but a good[a] wife only comes as a gracious gift from God!
15 Go ahead—be lazy and passive.
But you'll go hungry if you live that way.
16 Honor God's holy instructions
and life will go well for you.
But if you despise his ways and choose your own plans,
you will die.
17 Every time you give to the poor you make a loan to the
Lord.
Don't worry—you'll be repaid in full for all the good you've
done.
18 Don't be afraid to discipline your children
while they're still young enough to learn.
Don't indulge your children or be swayed by their protests.
19 A hot-tempered man has to pay the price for his anger.[b]
If you bail him out once,
you'll do it a dozen times.
20 Listen well to wise counsel
and be willing to learn from correction
so that by the end of your life
you'll be known for your wisdom.

---

a 19:14 Literally, "prudent" or "understanding" wife.

b 19:19 There is an implication in the Hebrew that he will get into legal trouble. An alternate translation of this verse could be "An evil-minded man will be injured; if you rescue him, his anger will only intensify."

21 A person may have many ideas concerning God's plan for
his life,
but only the designs of his purpose will succeed in the end.
22 A man is charming when he displays tender mercies to
others.
And a lover of God who is poor and promises nothing
is better than a rich liar who never keeps his promises.
23 When you live a life of abandoned love,
surrendered before the awe of God,
here's what you'll experience:
Abundant life. Continual protection.[a]
And complete satisfaction!
24 There are some people who pretend they're hurt—
deadbeats who won't even work to feed themselves.[b]
25 If you punish the insolent who don't know any better,
They will learn not to mock.
But if you correct a wise man,
he will grow even wiser.
26 Children who mistreat their parents
are an embarrassment to their family and a public disgrace.
27 So listen, my child.
Don't reject correction
or you will certainly wander from the ways of truth.[c]
28 A corrupt witness makes a mockery of justice,
for the wicked never play by the rules.[d]
29 Judgment is waiting for those who mock the truth,
and foolish living invites a beating.

---

a 19:23 Or "You will not be remembered for evil."

b 19:24 Or "The lazy man buries his fork in his plate and won't even lift it to his mouth."

c 19:27 Or "Stop listening to instruction that contradicts what you know is truth."

d 19:28 Or "The heart of the wicked feeds on evil."

Are You Living Wisely?

20 A drunkard is obnoxious, loud, and argumentative;
you're a fool to get intoxicated with strong drink.
2 The rage of a king is like the roar of a lion.
do you really want to go and make him angry?
3 A person of honor[a] will put an argument to rest.
Only the stupid want to pick a fight.
4 If you're too lazy to plant seed,
it's too bad when you have no harvest on which to feed.[b]
5 A man of deep understanding will give good advice,
drawing it out from the well within.
6 Many will tell you they're your loyal friends,
but who can find one who is truly trustworthy?[c]
7 The lovers of God will walk in integrity,
and their children are fortunate
to have godly parents as their examples.
8 A righteous king sits on his judgment seat.
He scatters evil away from his kingdom
by his wise discernment.
9 Which one of us can truly say,
"I am free from sin in my life,
for my heart is clean and pure"?[d]
10 Mark it down:
God hates it when you demonstrate a double standard:

---

a 20:3 Or "it is the glory of a man." It's better to keep a friend than to win a fight.

b 20:4 The Aramaic and the Septuagint read, "Rebuke a lazy man and he still has no shame, yet watch him go beg at harvest time."

c 20:6 Or "A compassionate man is hard to find, but it's even harder to find one who is faithful."

d 20:9 The Hebrew word translated "clean" can also mean "perfect" or "holy." The word translated "pure" can also mean "clear, bright, shining, unmixed." Through God's grace, by the blood of Jesus, believers have been purified, made holy, and set free from our sins.

One for "them" and one for "you."
11 Every child shows what they're really like by how they act—
you can discern their character,
whether they are pure or perverse.
12 Lovers of God have been given eyes to see
with spiritual discernment
and ears to hear from God.
13 If you spend all your time sleeping, you'll grow poor.[a]
So wake up, sleepyhead! Don't sleep on the job.
And then there will be plenty of food on your table.
14 The buyer says, as he haggles over the price,
"That's junk. It's worthless!"
Then he goes out and brags,
"Look at the great bargain I got!"
15 You may have an abundance of wealth,
piles of gold and jewels,
but there is something of far greater worth:
Speaking revelation words of knowledge.
16 Anyone stupid enough to guarantee a loan for a stranger[b]
deserves to have his property held as security.
17 What you obtain dishonestly may seem sweet at first,
but sooner or later you'll live to regret it.[c]
18 If you solicit good advice, then your plans will succeed.
So don't charge into battle without wisdom,
for wars are won by skillful strategy.
19 A blabbermouth will reveal your secrets,
so stay away from people who can't keep their mouths
shut.[d]

---

a 20:13 The Septuagint reads, "Don't love speaking evil."
b 20:16 Some manuscripts have "a promiscuous woman."
c 20:17 Or "The bread of falsehood may taste sweet at first, but afterward you'll have a mouth full of gravel."
d 20:19 The Aramaic adds a line: "One who is faithful in spirit hides a matter."

20 If you despise your father or mother,
your life will flicker out like a lamp,
extinguished into the deepest darkness.
21 If an inheritance is gained too early in life,
it will not be blessed in the end.
22 Don't ever say, "I'm going to get even with them
if it's the last thing I do!"
Wrap God's grace around your heart
and he will be the one to vindicate you.
23 The Lord hates double standards—
that's hypocrisy at its worst![a]
24 It is the Lord who directs your life,
for each step you take is ordained by God
to bring you closer to your destiny.
So much of your life, then, remains a mystery![b]
25 Be careful in making a rash promise before God,
or you may be trapped by your vow and live to regret it.
26 A wise king is able to discern corruption
and remove wickedness from his kingdom.[c]
27 The spirit God breathed into man[d] is like a living lamp,
a shining light—
searching into the innermost chamber of our being.
28 Good leadership[e] is built on love and truth,
for kindness and integrity
are what keep leaders in their position of trust.
29 We admire the young for their strength and beauty,

---

a 20:23 Or "The Lord hates differing weights, and dishonest scales are wicked."

b 20:24 The Aramaic reads, "So what man is capable of ordering his way?"

c 20:26 Or "A wise king winnows the wicked and turns his chariot wheel over them."

d 20:27 Implied by the Hebrew word *nishmat,* used in Gen. 2:7.

e 20:28 Or "a king's throne."

but the dignity of the old is their wisdom.[a]
30 When you are punished severely, you learn your lesson
well—
for painful experiences do wonders to change your life.

God Is the Source of Wisdom

21 It's as easy for God to steer a king's heart[b] for his
purposes
as it is for him to direct the course of a stream.[c]
2 You may think you're right all the time,
but God thoroughly examines our motives.
3 It pleases God more when we demonstrate godliness and
justice
than when we merely offer him a sacrifice.
4 Arrogance, superiority, and pride are the fruits of
wickedness[d]
and the true definition of sin.
5 Brilliant ideas pay off and bring you prosperity,
but making hasty, impatient decisions
will only lead to financial loss.[e]
6 You can make a fortune dishonestly,
but your crime will hold you in the snares of death![f]

---

a 20:29 Or "their gray hair."

b 21:1 Don't forget, we have been made kings and priests by the blood of the Lamb. See 1 Peter 2:9 and Rev. 1:6 and 5:10.

c 21:1 Because a leader's decisions affect so many people, God will intervene and steer them as a farmer steers the course of a stream to irrigate his fields.

d 21:4 Or "the tillage of the wicked." The Aramaic and the Septuagint has "the lamp of the wicked."

e 21:5 The Aramaic is "The thoughts of the chosen one are trusting, but those of the evil one lead to poverty." This verse is missing from the Septuagint.

f 21:6 As translated from the Aramaic and the Septuagint. The Hebrew is "The money will vanish into thin air."

7 Violent rebels don't have a chance,
for their rejection of truth and their love of evil
will drag them deeper into darkness.
8 You can discern that a person is guilty by his devious actions
and the innocence of a person by his honest, sincere ways.
9 It's better to live all alone in a rickety shack
than to share a castle with a crabby spouse![a]
10 The wicked always crave what is evil;
they'll show no mercy and get no mercy.[b]
11 Senseless people learn their lessons the hard way,
but the wise are teachable.
12 A godly, righteous person[c] has the ability
to bring the light of instruction to the wicked
Even though he despises what the wicked do.[d]
13 If you close your heart to the cries of the poor,
then I'll close my ears when you cry out to me!
14 Try giving a secret gift to the one who is angry with you
and watch his anger disappear.
A kind, generous gift goes a long way
to soothe the anger of one who is livid.[e]
15 When justice is served,
the lovers of God celebrate and rejoice,
but the wicked begin to panic.

---

a 21:9 The Septuagint reads, "It's better to live in the corner of an attic than in a large home plastered with unrighteousness."

b 21:10 The Hebrew is "They show no mercy," while the Septuagint reads, "They'll receive no mercy." The translator has chosen to merge both concepts.

c 21:12 The Hebrew is "a righteous one," which can also speak of God, "the Righteous One."

d 21:12 As translated from the Septuagint. There are many examples of this in the Bible: Daniel in Babylon, Joseph in Egypt, and the follower of Jesus today who is living among unbelievers.

e 21:14 The Aramaic and Septuagint translate this: "He who withholds a gift arouses anger."

16 When you forsake the ways of wisdom,
you will wander into the realm of dark spirits.[a]
17 To love pleasure for pleasure's sake
will introduce you to poverty.
Indulging in a life of luxury[b]
will never make you wealthy.
18 The wicked bring on themselves
the very suffering they planned for others,
for their treachery comes back to haunt them.[c]
19 It's better to live in a hut in the wilderness
than with a crabby, scolding spouse!
20 In wisdom's house you'll find delightful treasures
and the oil of the Holy Spirit.[d]
But the stupid[e] squander what they've been given.
21 The lovers of God who chase after righteousness
will find all their dreams come true:
An abundant life drenched with favor,
and a fountain that overflows with satisfaction.[f]
22 A warrior filled with wisdom ascends into the high place
and releases regional breakthrough,
bringing down the strongholds of the mighty.[g]
23 Watch your words and be careful what you say,
and you'll be surprised how few troubles you'll have.
24 An arrogant man is inflated with pride—
nothing but a snooty scoffer in love with his own opinion.

---

a 21:16 Or "the congregation of the Rephaim." The Rephaim were a pagan tribe of giants and have been equated with spirits of darkness. See Gen. 14:5 and Deut. 2:11.

b 21:17 Or "the lover of wine and oil."

c 21:18 Or "The evil become the ransom payment for the righteous and the faithless for the upright."

d 21:20 The Hebrew word for "oil" is an emblem of the Holy Spirit.

e 21:20 Or "a fool of a man."

f 21:21 Or "righteousness."

g 21:22 Or "demolishing their strength of confidence."

"Mr. Mocker" is his name![a]
25–26 Taking the easy way out is the habit of a lazy man,
and it will be his downfall.
All day long he thinks about all the things that he craves,
for he hasn't learned the secret that the generous man has learned:
Extravagant giving never leads to poverty.[b]
27 To bring an offering to God with an ulterior motive is detestable,
for it amounts to nothing but hypocrisy.
28 No one believes a notorious liar,
but the guarded words of an honest man stand the test of time.
29 The wicked are shameless and stubborn,
but the lovers of God have a holy confidence.
30 All your brilliant wisdom and clever insight
will be of no help at all if the Lord is against you.
31 You can do your best to prepare for the battle,[c]
but ultimate victory comes from the Lord God.

How to Live a Life of Wisdom

22 A beautiful reputation[d] is more to be desired than great riches,
and to be esteemed by others is more honorable
than to own immense investments.[e]

---

a 21:24 The Septuagint adds a line: "He who holds a grudge is a sinner."
b 21:25–26 This is implied in the context and is necessary to complete the meaning of the proverb. The last line of this verse reads in the Septuagint, "The righteous lavish on others mercy and compassion."
c 21:31 Or "The horse is prepared for the battle."
d 22:1 The Hebrew is simply "name preferred to wealth." The Aramaic indicates it could be "the Name [of God]."
e 22:1 Or "silver and gold." Remember, it is Solomon, one of the richest men to ever live, who penned these words.

2 The rich and the poor have one thing in common:
The Lord God created each one.
3 A prudent person with insight foresees danger coming
and prepares himself for it.[a]
But the senseless rush blindly forward
and suffer the consequences.
4 Laying your life down in tender surrender before the Lord
will bring life, prosperity, and honor as your reward.
5 Twisted and perverse lives are surrounded by demonic
influence.[b]
If you value your soul, stay far away from them.
6 Dedicate your children to God
and point them in the way that they should go,[c]
and the values they've learned from you will be with them
for life.
7 If you borrow money with interest,
you'll end up serving the interests of your creditors,[d]
for the rich rule over the poor.
8 Sin is a seed that brings a harvest;
you'll reap a heap of trouble with every seed you plant.
for your investment in sins pays a full return—
the full punishment you deserve![e]
9 When you are generous[f] to the poor,
you are enriched with blessings in return.

---

a 22:3 Wise people solve problems before they happen.

b 22:5 Or "thorns and snares." This becomes a metaphor of demonic curses and troubles. Thorns are associated with the fall of Adam. Jesus wore a crown of thorns and took away our curse. The snares picture the temptations of evil that the Devil places in our path.

c 22:6 Or "Train them in the direction they are best suited to go." Some Jewish scholars teach this means understanding your children's talents and then seeing that they go into that field.

d 22:7 The Septuagint reads, "The servant will lend to his own master."

e 22:8 As translated from the Septuagint.

f 22:9 The Hebrew word translated as "generous" here actually means

10 Say goodbye to a troublemaker and you'll say goodbye
to quarrels, strife, tension, and arguments,
for a troublemaker traffics in shame.[a]
11 The Lord loves those whose hearts are holy,
and he is the friend of those whose ways are pure.[b]
12 God passionately watches[c] over
his deep reservoir[d] of revelation-knowledge,
but he subverts the lies of those who pervert the truth.
13 A slacker always has an excuse for not working—
like, "I can't go to work. There's a lion outside!
And murderers too!"[e]
14 Sex with an adulteress is like falling into the abyss.
Those under God's curse jump right in to their own
destruction.
15 Although rebellion is woven into a young man's heart,[f]
tough discipline can make him into a man.
16 There are two kinds of people headed toward poverty:
Those who exploit the poor
and those who bribe the rich.[g]

"to have a bountiful eye." It is a figure of speech for generosity, a life of helping others.

a 22:10 As translated from the Aramaic.

b 22:11 As translated from the Septuagint. Followers of Jesus enjoy a relationship with our holy King as we live in the light and love to please him.

c 22:12 Or "the eyes of the Lord." In the church today, prophets become eyes in the body of Christ. They see and reveal God's heart for his people.

d 22:12 Although the concept of a reservoir is not found in the Hebrew, it is added by the translator for poetic nuance.

e 22:13 This humorous verse uses both satire and a metaphor. There's always an excuse for not working hard. The Aramaic text adds, "and a murderer too!"

f 22:15 The Aramaic word used here means "senseless."

g 22:16 The Hebrew is literally "Oppressing the poor is gain; giving to the rich is loss. Both end up only in poverty."

4 Don't compare yourself to the rich.[a]
Surrender your selfish ambition and evaluate them
properly.
5 For no sooner do you start counting your wealth
than it sprouts wings and flies away like an eagle in the
sky—
here today, gone tomorrow!
6 Be sensible when you dine with a stingy man[b]
and don't eat more than you should.[c]
7 For as he thinks within himself, so is he.[d]
He will grudgingly say, "Go ahead and eat all you want,"
but in his heart he resents the fact that he has to pay for
your meal.
8 You'll be sorry you ate anything at all,[e]
and all your compliments will be wasted.
9 A rebellious fool will despise your wise advice,
so don't even waste your time—save your breath!
10 Never move a long-standing boundary line
or attempt to take land that belongs to the fatherless.
11 For they have a mighty protector,
a loving redeemer,[f] who watches over them,
and he will stand up for their cause.
12 Pay close attention to the teaching that corrects you,

---

a 23:4 As translated from the Septuagint.
b 23:6 The Hebrew here literally means "an evil eye," which is a metaphor for a stingy man.
c 23:6 Or "Don't crave his delicacies."
d 23:7 The Aramaic, the LXX, and a few Hebrew manuscripts read: "Eating with him is like eating with someone with a hair in his throat—his mind is not with you!"
e 23:8 Or "You'll vomit up the little you've eaten."
f 23:11 The Hebrew word here is *goel*, which means "kinsman-redeemer." The Aramaic word means "Savior." This shows powerfully how God will take up the grievances of the oppressed.

and open your heart to every word of instruction.
13 Don't withhold appropriate discipline from your child.
Go ahead and punish him when he needs it.[a]
Don't worry—it won't kill him!
14 A good spanking could be the very thing
that teaches him a lifelong lesson![b]
15 My beloved child, when your heart is full of wisdom,
my heart is full of gladness.
16 And when you speak anointed words,[c]
we are speaking mouth to mouth![d]
17 Don't allow the actions of evil men
to cause you to burn with anger.[e]
Instead, burn with unrelenting passion
as you worship God in holy awe.
18 Your future is bright and filled with a living hope
that will never fade away.
19 As you listen to me, my beloved child,
you will grow in wisdom and your heart
will be drawn into understanding,
which will empower you to make right decisions.[f]
20 Don't live in the excesses of drunkenness or gluttony,
or waste your life away by partying all the time,[g]
21 Because drunkards and gluttons sleep their lives away

---

a 23:13 The Hebrew is "strike them with the rod."

b 23:14 Or "rescues him from death." The Hebrew word is *Sheol*.

c 23:16 Or "speak what is right."

d 23:16 This is taken from the Septuagint, and it literally means, "Your lips shall speak with my lips." The Hebrew is "My kidneys (soul) will rejoice." See Num. 12:6–8, which reveals that God spoke with Moses mouth to mouth (literal Hebrew).

e 23:17 The Hebrew word used here describes an emotion of intense passion. Many translate it "envy" ("Do not envy the sinner"), but that does not describe it fully. Another possible translation would be "zeal."

f 23:19 The Aramaic is "Set up my doctrines in your heart."

g 23:20 Translated from the Aramaic and the Septuagint.

and end up broke!
22 Give respect to your father and mother,
for without them you wouldn't even be here.
And don't neglect them when they grow old.
23 Embrace the truth[a] and hold it close.
Don't let go of wisdom, instruction, and life-giving
understanding.
24 When a father observes his child living in godliness,
he is ecstatic with joy—nothing makes him prouder!
25 So may your father's heart burst with joy
and your mother's soul be filled with gladness because of
you.
26 My son, give me your heart
and embrace fully what I'm about to tell you.
27 Stay far away from prostitutes
and you'll stay far away from the pit of destruction.
For sleeping with a promiscuous woman is like falling into
a trap
that you'll never be able to escape!
28 Like a robber hiding in the shadows
she's waiting to claim another victim—
another husband unfaithful to his wife.
29 Who has anguish? Who has bitter sorrow?
Who constantly complains and argues?
Who stumbles and falls and hurts himself?
Who's the one with bloodshot eyes?
30 It's the one who drinks too much
and is always looking for a brew.
Make sure it's never you!

---

a 23:23 The Hebrew word here literally means "create the truth" or "give birth to truth" or "possess the truth." This Hebrew word is also used for God as the Creator. See Gen. 14:19 and 22.

31 And don't be drunk with wine[a]
but be known as one who enjoys the company
of the lovers of God,[b]
32 For drunkenness brings the sting of a serpent,
like the fangs of a viper[c] spreading poison into your soul.
33 It will make you hallucinate, mumble,
and speak words that are perverse.
34 You'll be like a seasick sailor being tossed to and fro,
dizzy and out of your mind.
35 You'll awake only to say, "What hit me?
I feel like I've been run over by a truck!"
Yet off you'll go, looking for another drink!

Wisdom's Warning

24 Don't envy the wealth of the wicked or crave their company.
2 For they're obsessed with causing trouble
and their conversations are corrupt.
3 Wise people are builders—[d]
they build families, businesses, communities.
And through intelligence and insight
their enterprises are established and endure.

---

a 23:31 As translated from the Septuagint.

b 23:31 As translated from the Septuagint and a marginal reading of the Hebrew. The Aramaic is "Meditate on righteousness." The Septuagint adds a line not found in Hebrew or Aramaic that describes the unflattering life of a drunk: "You will walk around naked as a pestle!"

c 23:32 Or "horned serpent," or "dragon." This is the Hebrew word *basilisk,* which comes from a root word meaning "little king." It becomes an emblem of the poison of demonic power that can cause addictions and rule over the soul like a "little king."

d 24:3 Or "A house is built by wisdom." The house is more than a structure with roof and a floor. It becomes a metaphor of families, churches, businesses, and enterprises.

4 Because of their skilled leadership
the hearts[a] of people are filled with the treasures of wisdom
and the pleasures of spiritual wealth.
5 Wisdom can make anyone into a mighty warrior,[b]
and revelation-knowledge increases strength.
6 Wise strategy is necessary to wage war,
and with many astute advisers
you'll see the path to victory more clearly.
7 Wisdom is a treasure too lofty[c] for a quarreling fool—
he'll have nothing to say when leaders gather together.
8 There is one who makes plans to do evil—
"Master Schemer" is his name.
9 If you plan to do evil, it's as wrong as doing it.
And everyone detests a troublemaker.
10 If you faint when under pressure,
you have need of courage.[d]
11 Go and rescue the perishing! Be their savior!
Why would you stand back and watch them stagger to their death?
12 And why would you say, "But it's none of my business"?
The one who knows you completely and judges your every motive
is also the keeper of souls—and not just yours!
He sees through your excuses and holds you responsible

---

a 24:4 Or "inner chambers."

b 24:5 Or "Wisdom makes anyone into a hero." The Aramaic and the Septuagint read, "It's better to be wise than to be strong."

c 24:7 The Hebrew is actually "Wisdom is coral to a fool." That is, it is unattainable, deep and hidden.

d 24:10 Or "Your strength is limited." Our weakness often becomes an excuse to quit, but strength and courage come as the result of faithfulness under pressure. Some interpret this to mean "If you fail to help others in their time of need, you will grow too weak to help yourself."

for failing to help those whose lives are threatened.
13 Revelation-knowledge is a delicacy,
sweet like flowing honey that melts in your mouth.
Eat as much of it as you can, my friend!
14 For then you will perceive what is true wisdom,
your future will be bright,[a]
and this hope living within will never disappoint you.
15 Listen up, you wicked, irreverent ones—
don't harass the lovers of God[b]
and don't invade their resting place.
16 For the lovers of God may suffer adversity
and stumble seven times,
but they will continue to rise over and over again.
But the unrighteous are brought down by just one calamity
and will never be able to rise again.[c]
17 Never gloat when your enemy meets disaster
and don't be quick to rejoice if he falls.
18 For the Lord, who sees your heart,
will be displeased with you and will pity your foe.
19 Don't be angrily offended over evildoers or be agitated by
them.[d]
20 For the wicked have no life and no future—
their light of life will die out.[e]
21 My child, stand in awe of the Lord Jehovah!
Give counsel to others,
but don't mingle with those who are rebellious.
22 For sudden destruction will fall upon them

---

a 24:14 The Septuagint is "Your death will be good."
b 24:15 Or "the righteous."
c 24:16 Implied in the text as it completes the parallelism.
d 24:19 The Septuagint is, "Don't rejoice with those who do evil or be jealous of them."
e 24:20 Not only will they die out, but the implication is they will have no posterity.

and their lives will be ruined in a moment.
And who knows what retribution they will face![a]

Revelation from the Wise

23 Those enlightened with wisdom have spoken these
proverbs:
Judgment must be impartial,
for it is always wrong to be swayed by a person's status.
24 If you say to the guilty, "You are innocent,"
the nation will curse you and the people will revile you.
25 But when you convict the guilty,
the people will thank you and reward you with favor.
26 Speaking honestly is a sign of true friendship.[b]
27 Go ahead, build your career and give yourself to your work,
but if you put me first, you'll see your family built up![c]
28 Why would you be a false accuser and slander with your
words?
29 Don't ever spitefully say, "I'll get even with him!
I'll do to him what he did to me!"
30–31 One day I passed by the field of a lazy man
and I noticed the vineyards of a slacker.
I observed nothing but thorns, weeds, and broken-down
walls.
32 So I considered their lack of wisdom,
and I pondered the lessons I could learn from this:
33–34 Professional work habits prevent poverty from becoming
your permanent business partner. And—
If you put off until tomorrow the work you could do today,
tomorrow never seems to come.

---

a 24:22 Verses 21 and 22 are translated from the Aramaic.

b 24:26 The Hebrew is literally, "An honest answer is like a kiss on the lips." In the culture of the day, kissing was a sign of authentic friendship and a mark of relationship, which was often expressed in public among friends.

c 24:27 As translated from the Septuagint.

25 Solomon's proverbs published by the scribes of King Hezekiah:

2 God conceals the revelation of his Word[a]
in the hiding place of his glory.[b]
But the honor of kings[c] is revealed
by how they thoroughly search out
the deeper meaning of all that God says.
3 The heart of a king is full of understanding,
like the heavens are high and the ocean is deep.
4 If you burn away the impurities from silver,
a sterling vessel will emerge from the fire.
5 And if you purge corruption from the kingdom,
a king's reign will be established in righteousness.
6 Don't boast in the presence of a king
or promote yourself by taking a seat at the head table
and pretend that you're someone important.
7 For it is better for the king to say to you,
"Come, you should sit at the head table,"
than for him to say in front of everyone,
"Please get up and move—
you're sitting in the place of the prince."
8 Don't be hasty to file a lawsuit.
By starting something you wish you hadn't,
you could be humiliated when you lose your case.
9 Don't reveal another person's secret
just to prove a point in an argument,

---

a 25:2 Many translate this "a matter," whereas the Hebrew is *dabar*, which is translated more than eight hundred times in the Old Testament as "word."

b 25:2 There is beautiful poetry in the Hebrew text. The word for "hide" is *cathar* and the word for "word" is *dabar*. The Hebrew is actually "*Kabod* (glory) *cathar* (hidden) *dabar* (word)."

c 25:2 We have been made kings and priests, royal lovers of God, because of God's grace and Christ's redeeming blood. See 1 Peter 2:9 and Rev. 5:8–10.

or you could be accused of being a gossip
10 And gain a reputation of being one
who betrays the confidence of a friend.
11 Winsome words spoken at just the right time [a]
are as appealing as apples gilded in gold
and surrounded with silver. [b]
12 To humbly receive wise correction
adorns your life with beauty [c]
and makes you a better person.
13 A reliable, trustworthy messenger
refreshes the heart of his master, [d]
like a gentle breeze blowing at harvest time—
cooling the sweat from his brow.
14 Clouds that carry no water
and a wind that brings no refreshing rain— [e]
that's what you're like when you boast
of a gift that you don't have. [f]

---

a 25:11 The Aramaic reads, "The one who speaks the Word is an apple of gold in a setting of silver." The Septuagint is "A wise word is like a golden apple in a pendant of rubies."

b 25:11 Each one of God's promises are like apples gilded in gold. When we are full of his Spirit we can speak and prophesy words of encouragement that are spoken at the right time for the blessing of others.

c 25:12 Or "an earring of gold, an ornament of fine gold." An earring pierces the ear and is an emblem of a listening heart.

d 25:13 Or "employer."

e 25:14 The symbols of clouds, wind, and rain are significant. Clouds are often a metaphor for the people of God filled with glory (Heb. 12:1; Rev. 1:7). Wind is an emblem of the Holy Spirit bringing new life (John 3:6–8). Rain often points to teaching the revelation truths that refresh and water the seeds of spiritual growth (Isa. 55:8–11). God's anointed people are to be clouds carried by the wind of the Holy Spirit that bring refreshing truths to his people. When we are empty and false, we are clouds without rain. See 2 Peter 2:17 and Jude 1:12.

f 25:14 Or "boast of a promised gift you never intend to give." The Hebrew is literally "to make yourself shine in a gift of falsehood."

Wisdom Practices Self-control

15 Use patience and kindness when you want to persuade
leaders
and watch them change their minds right in front of you.
For your gentle wisdom will quell the strongest resistance.[a]
16 When you discover something sweet,
don't overindulge and eat more than you need,
for excess in anything can make you sick of even a good
thing.
17 Don't wear out your welcome
by staying too long at the home of your friends,
or they may get fed up with always having you there
and wish you hadn't come.
18 Lying about and slandering people
are as bad as hitting them with a club,
or wounding them with an arrow,
or stabbing them with a sword.
19 You can't depend on an unreliable person
when you really need help.
It can be compared to biting down on an abscessed tooth
or walking with a sprained ankle.
20 When you sing a song of joy to someone suffering
in the deepest grief and heartache,
it can be compared to disrobing in the middle of a blizzard
or rubbing salt in a wound.
21 Is your enemy hungry? Buy him lunch.
Win him over with your kindness.[b]
22 Your surprising generosity will awaken his conscience[c]
and God will reward you with favor.
23 As the north wind brings a storm,

---

a 25:15 Or "Soft words break bones."

b 25:21 Or "Is he thirsty? Give him a drink."

c 25:22 Or "You will heap coals of fire on his head." His heart will be moved and his shame exposed.

saying things you shouldn't[a] brings a storm to any
relationship.
24 It's better to live all alone in a rundown shack
than to share a castle with a crabby spouse![b]
25 Like a drink of cool water to a weary, thirsty soul,
so hearing good news revives the spirit.
26 When a lover of God gives in and compromises with
wickedness,
it can be compared to contaminating a stream with sewage
or polluting a fountain.
27 It's good to eat sweet things,
but you can take too much.
It's good to be honored,
but to seek words of praise[c] is not honor at all.
28 If you live without restraint
and are unable to control your temper,
you're as helpless as a city with broken-down defenses,
open to attack.

Don't Be a Fool

26 It is totally out of place to promote and honor a fool,
just like it's out of place to have snow in the summer
and rain at harvest time.[d]
2 An undeserved curse will be powerless to harm you.
It may flutter over you like a bird,

---

a 25:23 Or "words of gossip."

b 25:24 With the exception of one Hebrew letter, this verse is identical to 21:9. See footnote. The Aramaic reads, "than to live with a contentious woman in a house of divisions."

c 25:27 This line is translated from the Aramaic.

d 26:1 Both snow and rain are good in their proper season but harmful in the wrong season. So is it harmful to the fool if you affirm him and honor him prematurely.

but it will find no place to land.[a]

3 Guide a horse with a whip,
direct a donkey with a bridle,
and lead a rebellious fool with a beating on his backside!

4 Don't respond to the words of a fool with more foolish words,
or you will become as foolish as he is!

5 Yet, if you're asked a silly question,
answer it with words of wisdom[b]
so the fool doesn't think he's so clever.

6 If you choose a fool to represent you,
you're asking for trouble.
It will be as bad for you as cutting off your own feet!

7 You can never trust the words of a fool,
just like a crippled man can't trust his legs to support him.[c]

8 Give honor to a fool and watch it backfire—
like a stone tied to a slingshot.

9 The statements of a fool will hurt others[d]
like a thorn bush brandished by a drunk.

10 Like a reckless archer shooting arrows at random
is the impatient employer
who hires just any fool who comes along—
someone's going to get hurt![e]

---

a 26:2 There is an implication in some Hebrew manuscripts that the curse will go back and land on the one who wrongly spoke it, like a bird going back to its nest.

b 26:5 As translated from the Aramaic.

c 26:7 As translated from the Aramaic.

d 26:9 As translated from the Aramaic.

e 26:10 Implied in the context. This is a difficult verse to translate and it reads quite differently in the Aramaic and the Septuagint. The Aramaic is "A fool suffers much like a drunkard crossing the sea." The Septuagint reads, "Every fool endures much hardship and his fury comes to nothing."

11 Fools are famous for repeating their errors,
like dogs are known to return to their vomit.
12 There's only one thing worse than a fool,
and that's the smug, conceited man
always in love with his own opinions.

Don't Be Lazy

13 The lazy loafer says,
"I can't go out and look for a job—
there may be a lion out there roaming wild in the streets!"
14 As a door is hinged to the wall,
so the lazy man keeps turning over, hinged to his bed!
15 There are some people so lazy
they won't even work to feed themselves.
16 A self-righteous person[a] is convinced he's smarter
than seven wise counselors who tell him the truth.
17 It's better to grab a mad dog by its ears
than to meddle and interfere in a quarrel[b]
that's none of your business.

Watch Your Words

18–19 The one who is caught lying to his friend
and says, "I didn't mean it, I was only joking,"
can be compared to a madman
randomly shooting off deadly weapons.
20 It takes fuel to have a fire—
a fire dies down when you run out of fuel.
So quarrels disappear when the gossip ends.
21 Add fuel to the fire and the blaze goes on.
So add an argumentative man to the mix

---

a 26:16 Or "sluggard." This speaks of a person who lives in fantasy and not reality.

b 26:17 Or "to become furious because of a quarrel that's not yours."

and you'll keep strife alive.
22 Gossip is so delicious, and how we love to swallow it!
For slander[a] is easily absorbed into our innermost being.
23 Smooth talk[b] can hide a corrupt heart
just like a pretty glaze covers a cheap clay pot.
24 Kind words can be a cover to conceal hatred of others,
for hypocrisy loves to hide behind flattery.
25 So don't be drawn in by the hypocrite,
for his gracious speech is a charade,
nothing but a masquerade covering his hatred and evil on parade.[c]
26 Don't worry—he can't keep the mask on for long.
One day his hypocrisy will be exposed before all the world.
27 Go ahead, set a trap for others—
and then watch as it snaps back on you!
Start a landslide and you'll be the one who gets crushed.
28 Hatred is the root of slander[d]
and insecurity the root of flattery.[e]

Heed Wisdom's Warnings

27 Never brag about the plans you have for tomorrow,
for you don't have a clue what tomorrow may bring to you.
2 Let someone else honor you for your accomplishments,
for self-praise is never appropriate.

---

a 26:22 Or "complaining."

b 26:23 As translated from the Septuagint. The Hebrew is "burning words."

c 26:25 The Hebrew is "Seven abominations hide in his heart." This is a figure of speech for the fullness of evil, a heart filled to the brim with darkness.

d 26:28 Or "A slanderer hates his victims."

e 26:28 Implied in the text. The Aramaic is "Malicious words work trouble."

[3] It's easier to carry a heavy boulder and a ton of sand
than to be provoked by a fool and have to carry that burden!
[4] The rage and anger of others can be overwhelming,
but it's nothing compared to jealousy's fire.
[5] It's better to be corrected openly,
if it stems from hidden love.
[6] You can trust a friend who wounds you with his honesty,[a]
but your enemy's pretended flattery[b] comes from insincerity.
[7] When your soul is full, you turn down even the sweetest honey.
But when your soul is starving,
every bitter thing becomes sweet.[c]
[8] Like a bird that has fallen from its nest
is the one who is dislodged from his home.[d]
[9] Sweet friendships[e] refresh the soul and awaken our hearts with joy,
for good friends are like the anointing oil
that yields the fragrant incense *of God's presence.*[f]
[10] So never give up on a friend or abandon a friend of your father—
for in the day of your brokenness[g]
you won't have to run to a relative for help.

---

a 27:6 Or "Wounds by a loved one are long lasting (effective and faithful)."
b 27:6 Or "kisses."
c 27:7 When we are full of many things and many opinions, the sweet Word of God, like revelation honey, is spurned. Instead, we eat and fill our souls with things that can never satisfy.
d 27:8 Or "banished from his place." As translated from the Aramaic.
e 27:9 Or "counsel."
f 27:9 The Hebrew text refers to the sacred anointing oil and the incense that burns in the Holy Place.
g 27:10 As translated from the Aramaic.

A friend nearby is better than a relative far away.
11 My son, when you walk in wisdom,
my heart is filled with gladness,
for the way you live is proof
that I've not taught you in vain.[a]
12 A wise, shrewd person discerns the danger ahead
and prepares himself,
but the naïve simpleton never looks ahead
and suffers the consequences.
13 Cosign for one you barely know and you will pay a great price!
Anyone stupid enough to guarantee the loan of another
deserves to have his property seized in payment.
14 Do you think you're blessing your neighbors
when you sing at the top of your lungs early in the morning?
Don't be fooled—
they'll curse you for doing it![b]
15 An endless drip, drip, drip, from a leaky faucet[c]
and the words of a cranky, nagging wife have the same effect.
16 Can you stop the north wind from blowing
or grasp a handful of oil?
That's easier than to stop her from complaining.
17 It takes a grinding wheel to sharpen a blade,
and so a friendly argument can sharpen a man.[d]
18 Tend an orchard and you'll have fruit to eat.

---

a 27:11 Or "that I may answer those who reproach me."

b 27:14 Or "He who sings in a loud voice early in the morning, thinking he's blessing his neighbor is no different from he who pronounces a curse."

c 27:15 Or "a constant drip on a rainy day."

d 27:17 Or "a man's face."

Serve the Master's interests
and you'll receive honor that's sweet.
19 Just as no two faces are exactly alike,
so every heart is different.[a]
20 Hell and destruction are never filled,
and so the desires of men's hearts are insatiable.
21 Fire is the way to test the purity of silver and gold,
but the character of a man is tested
by giving him a measure of fame.[b]
22 You can beat a fool half to death
and still never beat the foolishness out of him.[c]
23 A shepherd should pay close attention to the faces of his flock
and hold close to his heart the condition of those he cares for.
24 A man's strength, power, and riches[d] will one day fade away,
not even nations[e] endure forever.
25–27 Take care of your responsibilities
and be diligent in your business
and you will have more than enough—
an abundance of food, clothing, and plenty for your household.[f]

---

a 27:19 As translated from the Aramaic and the Septuagint.

b 27:21 Or "by the things he praises."

c 27:22 Or "If you pound a fool in a mortar like dried grain with a pestle, still his foolishness will not depart from him."

d 27:24 The Hebrew says merely, "riches," while the Aramaic adds, "power (dominion)" and the Septuagint adds, "strength." The translator has chosen to combine them.

e 27:24 Or "a crown (dominion)."

f 27:25–27 An agricultural analogy is used in the Hebrew and Aramaic. The analogy of a farming enterprise has been changed to business here in order to transfer meaning. It is literally, "Gather the hay of the field and hills, and new grass will appear. Lambs will provide clothing, goats

Lovers of God

28 Guilty criminals experience paranoia
even though no one threatens them.
But the innocent lovers of God,
because of righteousness,
will have the boldness[a] of a young, ferocious lion!
2 A rebellious nation is thrown into chaos,[b]
but leaders anointed with wisdom will restore law and
order.
3 When a pauper[c] oppresses the destitute,
it's like a flash flood that sweeps away their last hope.
4 Those who turn their backs on what they know is right[d]
will no longer be able to tell right from wrong.
But those who love the truth strengthen their souls.[e]
5 Justice never makes sense to men devoted to darkness,
but those tenderly devoted to the Lord
can understand justice perfectly.
6 It's more respectable to be poor and pure than rich and
perverse.
7 To be obedient to what you've been taught[f]
proves you're an honorable child,
but to socialize with the lawless brings shame to your
parents.
8 Go ahead and get rich on the backs of the poor,

---

will pay for the price of the field, and there will be enough goat's milk for you, your family, and your servant girls."

a 28:1 Or "confidence."

b 28:2 Or "A rebellious nation will have one leader after another."

c 28:3 This pauper can also be one who is spiritually poor. Some Jewish expositors believe it refers to corrupt judges.

d 28:4 The Hebrew word is "the Torah." See also verses 7 and 9.

e 28:4 As translated from the Aramaic. The Septuagint is "build a wall to protect themselves."

f 28:7 Or "the Torah."

but all the wealth you gather will one day be given
to those who are kind to the needy.
9 If you close your heart and refuse to listen to God's
instruction,[a]
even your prayer will be despised.
10 Those who tempt the lovers of God with an evil scheme
will fall into their own trap.
But the innocent who resist temptation will experience
reward.
11 The wealthy in their conceit presume to be wise,
but a poor person with discernment can see right through
them.
12 The triumphant joy of God's lovers releases great glory.[b]
But when the wicked rise to power, everyone goes into
hiding.[c]
13 If you cover up your sin you'll never do well.
But if you confess your sins and forsake them,
you will be kissed by mercy.
14 Overjoyed is the one who with tender heart trembles before
God,
but the stubborn, unyielding heart will experience even
greater evil.
15 Ruthless rulers can only be compared
to raging lions and roaming bears.[d]
16 Abusive leaders fail to employ wisdom,
but leaders who despise corruption[e]

---

a 28:9 Or "the Torah."

b 28:12 As translated from the Aramaic.

c 28:12 Or "people become victims."

d 28:15 David, before he killed Goliath, went after the lion and the bear. See 1 Sam. 17:34–37. These beasts represented demonic forces of evil over the land. Daniel also mentions the world's ruthless leaders as lions and bears. See Dan. 7:1–8

e 28:16 Or "injustice."

will enjoy a long and full life.[a]

17 A murderer's conscience will torment him—
a fugitive haunted by guilt all the way to the grave
with no one to support him.

18 The pure will be rescued from failure,
but the perverse will suddenly fall into ruin.

19 Work hard and you'll have all you desire,
but chase a fantasy[b] and you could end up with nothing.

20 Life's blessings drench the honest and faithful person,
but punishment rains down upon the greedy and dishonest.

21 Giving favoritism to the rich and powerful is disgusting,
and this is the type of judge who would betray a man for a bribe.[c]

22 A greedy man[d] is in a race to get rich,
but he forgets that he could lose what's most important
and end up with nothing.[e]

23 If you correct someone with constructive criticism,
in the end he will appreciate it more than flattery.

24 A person who would reject[f] his own parents and say,
"What's wrong with that?" is as bad as a murderer.

25 To make rash, hasty decisions
shows that you are not trusting the Lord.

---

a 28:16 Or "enjoy a long reign."

b 28:19, Or "an empty dream." The Septuagint is "the one who pursues leisure."

c 28:21 As translated from the Aramaic.

d 28:22 Both the Aramaic and Hebrew have "the man with an evil eye." This is a figure of speech for a stingy or greedy man. A person who shuts his heart to the poor is said to have an evil eye. A person with a good eye is someone who looks on the poor with generosity.

e 28:22 As translated from the Aramaic. The Aramaic text sounds very similar to what Jesus says about gaining the world but losing our souls. See Mark 8:36.

f 28:24 As translated from the Septuagint. The Hebrew is "the one who steals from his own parents."

is to demonstrate justice for the poor.
15 Experiencing many corrections and rebukes will make you wise.
But if left to your own ways, you'll bring disgrace to your parents.[a]
16 When the wicked are in power, lawlessness abounds.
But the patient lovers of God will one day watch in triumph
as their stronghold topples!
17 Correct your child and one day you'll find he has changed
and will bring you great delight.
18 When there is no clear prophetic vision,[b]
people quickly wander astray.[c]
But when you follow the revelation of the Word,
heaven's bliss fills your soul.
19 A stubborn servant can't be corrected by words alone.
For even if he understands, he pays no attention to you.
20 There's only one kind of person who is worse than a fool:
The impetuous one who speaks without thinking first.
21 If you pamper your servants,
don't be surprised when they expect to be treated as sons.[d]
22 The source of strife is found in an angry heart,
for sin surrounds the life of a furious man.[e]

---

a 29:15 As translated from the Septuagint. The Hebrew is "your mother."

b 29:18 The Hebrew word used here can refer to "vision of the night," "dream," "oracle," or "revelation." The Septuagint reads, "Where there is no prophetic seer" or "interpreter."

c 29:18 Or "let loose, stripped, or made naked." The Septuagint reads, "The people become lawless."

d 29:21 Or "If you pamper your servant when he is young, he'll become a weakling in the end." The Septuagint reads, "If you live in luxury as a child, you'll become a domestic (servant) and at last will be grieved with yourself." The Aramaic states, "You'll be uprooted in the end."

e 29:22 The Hebrew word translated as "a furious man" can also mean "lord of fury" or "Baal of wrath."

23 Lift yourself up with pride and you will soon be brought low,[a]
but a meek and humble spirit will add to your honor.
24 You are your own worst enemy when you partner with a thief,
for a curse of guilt will come upon you
when you fail to report a crime.[b]
25 Fear and intimidation is a trap that holds you back.
But when you place your confidence in the Lord,
you will be seated in the high place.
26 Everyone curries favor with leaders.
But God is the judge, and justice comes from him.
27 The wicked hate those who live a godly life,
but the righteous hate injustice wherever it's found.

The Mysterious Sayings of Agur

30 These are the collected sayings of the prophet Agur, Jakeh's son[c]—
the amazing revelation[d] he imparted to Ithiel and Ukal.[e]

---

a 29:23 Or "to depression."

b 29:24 Or "when under oath to testify but you do not talk."

c 30:1 This section of Proverbs is attributed to Agur, who gave these oracles to his protégés Ithiel and Ukal. Agur means "to gather a harvest." He was the *son of* Jakeh, which means "blameless" or "obedient." Jakeh could be another name for David, Solomon's father. Many Jewish expositors believe that Agur was a pseudonym for Solomon. Nothing more is mentioned about Agur in the Bible than what we have here, which is typical for other prophets mentioned in the Scriptures. Some believe he could be the "master of the collection of sayings" referred to in Eccl. 12:11. Agur (taken from Agar) means "collector."

d 30:1 Or "mighty prophecy."

e 30:1 The name Ithiel can mean "God is with me" or "God has arrived." This was fulfilled by Christ, for his birth was the advent, the arrival of God to the earth in human form. Ukal means "I am able" or "I am

2 God, I'm so weary and worn out,
I feel more like a beast than a man.
I was made in your image,[a]
but I lack understanding.
3 I've yet to learn the wisdom
that comes from the full and intimate knowledge of you,
the Holy One.

Six Questions

4 Who is it that travels back and forth
from the heavenly realm to the earth?[b]
Who controls the wind as it blows[c] and holds it in his fists?
Who tucks the rain into the cloak of his clouds?
Who stretches out the skyline from one vista to the other?
What is his name?
And what is the name of his Son?
Who can tell me?

A Pure Heart Is Filled with God's Word

5 Every promise from the faithful God
is pure and proves to be true.
He is a wrap-around shield of protection for all his lovers
who run to hide in him.

---

strong and mighty." When placed together, the meaning of these Hebrew names could read, "Gather a harvest of sons who are blameless and obedient. They will have God with them, and they will be strong and mighty." This chapter contains some of the most mystical and mysterious sayings found in Proverbs, with hints of revelation from the book of Job.

a 30:2 Implied in the text, which is extraordinarily difficult to translate with certainty.

b 30:4 Jesus solves this riddle in John 3:13. Only Jesus Christ is the master of heavenly knowledge and wisdom. See also Eph. 4:7–10.

c 30:4 The Hebrew word *ruach* (wind) is also the term used for the Holy Spirit.

6 Never add to his words,
or he will have to rebuke you and prove that you're a liar.
7 God, there are two things I'm asking you for before I die,
only two:
8 Empty out of my heart everything that is false—
every lie, and every crooked thing.
And give me neither undue poverty nor undue wealth—
but rather, feed my soul with the measure of prosperity
that pleases you.
9 May my satisfaction be found in you.
Don't let me be so rich that I don't need you
or so poor that I have to resort to dishonesty
just to make ends meet.
Then my life will never detract from bringing glory to your
name.
10 Never defame a servant before his master,
for you will be the guilty one
and a curse will come upon you.
11 There is a generation rising that curses their fathers
and speaks evil of their mothers.
12 There is a generation rising that considers themselves
to be pure in their own eyes,[a]
yet they are morally filthy,[b] unwashed, and unclean.
13 There is a generation rising that is so filled with pride.
They think they are superior and look down on others.
14 There is a generation rising that uses their words like swords
to cut and slash those who are different.
They would devour the poor, the needy, and the afflicted
from off the face of the earth!
15 There are three words to describe the greedy:
"Give me more!"

---

a 30:12 See Judg. 21:25.
b 30:12 The Hebrew uses the word *excrement*.

There are some things that are never satisfied.
Forever craving more, they're unable to say, "That's enough!"
Here are four:
16 The grave, yawning for another victim,
the barren womb, ever wanting a child,
thirsty soil, ever longing for rain,
and a raging fire, devouring its fuel.
They're all insatiable.
17 The eye that mocks his father and dishonors his elderly mother[a]
deserves to be plucked out by the ravens of the valley
and fed to the young vultures![b]

Four Mysteries

18 There are four marvelous mysteries
that are[c] too amazing to unravel—
who could fully explain them?[d]
19 The way an eagle flies in the sky,[e]
the way a snake glides on a boulder,[f]

---

a 30:17As translated from the Septuagint.

b 30:17 This is a figure of speech for demonic powers that will remove their vision. Ravens and vultures are unclean birds associated with demonic powers in Hebrew poetry.

c 30:18 The Hebrew uses a poetic style of saying there are three mysteries, then saying there are four in order to emphasize their great importance. There could be within this poetic device a pointing to the fourth as the key, or the most important.

d 30:18 Notice that each of these four examples have to do with movement and mystery.

e 30:19 This is a picture of the overcoming life that soars above our problems and limitations with the wings of an eagle. It could also be a hint of the prophetic revelation that comes to God's servants mysteriously and supernaturally. See Isa. 40:31 and 1 Cor. 2:9–13.

f 30:19 The serpent becomes a picture of our sin that was placed on the

the path of a ship as it passes through the sea,[a]
and the way a bridegroom falls in love with his bride.[b]
20 Here is the deceptive way of the adulterous woman:[c]
She takes what she wants and then says,
"I've done nothing wrong."

Four Intolerable Things

21 There are four intolerable events
that[d] are simply unbearable to observe:
22 When an unfaithful servant becomes a ruler,
when a scoundrel comes into great wealth,
23 When an unfaithful woman marries a good man,
and when a mistress replaces a faithful wife.

Rock, Jesus Christ. See Num. 21:6–9, John 3:14–15, and 2 Cor. 5:21.

a 30:19 This is a picture of the way our lives, like a ship, sail on the high seas of mystery until we reach our destiny. Our lives contain mysteries, such as where God decided that we were to be born, how we were raised, and the companions who join us, until we reach our desired haven. See Ps. 107:23–30.

b 30:19 The Hebrew word translated "bride" can also mean "virgin," pointing to a wedding, thus implying the use of "bridegroom" instead of "man." (Consider Ruth and Boaz.) More important, this is a beautiful metaphor of the mystery of the love of our heavenly Bridegroom (Jesus), who romances his bride and sweeps us off our feet. Love is a mystery. See also 2 Cor. 11:2 and Eph. 5:32.

c 30:20 The adulterous woman of Proverbs is a metaphor of the corrupt religious system. See Rev. 17–18.

d 30:21 See footnote for 30:18. These four events each depict a promotion undeserved, a displacing of one who is virtuous with one who is corrupt. Each promotion indicates that they will carry their corruption with them. The unfaithful servant will likely become a tyrant. The fool who becomes wealthy will squander his wealth. The unfaithful woman (or "hated woman") will continue her immorality even after she's married. The girlfriend who replaced the faithful wife will likely find another man one day.

Four Creatures Small and Wise

24 The earth has four creatures that are very small but very
wise:[a]
25 The feeble ant has little strength,
yet look how it diligently gathers its food in the summer
to last throughout the winter.[b]
26 The delicate rock-badger isn't all that strong,
yet look how it makes a secure home, nestled in the rocks.[c]
27 The locusts have no king to lead them,
yet they cooperate as they move forward by bands.[d]
28 And the small lizard[e] is easy to catch
as it clings to the walls with his hands,
yet it can be found inside a king's palace.[f]

Four Stately Things

29 There are four stately monarchs[g]
who are impressive to watch as they go forth:
30 The lion, the king of the jungle, who is afraid of no one,
31 The rooster strutting boldly among the hens,[h]
the male goat out in front leading the herd,
and a king leading his regal procession.[i]

---

a 30:24 Or "They are the epitome of wisdom."

b 30:25 To prepare for the future is a mark of true wisdom.

c 30:26 This becomes a picture of the believer. Though feeling weakness at times, we can make our home in the high place, inside the cleft of the Rock. See John 14:1–3.

d 30:27 The locust army points us to Joel 1 and 2. There is an awakening army coming to devour the works of the Enemy. Their King, though invisible, guides them from on high as one army.

e 30:28 Or "spider."

f 30:28 Though we may see ourselves as insignificant (like the small lizard), God can place us in significant places where we can be used for him.

g 30:29 See footnote on 30:18.

h 30:31 As translated from the Septuagint.

i 30:31 Or "a king surrounded by his band of soldiers." The Hebrew text

32 If you've acted foolishly by drawing attention to yourself,
or if you've thought about saying something stupid,
you'd better shut your mouth.
33 For such stupidity may give you a bloody nose! [a]
Stirring up an argument only leads to an angry
confrontation.

31 King Lemuel's [b] royal words of wisdom:
These are the inspired words my mother taught me. [c]
2 Listen, my dear son, son of my womb.
You are the answer to my prayers, my son.
3 So keep yourself sexually pure
from the promiscuous, wayward woman.
Don't waste the strength of your anointing
on those who ruin kings—
you'll live to regret it! [d]
4 For you are a king, Lemuel,
and it's never fitting for a king to be drunk on wine
or for rulers to crave alcohol.
5 For when they drink they forget justice
and ignore the rights of those in need,
those who depend on you for leadership.

---

is abstruse.

a 30:33 Or "Churning milk makes butter, and punching the nose brings blood, so stirring up anger produces quarrels." The Hebrew contains a word play with the word *anger*, which is almost identical to the word for "nose."

b 31:1 Jewish legend is that King Lemuel was a pseudonym for Solomon, which would make his mother mentioned here to be Bathsheba. There is no other mention of Lemuel in the Scriptures. The Hebrew word translated "inspired words" is *massa*, which some have surmised was a place, meaning "Lemuel, King of Massa."

c 31:1 The Septuagint is "These are words spoken by God, and through a king came an answer divine."

d 31:3 As translated from the Septuagint.

6–7 Strong drink is given to the terminally ill,
who are suffering at the brink of death.
Wine is for those in depression
in order to drown their sorrows.
Let them drink and forget their poverty and misery.
8 But you are to be a king who speaks up on behalf
of the disenfranchised,
and pleads for the legal rights of the defenseless
and those who are dying.
9 Be a righteous king, judging on behalf of the poor
and interceding for those most in need.[a]

The Radiant Bride

10 Who could ever find a wife like this one—[b]
she is a woman of strength and mighty valor![c]

---

a 31:9 See James 1:27.

b 31:10 Starting with verse 10 through the end of the book, we have a Hebrew acrostic poem. It is alphabetical in structure, with each of the twenty-two verses beginning with a consecutive Hebrew letter of the alphabet. The implication is that the perfections of this woman would exhaust the entire language. The subject is the perfect bride, the virtuous woman. This woman is both a picture of a virtuous wife and an incredible allegory of the end-time victorious bride of Jesus Christ, full of virtue and grace.

c 31:10 The Hebrew word used to describe this virtuous wife is *khayil.* The meaning of this word cannot be contained by one English equivalent word. It is often used in connection with military prowess. This is a warring wife. *Khayil* can be translated "mighty; wealthy; excellent; morally righteous; full of substance, integrity, abilities, and strength; mighty like an army." The wife is a metaphor for the last-days church, the virtuous, overcoming bride of Jesus Christ. The word *khayil* is most often used to describe valiant men. See Ex. 18:21, where it is used for the mighty ones Moses was to commission as elders and leaders among the people. Because many of the cultural terms and metaphors used in this passage are not understood or even used in today's English-speaking world, the translator has chosen to make them explicit.

She's full of wealth and wisdom,
the price paid for her was greater[a] than many jewels.
11 Her husband has entrusted his heart to her,[b]
For she brings him the rich spoils of victory.
12 All throughout her life she brings him what is good, and not evil.[c]
13 She searches out continually to possess
that which is pure and righteous.[d]
She delights in the work of her hands.[e]
14 She gives out revelation truth[f] to feed others.
She is like a trading ship bringing divine supplies[g]
from the merchant.[h]

---

a 31:10 Or "her worth." The price paid for her was the sacred blood of the Lamb of God, her Bridegroom.

b 31:11 Or "has great confidence in her."

c 31:12 The virtuous bride will not bring disgrace to his name. Jesus will not be ashamed to display her to the world.

d 31:13 Or "wool and linen (flax)." Wool is a metaphor often used as a symbol of what is pure. See Isa. 1:18, Dan. 7:9, and Rev. 1:14. Linen was made from flax and always speaks of righteousness. The priests of the Old Testament wore linen garments as they went before God's presence to offer sacrifices. The curtains of the tabernacle were likewise made of linen, signifying God's righteousness. See Ex. 28:39–43 and Rev. 19:8. The virtuous bride of Christ in the last days will be seeking for only what is pure and righteous in the eyes of her Bridegroom.

e 31:13 Or "eagerly works with her hands." The hands, with their five fingers, speak of the five ministries of the present work of Christ on the earth: apostles, prophets, evangelists, pastors, and teachers. These are often referred to as the five-fold ministries. Her delight is to equip others and help those in need.

f 31:14 Or "bread." This is a consistent emblem of spiritual food.

g 31:14 Or "supplies from far away." The implication is from another realm. She is bringing heavenly manna for those she feeds.

h 31:14 Or "like merchant ships bringing goods." Like a ship loaded with cargo, the bride of Christ brings heavenly treasures to others. The use of the term *merchant* points to Jesus Christ. He is described as a merchant in

15 Even in the night season[a] she arises[b] and sets food on the
table
for hungry ones in her house and for others.[c]
16 She sets her heart upon a nation[d] and takes it as her own,
carrying it within her.
She labors there to plant the living vines.[e]
17 She wraps herself in strength,[f] might, and power in all her
works.
18 She tastes and experiences a better substance,[g]
and her shining light will not be extinguished,
no matter how dark the night.[h]
19 She stretches out her hands to help the needy[i]

Matt. 13:45 in the parable of the costly pearl. The "pearl" is the church or the believer, which cost all that Jesus had (his blood) to purchase us.

a 31:15 She is interceding in the night, laboring in a night season to help others.

b 31:15 The Hebrew word translated "arise" can also mean "to rise up in power." We are told to "arise and shine, for our light has come." See Isa. 60:1, which uses the same Hebrew word for "arise." The bride of Christ will arise with anointing to feed and bless the people of God.

c 31:15 Or "female servants." The servants are a metaphor of other churches and ministries.

d 31:16 Or "a land, a country."

e 31:16 Or "By the fruit of her hands she plants a vineyard." (The Septuagint is "possession.") For the hands, see 31:13 footnote. This vineyard becomes a metaphor for the local church. We are the branches of the vine (Christ). See John 15. She is passionate about bringing forth fruit. She becomes a missionary to the nations, planting churches and bringing new life.

f 31:17 Or "She girds her loins with strength and makes her shoulders strong." This is a figure of speech for being anointed with power to do the works of Jesus. See John 14:12.

g 31:18 Or "good merchandise."

h 31:18 Her prayer life (lamp) overcomes her circumstances, even in a culture where darkness prevails.

i 31:19 As translated from the Septuagint. The Hebrew uses a term for "distaff" (a weaver's staff), which is taken from a root word for

and she lays hold of the wheels of government.[a]
20 She is known by her extravagant generosity to the poor,
for she always reaches out her hands[b] to those in need.
21 She is not afraid of tribulation,[c]
for all her household is covered in the dual garments[d]
of righteousness and grace.
22 Her clothing is beautifully knit together[e]—
a purple gown of exquisite linen.
23 Her husband is famous and admired by all,
sitting as the venerable judge of his people.[f]
24 Even her works of righteousness[g]
she does[h] for the benefit of her enemies.[i]
25 Bold power and glorious majesty[j] are wrapped around her

"prosperity." The poetic nuance of this phrase is that she uses her prosperity to bless the needy.

a 31:19 Or "Her hands grasp the spindle." The word translated as "spindle" can also mean "governmental circuits" or "wheels." There is a hint here of the wheels mentioned in Ezek. 1. The throne of God's government sits on flaming wheels. See Dan. 7:9.

b 31:20 Notice the mention of her hands. See footnote on 31:13.

c 31:21 Or "snow." This is a figure of speech for the fear of a cold winter season.

d 31:21 As translated from the Septuagint. The Hebrew is "Everyone is covered in scarlet (blood)." Grace has brought righteousness to those in her house (under her ministry).

e 31:22 This garment speaks of the ministries of the body of Christ, woven and knit together by the Holy Spirit. See Eph. 4:15–16 and Col. 2:2.

f 31:23 Or "sitting at the city gates among the elders of the land." Judgment was rendered at the gates of a city in that day. It was their courtroom. Our heavenly King is also the Judge. So famous, so glorious, yet he is our Bridegroom.

g 31:24 Or "linen." See footnote for 31:13 regarding linen as a symbol for righteousness.

h 31:24 Or "sells them." The root word for "sell" can also mean "surrender."

i 31:24 Or "aprons or belts for the Canaanites." The Canaanites were the traditional enemies of the Hebrews.

j 31:25 Or "beauty, honor and excellence."

as she laughs with joy over the latter days.[a]
26 Her teachings are filled with wisdom and kindness,
as loving instruction pours from her lips.[b]
27 She watches over the ways of her household[c]
and meets every need they have.
28 Her sons and daughters arise[d] in one accord to extol her
virtues,[e]
and her husband arises to speak of her in glowing terms.[f]
29 "There are many valiant and noble ones,[g]
but you have ascended above them all!"[h]
30 Charm can be misleading,
and beauty is vain and so quickly fades,
but this virtuous woman lives in the wonder, awe,
and fear of the Lord.
She will be praised *throughout eternity*.
31 So go ahead and give her the credit that is due,
for she has become a radiant woman,

---

a 31:25 The virtuous and victorious bride has no fear for the days to come. She contemplates eternity and her forever union with the Bridegroom.

b 31:26 The Septuagint is "She opens her mouth carefully and lawfully."

c 31:27 Or "She is a watchman over her house (family)."

d 31:28 The Hebrew word translated "arise" can also mean "to rise up with power." The Septuagint is "She raises her children so they will grow rich."

e 31:28 Or "Hooray, hooray for our mother!"

f 31:28 For more of how the heavenly Bridegroom loves his bride, read the Song of Songs.

g 31:29 Or "Many daughters have obtained wealth because of her." These valiant and noble ones (daughters) represent the church of previous generations who remained faithful in their pursuit of Jesus. But this final generation will be the bridal company of the lovers of God who do mighty exploits and miracles on the earth.

h 31:29 Or "You are first in his eyes." See Song 6:8–9.

and all her loving works of righteousness deserve to be
admired[a]
at the gateways of every city!

a 31:31 The Septuagint could be translated, "Her husband is praised at the city gates."

Passionate Praying

Day 1 - Psalm 5

Have you ever noticed how passionate David is in the Psalms? His words are not religious and ritualistic, devoid of emotion and sincerity. They are full of raw honesty. Look at Psalm 5: "Listen to my passionate prayer! Can't you hear my groaning?" (v. 1). David prays with fire in his bones. As a result, God answers in kind with fire. This is why David declares, "Every morning I lay out the pieces of my life on the altar and wait for your fire to fall upon my heart" (v. 3). David knows that his passion attracts the Father's presence. Will you open up your heart to the fire of God today?

Consider the intimacy David shows with the Father. In what way does this inspire you to build the same intimacy with your Father?

Responding to Injustice

Day 2 - Psalm 9

When you're in the valley of oppression, it is so easy to react based on circumstances rather than responding according to the realities of heaven. One way to respond in the Spirit is to thank God. In Psalm 9, King David explodes with thanksgiving. Even though David is feeling oppressed, he thanks God for his marvelous miracles, for his wonderful vindication, and for his perfect protection. Above all, he thanks God that he doesn't forget those who are forgotten by others and that he will punish those who commit acts of injustice against the weak. That's a great response. Make this your declaration today: I will always express my heartfelt gratitude to God, even in times of trouble.

What situations in your life and in the world do you find perplexing right now? Bring these situations to the Father in a spirit of thanksgiving and intercession.

From Depression to Delight

Day 3 - Psalm 13

Sometimes it's really difficult to pray with passion when your soul is downcast and you're feeling depressed. David was clearly in this situation in Psalm 13. What is so admirable is that he didn't give up on his conversations with God. He kept choosing to pray. More admirable still, he makes a choice to ask God for light rather than focusing on the darkness. He prays, "Bring light to my eyes in this pitch-black darkness" (v. 3). Most admirable of all, David positions himself in his spirit on the far side of God's answer to his prayer. He decrees, "I will sing my song of joy" (v. 6). If you are in a dark place right now, let God transport your heart and focus to his place of light.

If you feel like you're in a wilderness right now, consider what new song you would sing to the Lord, as David did. Choose to look up rather than down. Encourage your soul to soar!

God's Holy Lovers

Day 4 - Psalm 17

Have you ever been woken up in the night and felt the fire of God cleanse you through and through? From Psalm 17, we can see that David knew this experience. "In a visitation of the night you inspected my heart and refined my soul in fire" (v. 3). Loving our Father passionately draws us near to his fire of love that refines us, not by our trying extra hard to be righteous, but by his fire removing impurities from within. He melts down strongholds of deception and burns away addictions to sin, leaving us free to express our devotion to him. The whole focus is love, and love is the end result—purer love experienced by us and expressed by us.

Which of the descriptions of God found in Psalm 17 are the most dear to you? Why? (my Power; Bedrock beneath my feet; Castle on a cliff; my forever firm Fortress; my Mountain of hiding; my Pathway of escape; my Tower of rescue; my secret Strength and Shield; Salvation's Ray of Brightness; always the Champion of my cause)

The Shepherd King

Day 5 - Psalm 23

When he composed Psalm 23, David reached the highest heights of lyrical beauty and spiritual adoration. Having been a shepherd himself, David gives eloquent praise to the Shepherd Lord. The Shepherd Lord extolled by David offers him a resting place in his luxurious love and leads him to oases of peace, brooks of bliss. All this is true for us too. As followers of the Messiah Jesus (the Good Shepherd to whom David is pointing), we too can say, "I'll never be lonely, for you are near" (v. 4). We too can say that we are pursued by love. Worship the Good Shepherd today.

"You anoint me with the fragrance of your Holy Spirit" (Psalm 23:5). Let your heart cry out like David's to be covered in the perfume of the Glory King!

Orphans No More

Day 6 - Psalm 27

In Psalm 27:10, David says, "My father and mother abandoned

me. I'm like an orphan." Then he goes on to say to God, "But you took me in and made me yours." God became a Father to David, giving him the four things every child needs from a parent: acceptance, attention, direction, and protection. All these things David describes in verses 7–14. Above all, he declares that he has found "the privilege of living with him every moment in his house" (v. 4). He has found home. Thanks to Jesus, the same is true for us. We are no longer orphans. We have found our heart's true home in him. Praise God you're not an orphan anymore (John 14:18).

If you have not yet truly found your home in God's presence, ask the Holy Spirit to fill you afresh, take you deeper into himself, and reveal to you the truth that you are his child.

My Hiding Place on High

Day 7 - Psalm 32

According to Psalm 32, the key to God's hiding place is integrity. David had broken the commandments when he committed adultery with Bathsheba and then murdered her husband. After refusing to repent, he eventually surrendered to God. God's hand of conviction had been heavy on David's heart, causing him no end of inner turmoil, but when David relented and repented, God completely forgave him and wiped the slate clean. David now knew for sure that he would be kept safe when the storms of life threatened. Only those who exhibit integrity and transparency before God can declare, "You are my secret Hiding Place" (v. 7). Make a new commitment to being real before God today.

> Are you carrying any burdens in your soul right now—burdens caused by unconfessed sin? Let go of them by telling God about them and enjoy the feeling of your burdens being removed and God becoming your Hiding Place once again.

From Weeping to Rejoicing

Day 8 - Psalm 39

Have you ever been so deeply moved by your frailty and failures that you've wept before the Lord? If you have, you're in good company. If Psalm 39 is anything to go by, David went through times like these. In this psalm it is the sense of his mortality that has overwhelmed him. The life of a human being is a puff of air, a fleeting shadow. All our energy is invested in things that are here today, gone tomorrow. Recognizing his own weakness, David offers up his tears as liquid prayers. He ends by asking that God would not let him die before experiencing joy once again. Moments like these help us keep perspective on what's really important—those things that last forever. Don't wait for difficulties to remember that our time on earth is short. Consider it now, and focus your heart on heavenly things.

Nearly every great revival in history has begun with someone somewhere weeping before the Lord. Their personal revival so often led to a corporate revival in their community. Ask the Holy Spirit to give you the gift of tears.

Encouraging Yourself in the Lord

Day 9 - Psalm 43

Did David have access to uplifting podcasts? No, nor were any other modern resources available to him—Christian TV, DVDs, books, Bible study apps, and so forth. As Psalm 43 vividly shows, David had only one way of turning his downcast soul into a rejoicing soul. He had to encourage and strengthen himself in the Lord. When David felt oppressed and depressed, he spoke to his own soul, telling himself not to be disturbed but to expect God to break through. Perhaps we have a lot to learn about the art of encouraging ourselves in the Lord from David. Let's cultivate a lifestyle of speaking to the soul within, calling it into strength and encouragement in the Lord.

Practice speaking to your own soul right now. Command it to be encouraged in the Lord. Remind yourself of the greatest displays of God's power you've seen.

Adoring Our King

Day 10 - Psalm 47

How passionate is your praise? How effusive is your worship? In both your private encounters with God and in public worship in the church, we should express our adoration with our hearts, hands, feet, and voices. This is certainly what Psalm 47 encourages. We are urged to clap our hands and utter raucous shouts of joy! The Messiah is the most formidable of kings. He is the triumphant King who rules over the nations. How can we remain passive and indifferent in the light of such a royal revelation? God never said that he inhibited the praises of his people. He said that he inhabited them. Maybe, like David, we can become a whole lot more passionate—more undignified than we have been in the past

What does "undignified" look like to you? Do something to worship your Father with unrestrained passion today! You may feel foolish, but let loose!

The Place of Rest and Peace

Day 11 - Psalm 55

There is a place of Shabbat and shalom in the presence of the Lord. Shabbat means "rest." Shalom means "peace." In Psalm

55, David is trembling because he is encircled by fearsome enemies. He wants to run away to a safe place. Then he realizes that there's a place he can access anytime in God's presence—the place of everlasting Shabbat and shalom. This is the higher place, a place secure from the raging storm of intimidation and oppression. This is his Shelter, the protective and majestic presence of "God-Enthroned" (v. 19). This is the place to which David moves his soul (v. 17), committing to run to it rather than away from his problems. Enter that place and hear God greet you with Shabbat shalom!

What are the things that you're tempted to run from right now? Bring them in heartfelt prayer before the Lord. Run into the arms of your Father instead, your true place of rest and peace.

Strengthening Yourself in the Lord

Day 12 - Psalm 60

When you draw near to your Father in prayer, do you find strangely encouraging thoughts pass through your mind? This is God speaking to you, just as we see in Psalm 60. David is impacted here by a sense of God's absence, not his presence. Rather than wallow in doubt, David contends for the presence of God. He presses in and cries out, "Come to your beloved ones" (v. 5). Then the sanctuary doors to God's presence spring open, and the Father begins to speak prophetically about the future of his people. These prophetic words not only release hope but they also awaken a heroic spirit in David (v. 12). Activating the prophetic strengthens and emboldens us.

Ask the Father to help you hear his voice with greater clarity and activate the prophetic in your life with greater frequency.

Strengthening Yourself in the Lord: Part 2

Day 13 - Psalm 62

In Psalm 62 we discover one of the great secrets of strengthening yourself in the Lord. It is the simple prayer, "More, Lord." The people who remain perpetually strong in God are those who rely on the power of God and who pursue the presence of God. They know that all the love they need is found in him. Therefore they stand perpetually before God, the One they love. They wait faithfully for God to manifest his glory, and they do this because they believe the promise: "The greater your passion for more—the greater reward I will give" (v. 12). Waiting, therefore, doesn't involve passivity. It involves passion. Always position yourself to cry, "More, Lord." The proud despise this place, but the humble camp there continually.

Spend some time applying the principle articulated in Psalm 62:12, expressing your passion for "more."

Blessing the Nations

Day 14 - Psalm 67

It's important to remember that God blesses us in order to bless the world. Those who only pray, "Bless me, God," miss the point. What's radical in Psalm 67 is how David connects the nations coming to know God to God blessing us. We should forget neither God's desire to bless us nor the nations that have yet to taste his blessing, but instead remember the power of our blessing is that it testifies his heart to the nations so that they may be saved. Let's embrace a mind-set that says, "Bless me at your fountain, O God, so that I may go to the nations and bless them," and, "How glad the nations will be when you are their king!"

> One group of nations specifically mentioned in these psalms is Africa. "Africa will send her noble envoys to you, O God. They will come running, stretching out their hands in love to you" (Psalm 68:31). Bless Africa today and claim that beautiful promise in prayer.

You're All I Need

Day 15 - Psalm 74

God's visitation always occurs within the context of our

desperation. When God's people cry, "You're all I need," the Holy Spirit is irresistibly drawn to the sound of our desperation. This is very much the theme of Psalm 74. In a time of great distress, the composer sings a song of passionate pleading for God to "wrap us back into your heart again" (v. 2). In the place of devastation, the writer expresses his longing for God. "Come running to bring your restoring grace to these ruins," he cries (v. 3). What a phrase that is—restoring grace! Maybe you feel like your life is in shambles right now. Cry out to God, "You're forever all I need." Ask for his restoring grace so that you might rebuild a godly life amidst the rubble.

Take that phrase, "You're all I need," and turn it now into a prayer or a song of worship to God.

The Fearsome One

Day 16 - Psalm 76

As soon as we start talking about fearing the Lord, some are turned off. "All this talk of the fear of the Lord is toxic," they say. But the biblical idea of fearing God does not mean a cowering, miserable submission to a divine terrorist. It means being so filled with awe at the majestic otherness and radiant holiness of God that we long to do his will and please his heart. This is very much the stance taken by the songwriter in Psalm 76. His heart is full of passionate praise for the resplendent majesty and incomparable glory of the Living God. This God roars his rebuke, felling and stunning his enemies. This

God is greatly to be feared. We ought to hold our breath in awe of him. He is not just the Near One. He is the Awesome One.

> Does your worship focus more on awe of God or affection for God? Draw near to your Father today and allow him to reveal himself to you in that radical middle between awe and affection.

Learning to Dig Deep

Day 17 - Psalm 84

Have you ever traveled through the dark valley of tears? If you have, Psalm 84 is for you. In this magnificent song, the psalmist gives voice to that lovesick longing for God that comes when we experience testing times of pain. He knows that dwelling close to the presence of God is his strength. His call to us is "dig deep" when your path winds through the valley of tears (v. 6). Don't let the pain become your preoccupation. Make it your priority to dig deep until you find that secret brook of blessing filled by the rain of revival outpourings. Then you will grow stronger with every step forward, because just one day of intimacy in God's presence is like a thousand days of joy rolled into one. In times of trouble, let's dig deep—deep into the past (Psalm 83) and deep into the presence (Psalm 84).

What would it mean for you to dig deep? Turn those thoughts into passionate prayer and specific action.

Christ the King

Day 18 - Psalm 88

When we think of Christ the King, we must never forget that he chose to reveal himself as the suffering Servant King. He did not come as a triumphant, militaristic king. Psalm 88 is a vivid reminder of this. As you read it, imagine Christ on the cross speaking these words. They go deep into the heart of Christ's sense of abandonment by his Father at Calvary. In his human heart, Christ's life is ebbing from him as spectators consider him pierced and abandoned. Christ feels the heavy weight of his Father's wrath over sin. All his friends have deserted him. His arms are opened wide as he hangs upon the cross, humiliated and broken. In his first coming, Christ revealed himself as the Suffering King. In his second coming, he will return as the Conquering King.

How different Christ is from the kings of the earth! Spend time in passionate praise of Christ, the Returning King of all the earth.

The Protected Life

Day 19 - Psalm 91

While life on earth has many profound challenges and perplexing mysteries, God's lovers are destined to live under the covering of God's protection. Psalm 91 is a magnificent praise song about God's protective love. His massive arms are wrapped perpetually around us, shielding us from demonic attacks by day and by night. Even in a time of national disaster, thousands may be killed but we will remain unharmed. God sends his angels with special orders to protect us wherever we go. As God's royal lovers, we live our lives within the protective shadow of God Most High. We find and feel his presence even when we are greatly under pressure. We enjoy a feast that perpetually satisfies because God is our glorious Hero. Let's hide our lives in God, our secret Hiding Place.

> Here's a great promise to turn into praise. "Because you have delighted in me as a great lover, I will greatly protect you. I will set you in a high place, safe and secure before my face" (Psalm 91:14).

When God's Glory Falls

Day 20 - Psalm 97

The writer of Psalm 97 is consumed with the revelation of God's righteousness. He sees it so clearly, and really, he sees our God so clearly, that he laughs at the idea of anyone worshiping an idol they crafted with their own hands. It's as though he says, "Really? You have worshiped what your own hands made? You will feel ashamed when you see the real God." This is what births true worship—a true revelation of God himself. No obligation, no laws, no list of rules can produce the true fear of the Lord in our hearts that produces genuine worship. Only a revelation of God himself produces such abandon. What a blessing that this revelation also teaches us righteousness in a way that all our efforts to obey laws have failed to do. Will you seek a true revelation of God in his righteousness today?

Psalm 97 says that God sows seeds of light within his lovers, releasing a harvest of righteousness. Welcome seeds of light into your heart and pray for a great harvest of righteousness.

The Faithful Father

Day 21 - Psalm 105

Many people have been fathered by someone who didn't keep his promises. This is tragic and causes children to doubt their father's words. Psalm 105 says our Father is true to his word. He made promises to Abraham, Isaac, and Jacob, and he has kept all of them. Even though the Hebrew people were originally nomadic and few, eventually they entered the land of promise and became numerous and abundant. Even when they found themselves enslaved for a time in Egypt, the Father remembered his promises and brought them out of servitude through his servant Moses, performing signs and wonders as he set the captives free. When they left they were laden with the gold and silver of Egypt! This is a Father who keeps his promises. Let the whole world shout, "Hallelujah!"

Celebrate God's promise-keeping love today. Consider an area in which you find the most difficulty remaining faithful. Ask the Holy Spirit to reveal his faithfulness to you in such a way that it transforms this area of your life.

I Am Prayer

Day 22 - Psalm 110

Heartfelt prayer is a gateway into the courts of heaven. Never forget that you and I are the adopted sons and daughters of the High King of heaven. We are, by God's grace, kings and lords. When we start to pray in the Spirit, heaven's door opens and we are shown glorious things in the throne room of God. This was David's experience in Psalm 110, the Old Testament passage most quoted by the New Testament authors. In the spirit of prayer, David sees the Father and the Son in heaven (Jehovah God and the Lord Messiah), and he hears the Father telling his Son that all enemies will one day be under his footstool. David calls the Messiah, "Adonai," which means "Lord of Lords." We are the lords over whom Jesus is Lord! As we grow in prayer, we see more and more who Christ is, and we catch a glimpse of who we are in Christ as well.

The Father loves it when we converse with him naturally, honestly, and passionately. In what ways could you become more raw and real in prayer?

Passionate Love

Day 23 - Psalm 115

Psalm 115 begins: "You are the One who loves us passionately" (v. 1). Once a person has encountered this divine love, they have a testimony no unbeliever can destroy. Unbelievers worship the created, not the Creator, and as such, the object of their idolatry cannot speak to them or hear them. We, on the other hand, worship the Creator, and he is personal and loving; he hears and answers us. This God wraps his presence around his lovers and gives them not only a great intimacy but a great authority: the heavens belong to him, but the earth belongs to us (v. 16). Let's welcome the fire of God's passionate love into our hearts every day.

> "I am passionately in love with God." Turn this phrase into your own cry of worship and allow the Holy Spirit to blow upon the embers of your heart until you are aflame with love again.

Passion for His Precepts

Day 24 - Psalm 119

One of the hallmarks of a genuine move of the Holy Spirit is a love for God's Word among his people. In Psalm 119, King David articulates his love for the Scriptures. God's Word is perfect and infallible. It is the greatest treasure, a shining light for those with open hearts. Those who walk in alignment with God's Word experience strength, honor, abundance, and joy. They experience revival as they read and apply the Scriptures. David was passionate for God's precepts; he yearned for revelation light. He knew that God's Word is fastened to eternity (v. 89), so he filled his heart with its truth. "I'm a lover of your Word," he proclaimed. Those who can say that with passion will live constantly in an atmosphere of revival.

> "My passion and delight is in your Word, for I love what you say to me! I long for more revelation of your truth, for I love the light of your Word as I meditate on your decrees" (Psalm 119:47–48). Turn these verses into your own prayer today.

The True Place of Peace

Day 25 - Psalm 121

Psalms 120 to 134 are known as songs of "ascent" or "songs to take you higher." If ever there was a song designed to lift us up, Psalm 121 is it. The original context was probably the pilgrim's journey up to Jerusalem for the Feasts of the Lord: Passover, Pentecost, and Tabernacles. The pilgrim may even have recited these songs climbing up the steps toward the temple. As the pilgrim looked up, he realized once again that his protection did not come from the mountains and hills but from

God, who tirelessly watches over us all day and night. Let's never forget that God is by our side at all times. He watches over us and shelters us. Guarded by God himself, we find a place of peace under the canopy of his vigilant love.

> Our peace is found in the arms of Jesus, who is the Prince of Peace. Bring all your troubles and cares to him and ask him for the heavenly peace that passes all understanding–a peace that the world cannot give.

The Miracle That Is Israel

Day 26 - Psalm 129

There are many views held by Christians about Israel, but one thing we can all marvel at is the extraordinary durability of this tiny nation. While far greater empires have come and gone, Israel has somehow miraculously survived. This is a thought that grips the songwriter in Psalm 129. From the beginning Israel has experienced persecution and discrimination, and yet she has survived. "We're still here!" the psalmist cries (v. 2). God has always stood to defend his people against those who hate the Jews. What's the secret? Psalm 129 answers the question. God's supernatural, covenant love is the secret.

> God is breathing his Holy Spirit into many Jewish people today, inside and outside of Israel. Pray

with passion for Jewish people you know to come to know who Jesus really was and is.

Dripping with God's Blessing

Day 27 - Psalm 133

Have you ever wondered if there's a way you can secure the release of God's blessing over your life? If so, Psalm 133 provides at least one answer. When brothers and sisters in Christ live together in sweet unity, then God releases his blessing. This blessing is like the anointing oil that dripped from the top of Aaron's head to the hem of his robes. It's like the dew that drips from the heavens and brings refreshment to the slopes of Mount Hermon. If we want to receive the blessing of God, we could start by committing ourselves to sweet unity with other believers. Disunity and division drive God's blessings away. But when unity is restored, the anointing is released and drips from heaven onto our heads until we are covered in its fragrance.

The next time you are up at night, bring your expressions of affection to God as a loving priest. What might you say?

A Lofty and Lowly Love

Day 28 - Psalm 136

Everyone loves to be thanked, and God is no exception. Psalm 136 begins, "Let everyone thank God, for he is good." The songwriter then lists reasons why we should be grateful: God is king over all gods, he is Lord of Lords, the miracle-working Lord, the Creator who has filled the heavens with revelation, the Deliverer of his children, the Leader of his people, the Vanquisher of his enemies, and the Great Provider. Above all, he is the one "who chose us when we were nothing!" (v. 23). You were nothing, but God came looking for you, rescued you, adopted you, and made something out of you. Let's live in constant gratitude.

Listen to God's word of affirmation over you: "You're my special treasure." How does it make you feel to be so treasured by the infinite and all-powerful God? Turn your response into heartfelt thanksgiving.

The Only One

Day 29 - Psalm 141

In biblical times, a woman who had become betrothed to a man went around in public wearing a veil. That veil was a code; in Hebrew it said *mekudheshet*, or "I'm spoken for." It was her way of saying that her eyes were now reserved exclusively for her bridegroom. In Psalm 141, King David makes this passionate statement: "You are my Lord and my God; I only have eyes for you" (v. 8). David utters this cry in a time of difficulty and danger. He is surrounded by "experts in evil" who want to entice and entrap him. But David resolves to keep his eyes fixed on the Lord. He will not fall into their traps. He knows how a person's eyes can lead them into sin. So he fixes his attention and affection in an exclusive way on God. In the same way, guard your eyes and say, "I only have eyes for you."

God wants an exclusive love. He wants us to have eyes only for him. Ask him if there are any areas in your life that draw your affection away from him alone. Confess those areas and ask him to remove those idols from your heart. Then say to him, "You're the only One."

Praise and High Praise

Day 30 - Psalm 145

There's praise and then there's high praise. Praise is a discipline. High praise is a delight. In Psalm 145, David moves from the duty of praise into the ecstasy of high praise. He says that his heart explodes with praise. He cannot take in how utterly and indescribably great God is. He is overwhelmed with

God's goodness, his glory, and his awe-inspiring acts of power. David's heart bubbles over as he meditates on God's "excellent greatness" and his "marvelous beauty" (vv. 6–7). God's love is like a river of kindness that constantly overflows its banks. In fact, God manifests himself as kindness in everything he does. See how the heart explodes in this psalm? When we are wrecked by the revelation of God's greatness, we move from sacrificial duty to euphoric delight. We move from praise to high praise.

Draw near afresh to God. He will reveal himself to you afresh. Then let your heart bubble over in high praise and move from duty to delight.

Enthused with Joy

Day 31 - Psalm 150

The book of Psalms ends with an invitation to ecstatic praise (Psalm 150). The contexts for praise are ubiquitous. Praise can be given to God anytime and anywhere, whether on earth in God's house or in heaven in his stronghold. The reasons for praise are manifold. You can praise God for anything or everything, from his miracles of might to his magnificent greatness. The instruments for praise are endless—ranging from pianos and guitars to drums and trumpets. The methods of praise are varied too, whether you are dancing before the Lord or making music and song. Everyone, everywhere, can bring God ecstatic praise. Let them be a crescendo—an ever-increasing, ever-expanding shout of praise. Let them above all be characterized by this one great thing: that they are "enthused with joy."

Ask the Holy Spirit to enthuse you with joy. Release your ecstatic praise to God. Let your awe and thankfulness and celebration of his goodness burst forth from you in every way you can imagine!

Proverbs

31-Day Devotional

Wisdom to Reign in Life

Day 1 - Proverbs 1:1–7

Great authors always begin with a great hook—something that catches your attention and lures you into reading on. The author of the book of Proverbs, King Solomon, is no exception. He starts with a memorable decree in Proverbs 1:1: "Here are kingdom revelations, words to live by, and words of wisdom given to empower you to reign in life."

The book of Proverbs is full of wisdom from heaven designed to help us reign on earth. These revelations are "words of wisdom." Like the "word of wisdom" in 1 Corinthians 12:8 (one of the gifts of the Holy Spirit), these proverbs are brief, memorable, and truth-packed statements that have a supernatural source and power.

What is the impact of such words of wisdom? They have the capacity to enable us to "reign in life." This is the true potency of kingdom proverbs; they have the heaven-sent power to help us bring heaven to earth in every relationship and in every situation. They release heaven's strategies and destinies in every context.

Even in contexts outside the church (such as in a company boardroom), such wisdom can provide brilliant strategies for leadership.

As you embark on this book, stir up your passion to receive and understand the Father's heavenly wisdom.

What does reigning in life look like to you?

The Treasure Hunt

Day 2 - Proverbs 2:1–5

Every son or daughter of God has a calling upon his or her life to honor and remember the Father's timeless wisdom. Only if we are hungry for this wisdom will we receive it. Only if we remember it will we apply it.

This spiritual wisdom comes to receptive searching hearts. So the calling upon our lives is to "cry out for comprehension and intercede for insight" (v. 3). It is to engage in a spiritual treasure hunt in which we look for true wisdom.

God's perfect wisdom is like sterling silver. What man or woman, hearing that there is a huge chest full of silver in a dark cave in the tallest mountains, wouldn't do everything and anything to discover it?

We cherish such treasure in the natural. We should do the same in the spiritual.

If you think about it, when we were children we loved stories about hidden treasure. We loved playing games in which we hunted for treasure.

This is a key. If we are to find the treasure of God's wisdom, then we must have the mind of a child. We must come before the Father and hear him call us "my child" (v. 1).

Cultivate today a childlike spirit in which you long for the heavenly treasure of the Father's wisdom.

How great is your passion for the treasure of God's wisdom? Write a prayer in which you cry out for God's wisdom.

A Long Life

Day 3 - Proverbs 3:11–35

The person who develops a passion for the Father's wisdom is the person who lives a long and satisfying life. What are the hallmarks of the person who sets their heart on kingdom wisdom?

First of all, they welcome God's discipline when they depart from God's path. They understand that God is a loving Father, so they accept the correction of his heavenly wisdom when they need realigning to "the proper way to live" (v. 13).

Secondly, they revere heaven's wisdom as more precious than gold, silver, and gemstones. Nothing compares to God's wisdom, because it empowers and energizes a person and gives them abundance and promotion like nothing else.

Thirdly, they understand that it was the Father's wisdom that gave the blueprints for the creation of the universe. That being so, they know that this same wisdom is more than capable of giving them the blueprints for their own lives.

When a son or a daughter of God begins to nurture this kind of respect for wisdom, a number of benefits accrue. They find that they are refreshed and healed. They sleep well. They live free from fear and anxiety. They have money in the bank, and they pay their bills and taxes on time! What's not to like about the Father's wisdom?

If there's any realignment and correction needed in our lives, let's welcome it.

"Wisdom extends to you long life in one hand with wealth and promotion in the other" (v. 16). Compose a prayer expressing your longing for the benefits of God's wisdom.

Delighting the Father

Day 4 - Proverbs 4:20–27

Once again we hear the Father urging us to be attentive to his words of wisdom from heaven. How do we do this? By meditating upon these insights and memorizing them. When we contemplate the kingdom revelation contained within these verses, our thoughts become filled with the Father's words. When we memorize them, their truth penetrates deep into our spirits.

For this to happen, we cannot merely read these proverbs with the head alone. Our hearts need to be engaged too. If our hearts are not filled with warmth, then our heads are unlikely to be filled with light. This is why we must guard the affections of our hearts. If we come to God's Word and read it with fire in our hearts, then its truths will permeate and illuminate every part of us.

It is so important to read the Father's book as loving sons

and daughters rather than as dispassionate students of God. Lovers of God read the Word because they enjoy being close to the Father's heart, leaning on his chest, and hanging on every word from his mouth.

Those who have a heart-to-heart relationship with God delight him because they are the ones to whom he can most fully give his love. They are affectionate and attentive. Their reward is that his words bring life and health not only to their spirits, but also to their souls (their minds and hearts) and even their bodies.

If you're looking for "radiant health" (v. 22), make it your aim not to detour into darkness but to read God's Word as a lover and to stay on the highway of light.

> Many of us have not been trained to read the Bible as lovers (with our hearts) but as students (with our minds). God desires that we read his book with both. Write a prayer expressing your heart to read the Bible as a loving son or daughter.

Guarding Your Affections

Day 5 - Proverbs 5:1–14

Christians have traditionally focused on right beliefs and right behavior. These are extremely important because believing the right thing leads to behaving in the right way. This is why a spiritual father (the apostle Paul) was eager to warn his spiritual son (Timothy) to watch his life and doctrine closely. Living the right way and embracing the right doctrine is a key to reigning in life.

But there's another area where we need to be equally vigilant: the area of "right affections." If beliefs apply to the mind and behavior to the will, then affections, desires, and passions apply to the heart. In the book of Proverbs, the heart is just as important as the head and the will. The heart is the deep, inner core of our personality—the engine for all our decision making. Good hearts produce good choices.

In Proverbs 5, our Father makes it very clear that he wants holy passions and affections in us. This is especially true in our sexuality. He warns us not to be seduced into acts of sexual immorality because they lead down a slippery road to anguish and shame. Instead, we should run as far and as fast as possible from it.

Truly, our Father's wisdom leads to greater fulfillment than the temptations of the world. His perfection trumps every one of the world's perversions. Let the Father's wisdom enter your heart and align your sexuality to his perfect blueprint.

Write a prayer asking the Father to reveal his perfect will and ways for your sexual affections and passions. Listen to him and write what you feel he says.

Down-to-Earth Wisdom

Day 6 - Proverbs 6:16–35

Are you allowing the Father's wisdom to shape how you conduct your friendships? Are you reigning in life in the way you treat your friends? Are you being wise in your boundaries, especially in your relationship with people you find attractive?

These are critical and practical questions addressed by Solomon in this third section of Proverbs 6. After looking at finances and work, he moves to relationships, especially our friendships with others.

In Proverbs 6:16–19, Solomon says, "There are six things God hates, seven in fact." Seven is the number of completion. By including seven items, Solomon emphasizes that these are completely abominable.

All seven items have to do with relationships. The common thread throughout is harming others through patronizing, spreading gossip, violence, scheming, gloating, bearing false testimony, and stirring up enmity between friends.

In the next section, Solomon looks at the issue of lust. He warns us to keep our boundaries strong. If you lust after someone else's spouse and sleep with him or her, you may even pay for it with your life.

The lesson here is that our wrong choices today have dire consequences tomorrow. Solomon warns us to think about the future. "How can a man light his pants on fire and not be burned?" (v. 27). That's a great question.

Let's be wise in our relationships.

The issue of personal boundaries is so important, whether you're married or not. What areas of your life can you bring to your Father, asking him to help you strengthen your borders?

Protecting Your Spiritual Passion

Day 7 - Proverbs 7:15–27

Who is it that inspires the harlot to seduce the burning lovers of God? The answer is Satan. Satan hates it when anyone leaves a life of slavery. He is a slave master and a slave driver. He will do anything to keep us in chains to sin, the law (a works-based religious life), or some oppressive social system.

This is the Devil's greatest fear—that people will be filled with the spirit of sonship and adoption, crying out, "Abba," which means "Daddy" or "Papa" (see Romans 8:15–17). He will do anything to keep people in slavery and prevent them from entering their inheritance: intimate sonship.

And he will also go to any lengths to seduce those who have entered full sonship into reverting back to the life of slavery. This is why the harlot entices the young man in Proverbs 7:16 by saying that she has covered her bed with "lovely multicolored Egyptian linens." The word Egyptian is the clue. Egypt was the land in which the Israelites were enslaved, the land from which they were rescued. God wanted his firstborn son, Israel, to himself. When Moses delivered the Israelites from Egypt, they moved from slavery into sonship.

See how important it is to guard our hearts? The enemy wants to lure us away from passionate sonship into religious servitude. He wants to take us from the land of abundance into Egypt, the land of slavery.

Let's heed our Father's call. He is compassionate toward us and will save us as we diligently guard our hearts.

~

The harlot lists her various enticements, but we are called to not forget our Father's benefits. Write down God's attributes and offers that draw you near to his embrace. Let these things captivate your imagination as you allow yourself to slip more deeply into his arms.

Christ, the Wisdom of God

Day 8 - Proverbs 8:22–31

Prepare yourself to adore Christ, the wisdom of God! This section of Proverbs 8 is one of the most luminous and glorious in the entire book. Here Solomon, himself under the anointing of wisdom, goes back to the very beginning of time, to the creation of all things. There he sees prophetically the role of wisdom in the joyful act of creation. Speaking under a heavenly anointing of revelation knowledge, Solomon has the wisdom declare, "In the beginning I was there!" (v. 22).

We know from the opening verses of the gospel of John that Jesus Christ was present at the genesis of all things and that through him everything was created. Christ the wisdom of God was the one through whom God the Father made all things. From the tiniest atom to the brightest star, Christ was involved in the creative process. He was the Word with which the Father spoke everything visible and invisible into being.

Christ's part in all of this is filled out in Proverbs 8. "I was there dancing," he cries (v. 24). Have you ever thought of the Trinity "dancing together" as they brought all things into existence? What a picture! Before everything was made—from the ocean depths to the sculpted mountains—Christ performed the role of Master Artist, playfully fashioning the earth and the heavens with laughter and joy, finding his delight in the children of men (our first parents, Adam and Eve).

This is a breathtaking picture. Worship the dancing Messiah today and thank God for his divine creativity.

> Proverbs 8 brings out a rarely celebrated aspect of Christ's character—his creativity. Ask him today to increase in you that same playful and artistic sensibility that he exhibited at the genesis of all things. Express your longing as creatively as you can, maybe even by dancing.

The Teachable Spirit

Day 9 - Proverbs 9:1–6

The Father loves hearts that are receptive to his kingdom revelation and minds that are eager to learn heaven's wisdom.

This passionate desire for God's insights and understanding is what creates in us the fertile conditions in which divine wisdom can grow. The teachable heart is the spiritually hungry heart.

It is this hunger that Solomon celebrates at the beginning of Proverbs 9. Wisdom is portrayed once again as an elegant lady. This lady has prepared a sumptuous feast and sent out an invitation. The table is set and the wine has been poured. Now it's up to us. Are we hungry and thirsty enough to answer Lady Wisdom's invitation and head for her palace?

As we have seen before, Lady Wisdom is a type or a foreshadowing of Jesus. Jesus was called the wisdom of God (1 Corinthians 1:30). Jesus laid down his life so that we who were foolish and floundering could know God's wisdom and reign in life on the earth. It was the shedding of his blood that made this possible. As verse 2 says, "The sacrifice has been killed."

All that's needed now for us to acquire wisdom is to be humble and hungry. We have to be humble enough to lay aside our simple thoughts and agree with God's ways. We have to be hungry enough to want to feast at Wisdom's table and find God's righteousness there.

Our pursuit should be this: "I am going to cultivate a greater hunger for your wisdom, O God."

Imagine Lady Wisdom's invitation is in front of you right now, unanswered. In what area do you need to agree with God? Express a prayer with humility, asking for a teachable heart eager to receive wisdom from above.

Holy Restraint

Day 10 - Proverbs 10:8–19

Have you ever had the experience of the Holy Spirit preventing you from saying something that would have been extremely hurtful, destructive, or unwise? If you have, you'll know that there is great wisdom in thinking before you speak and sometimes in not speaking at all!

As our Father trains us in his wisdom, we will develop godly discipline in this area. We will learn over time when to speak and when not to speak, what to say and what not to say. In short, we will cultivate holy restraint, remembering that it is sometimes better to listen than to speak.

There are those, according to verse 8, who do not position themselves to listen to and learn from correction. They do all the talking so that no one can get a word in. Such people are unwise. Their lack of restraint will lead to them stumbling into the mess they've created.

There are also those, according to verse 14, who exhibit wisdom by not saying everything even when it's their turn to speak. They divulge just enough, while the fool blurts everything out. In this, the wise man or woman shows that they have learned the art of holy restraint.

One of wisdom's life lessons in this passage is therefore this: be as brief in your speech as Solomon is in his proverbs. If you go on talking, you'll end up saying something wrong, something you'll regret. So prove you're wise by holding your tongue and saying only what needs to be said.

The Holy Spirit is ever present to help us. Ask him to show you how you can become wiser in how you speak. Write your reflections about what you feel he says to you.

The Fruit of Righteousness

Day 11 - Proverbs 11

Why does Solomon talk so much about righteousness in Proverbs 11? It is because God knows that righteousness is what will lead us on the path of fullest life. As our good Father, he desires our lives to be truly filled with life and blessing.

Consider this—wisdom is what teaches us how to make righteous choices. Righteousness is one of the fruits of wisdom.

Every Christian knows that God calls us to be righteous, but many do not understand the role wisdom plays in enabling us to live righteously. This is why many children of God unfortunately look to rules and laws to teach them how to live instead of allowing the Spirit of Adoption to grow within them until they look and live just like their Father.

This Spirit of Adoption is the Holy Spirit, the very Spirit of Wisdom. He dwells within us, freeing us from needing the outward restriction and restraint of rules, instead transforming our hearts into his likeness.

To be trained in wisdom is to be trained to follow Jesus' example of life, and following Jesus' example of life means living righteously—not because we pursued a written standard, but because we became intimate with wisdom from the heart as children with a loving Father.

Our Father's love—the deepest expression of righteousness—partners with wisdom to perfect us in both love and wisdom, leading to righteousness and blessing.

In what way do you want to be transformed into his likeness? Let your heart write a prayer to the Holy Spirit, asking him to fulfill that desire.

Keeping a Lid on Our Lips

Day 12 - Proverbs 12:13–28

So much of the book of Proverbs focuses on our words. This part of Proverbs 12 is no exception. Here Solomon gives us some clues concerning reigning in life in our speaking: "When someone insults you, don't respond in kind. Keep quiet and shrug it off. The fool has a short fuse, but the wise person uses words with discretion when put under pressure."

The wise person chooses to tell the truth rather than to stretch or embellish it. Those who embrace heaven's wisdom are truth tellers. They avoid telling lies.

Those who reign in life use words carefully and kindly. While fools use words recklessly and hurtfully, the wise use words that comfort and heal.

The wise person doesn't use words to impress other

people with their knowledge. This is what fools do. Wise people are not addicted to the need for approval.

Wise people are skillful at bringing a life-giving word of encouragement to people who are struggling. Their words can do wonders to restore joy to a wounded heart.

Finally, wise people live in a constant flow of kingdom revelation. They know God's strategies for reigning in life. Therefore they always give good advice to others.

Do you see how important it is to be wise in our speaking?

How wonderful it is, then, that our Father who teaches us to speak is the One whose words are established forever!

If you have been given to words that tear others down, release that habit to Father God. Receive from him in exchange a heart filled with life-giving words to say. Practice by writing life-giving words to yourself, encouraging yourself with the good words that God says about you.

Dreams Fulfilled

Day 13 - Proverbs 13

We start dreaming at a very early age. Some dreams change as we change through life, but some dreams remain deep within us for the long haul.

Proverbs 13:12 says, "When hope's dream seems to drag on and on, the delay can be depressing." It's interesting to see this verse penned just after our Father taught us the wisdom of gradual increase.

The nature of dreams is that we desire the moment when they are fulfilled. We wish to jump straight to that day. But here is where our Father shows how intimate he is with our hearts—he knows our desire to have our dreams fulfilled even today, but he also wants our ability to be faithful to match the magnitude of our dreams.

It would break his heart and ours if our dream were to be fulfilled instantly, only to come crashing down around us. How much more wonderful is it to have the wisdom and ability to steward our dream once we have attained it?

Do not grow discouraged or depressed if your dream tarries. Instead, rest in intimacy with your Father who is steadily guiding you day by day toward your dream's grand fulfillment.

Then, when our dreams at last come true, life's sweetness satisfies our souls.

What dream are you waiting to be fulfilled in your life? Ask the Holy Spirit to show you steps you can take in this season of life so that you can progress toward the sweet and satisfying experience of a dream fulfilled.

In Praise of Messy Stables

Day 14 - Proverbs 14

Are you one of those who despises mess and makes strenuous and repeated efforts to keep everything tidy? Or are you one of those who create messes for others to clean up?

Everyone has a different perspective on mess. The truth is, there are messes to avoid (as in making a mess of your life) and messes to applaud.

In verse 4, Solomon gives us heavenly wisdom on the second of these. He declares, "The only clean stable is an empty one." In other words, if you don't want mess, don't have livestock!

Then he goes on to add this luminous truth: "If you want the work of an ox and enjoy an abundant harvest, you'll have a mess or two to clean up!"

This proverb is radiant with wisdom. Anyone who wants to see a visitation of God and a growth in God's people knows that this principle holds true: revival is messy.

Consider for a moment the most important event in history. When the Infinite became an infant, it was in a stable filled with animals. The Messiah was therefore born in a mess. You can't avoid the implications of all this.

Solomon was so right. Great awakenings are untidy. Many people prefer the order of the cemetery to the order of the nursery, so they miss out on their abundant harvest. Let's be numbered among those who don't mind cleaning up the mess.

Your dreams will not be fulfilled without making a mess or two along the way. Ask the Holy Spirit to show you what steps you can take toward the dreams he has put in your heart—even if it's messy—and write what he says.

Reigning in Life: Part 1

Day 15 - Proverbs 15:13–33

The book of Proverbs begins with the idea that a proverb is something designed to enable us to reign in life. Our original mandate in the garden of Eden was to relate to the Father with intimacy and to reign on the earth with authority. We lost that thanks to the first Adam. We have had it restored thanks to the last Adam, Jesus Christ.

In this next portion of Proverbs 15, we catch a glimpse of some of the characteristics of those who reign in life, or as the heading above verse 13 puts it, those who live the ascended life.

What is the ascended life? Think for a moment of Jesus. He was raised from the dead and ascended into heaven to sit at the right hand of the throne of God in glory. According to Ephesians 2:6, those of us who are in Christ are seated with him. There we reign in life with him.

In Proverbs 15, we are presented with some of the traits of the person who lives an ascended life. They choose to be cheerful, not depressed. They are thankful and content, as long as they have God and love, regardless of their wealth. They are calm and patient, not hot tempered. They make good rather than frivolous decisions. They seek out multiple counselors rather than acting unilaterally. Their advice is heavenly rather than worldly. They head constantly heavenward rather than being tugged downward.

Such a person can live in the heights of heaven where revelation knowledge is found. Keeping low before the Lord in humility, they are raised high to the place where they fall down under the heavy weight of the glory of God.

Let your heart rest in the truth that you are ascended with Christ. Let that become the place your heart considers home. As you do, living an ascended life will become natural.

Have you considered what it means that you are seated with Christ Jesus in heavenly places? Let Father God open the eyes of your heart to envision what surrounds you. What does it mean to live a heavenly life while still dwelling on earth?

Reigning in Life: Part 2

Day 16 - Proverbs 16:1–9

Our Father wants us to succeed. Why else would he give us an entire book full of wisdom to help us reign in life?

The fear of the Lord recognizes the vast difference between our limits and his infiniteness. He sees the end from the beginning and knows the outcome of every decision before it is made. Why, then, would we be so foolish as to make decisions on our own? If our Father has offered his perspective, insight, wisdom, and instruction to help guide us to good outcomes in our decisions, why would we ever strike out on our own?

Instead, we follow the advice of Solomon by committing our work to the Lord, seeking his purposes for our lives, and pursuing intimacy with him both in our heart and our actions.

When we do this, we have the promise of provision in our way. We also have assurance that our steps will not fail and that our Father will cause even those who hate us to be at peace with us.

We are not alone. We are part of a divine family! Let us not seek our own ways, but instead walk with our Father. He will establish us and give us success.

Are there any important plans for the future that you're making right now? Take time right now to sense his leading and commit those plans to the Lord. What do you feel him saying to you about your plans?

Wisdom's Heart Transplant

Day 17 - Proverbs 17

Whenever our Father speaks to us about our hearts, it is always an invitation to intimacy. He never expects us to isolate ourselves and somehow exert enough force on our hearts to make them acceptable to him.

He is not just our God, but also our Father and Maker. He understands the intricacies of our hearts, and he knows that we have no power to change them. Only he has that ability.

Our Father's method for transforming our hearts is not like the instructor who lectures and assigns homework to be done independently. Instead, he pulls us into his embrace and reveals his heart to us. That moment of revelation becomes our moment of transformation in which our heart becomes like his, not through our work, but through our relationship of love.

So when Proverbs 17 describes the kind of heart required for reigning in life, it also describes the heart of our Father. Here are some of the highlights:

- A "purified" heart (v. 3); a heart that has been refined through the fire of God's jealous love
- A "humble" heart (v. 10); a heart that delights in understanding
- A truthful rather than a "perverse" heart (v. 20); a heart that never lies and always tells the truth
- A "cheerful" heart (v. 22); joy in our hearts releases healing to our souls and bodies
- An "understanding" heart (v. 27); a heart filled with God's peace at all times

These descriptions are a gateway to revelation, but only intimacy with our Father will impart these virtues to our heart.

Choose one of these five virtues of the heart and meditate on how your Father embodies it to the fullest. Ask him to reveal himself to you in this way so that you may become more like him. Journal about your experience.

Experiencing Wisdom

Day 18 - Proverbs 18:20

The wisdom Solomon received was not a momentary gift of wisdom to solve an immediate problem. When Solomon asked for wisdom, he received a supernatural endowment from the Spirit of God. His wisdom was not situational, moment by moment, but rather deep, wide, and all-encompassing. He lived in a realm of wisdom and shaped his world to the wisdom God had given him.

This is the realm into which our Father invites us. It is a transformational place where the Spirit of Wisdom draws us into union with himself. The impartation of wisdom we receive from him in that place is so deep that the word learning hardly describes it. We learn it in the same sense that we learn to walk as a child—once we learn it, it becomes our way of living and we can imagine no other life.

The place of wisdom is always a place of intimacy with our Father, for he is wisdom. The place of wisdom is a place of blessing, for wisdom produces blessings. And the place of wisdom is as experiential as life itself, for wisdom encompasses and applies to all of life.

Wisdom like this that conforms us to the Spirit of Wisdom cannot remain trapped within us, but overflows into our words as we speak to those around us. How wonderful it is to have the guard of wisdom protecting our communication! As we see our words bring life to our relationships and occupations, our hearts are filled with satisfaction.

Recall a moment when you heard yourself say something so wise that it surprised you. This can happen for you every day. What would it look like if your words brought life and wisdom to all your relationships, at home and at work?

Wisdom in Friendships

Day 19 - Proverbs 19

God's love is expressed through wisdom. His mercy is expressed through wisdom. Everything he does is expressed through wisdom. Our Father's faithfulness is actually a matter of wisdom.

Consider how essential faithfulness is to God's nature—he is the same yesterday, today, and forever! His steadfast faithfulness is what makes him the rock upon which we can build our lives.

Now apply that faithfulness to our human friendships. Envision that faithfulness in marriage and family. Imagine that faithfulness in government and business. What impact could the wisdom of faithfulness have in our world?

Proverbs 19 reveals much about earthly friendships, most notably their remarkable lack of faithfulness when hardship comes. We see the fruit of this all around us as people choose ease over the stability of deep roots.

As much as we all desire faithfulness from our friends, none of us has the power to make anyone be faithful to us. The only one we are in charge of is ourselves, which means it is on us to be steady, faithful, and unchanging, and to demonstrate the heart we also desire from our friends.

As we become intimate with our Father, we will encounter his faithfulness and be changed. As we are changed to become more faithful, our world around us will change too.

How has the heavenly Father been faithful to you? If you've been hurt by the unfaithfulness of others in the past, ask your Father to bring healing to your heart.

Warnings Against Laziness

Day 20 - Proverbs 20

One of the most toxic and dangerous attitudes in many parts of the world today is the spirit of entitlement. People have come to believe the lie that others—whether it's the state or some more local institution—owe them. They believe that they are entitled to have every benefit for nothing. They expect regular income, housing, food, medical care, and other necessities of life even though they make absolutely no contribution in return for them.

Now there are cases where a person must have benefits for which they cannot directly and actively contribute. In such cases there must be provision. Throughout the book of Proverbs, Solomon talks about the importance of championing the causes of those who cannot speak or act for themselves. This is the character of God, who loves justice and hates it when the poor are disempowered.

But others become lazy and expect everything for nothing. To them, Solomon has some stern words of wisdom and warning: If you don't plant seeds in the ground, you won't have a harvest later. If you spend all your time sleeping, don't be surprised if you wake up poor.

To all those who have yielded to the spirit of entitlement and are living a life of indolence and inertia, Solomon's word is firm and loving. "Wake up, sleepyhead!" (v. 13). If a person becomes active and intentional about work again, there will be plenty of food on the table.

Has a spirit of entitlement crept into your heart, turning you from passionate to passive? What area of entitlement or inactivity is the Holy Spirit highlighting in your life?

Wisdom in Warfare

Day 21 - Proverbs 21

Many of us, when we were children, pictured ourselves as heroes, storming the gates of the enemy, setting the captives free. The good news is that this is an expression in fantasy of a calling we have in reality. In reality, we are all called to reign in life. As believers seated in the heavenly realms with Christ, we are called to bring the rule of heaven to earth and to destroy the works of the evil one.

For us to do this effectively, we must exercise wisdom in spiritual warfare. Verse 22 speaks of "a warrior filled with wisdom." Maybe you would have preferred to hear about "a warrior stocked with ammunition." But our weapons are heavenly weapons, and in Proverbs the greatest resource for reigning in life is God's eternal wisdom.

The next thing we hear about this warrior is that he or she "ascends the high place." This is tremendous! As people who live in Christ, we have access to heaven. We are seated with Christ in the heavenly places. We can ascend in our spirits any time to the realm where Christ reigns victorious over every demonic power. We can bring to earth the victory that is already secured in heaven.

Wisdom in warfare therefore simply agrees with what God has already established in heaven, beginning with our spirits agreeing with our Father's loving wisdom and continuing until the fruit of that wisdom has filled our world with life.

Maybe there is an area in your life with which you have been fighting for some time. Despite this experience, thankfully, we continually have victory because Jesus has already won. By accessing heaven's wisdom, you can see even mighty strongholds demolished.

Give any area of struggle over to God afresh. Ask the Holy Spirit to show you the victory he gives you in your area of struggle. Write down any new wisdom-based battle plans that the Holy Spirit is revealing to you.

Keys to Promotion

Day 22 - Proverbs 22

God is a loving Father who is deeply interested in all aspects of our lives, down to the smallest details. He wants to give us kingdom revelations that will equip us to prosper in our families, friendships, employment, everything.

When we look at work, what are God's kingdom secrets for success? Proverbs 22 contains a number of these secrets. Right at the top is "a beautiful reputation" (v. 1). The person who wants to prosper in the workplace must cultivate an honorable character. This takes time, so there are no shortcuts, but it begins with the child of God preferring a good reputation to a large bank account. As Solomon makes clear, it's more important to be esteemed by others than it is to own great investments.

Once a believer has made a conscious choice to value reputation above riches, there are some practical steps that

Solomon outlines. These all have to do with our character. The person of noble reputation steers well clear of people who are twisted and perverse and gives troublemakers a wide berth. This person has strong and abiding values worth passing on to their children. They are generous to the poor and work hard. They are people of discipline and ethical integrity.

Having a beautiful reputation at home and work is one of the keys to promotion. Trustworthy people are given greater entrustments.

Creating a beautiful reputation takes time. How much do you value your reputation? Ask God to show you steps you can take to establish a better reputation.

Unrelenting Passion

Day 23 - Proverbs 23

Proverbs 23:17 is a critical verse for those who are called to lead or manage other people well. Solomon tells us not to allow ourselves to burn with anger when we see others do evil things. We are not to give our hearts over to ranting and raging. That is a foolish use of passion.

If we allow anger to reign in us, we create a culture of anger through our influence; but if we instead cultivate loving justice and mercy, we will fill the world with these things.

It comes down to a question of where we place our focus. If we continually focus on those things that aggravate us and thereby cultivate anger, we will bring harm to ourselves and those around us. But if we continually choose to focus on our Father and the love he has for us, we will be filled with that love and in turn better love those around us.

Anger will never resolve injustice, just as darkness cannot displace darkness. Let us give our hearts over to forgiveness and releasing mercy to those who have done wrong. The act of forgiveness will release us from a prison of anger and free us to receive our Father's love like never before.

Embrace a vision of the Father and so be filled with the light of his love.

Write out a letter of release, forgiveness, and mercy to those who have wronged you and ask the Holy Spirit to heal your hurts and fill you afresh.

After the Fall

Day 24 - Proverbs 24

One of the greatest challenges we have today is to know how to respond wisely when someone falls, whether as a result of their own moral failure or because they have been struck down by some adversity. Proverbs 24 has some timely and heavenly wisdom on this subject both for those who experience the fall and indeed those who see it happen.

First of all, we learn from verse 16 that those who love God are unlikely to go through the whole of life without

thePassionTranslation.com

stumbling and falling. That is a given. We live in a fallen world, and there is a master schemer (v. 8) who plots the downfall of the ungodly. His desire is to fell God's lovers, either through temptation or affliction.

It's not whether we'll fall down that's the real issue here. It's whether we'll get back up again. Those who love God may fall seven times, but they will get right back up again every time. They know that the call is bigger than the fall, so they get up and press on. The unrighteous, on the other hand, are finished after just one calamity.

Secondly, we learn from verse 17 that God hates gloating. This is really a word of warning for those who are fascinated by or even take pleasure in another person's disaster. God says in verse 17 that this displeases him. This is especially true if the person concerned is an enemy.

God's wisdom here is, as usual, stunning. To the fallen he says, "Get up again!" To those who see the fall he says, "Don't gloat." Let's activate this kind of heavenly wisdom so that true restoration can happen every time God's lovers fall. That wisdom will restore fallen people into mighty warriors (v. 5).

The culture of heaven turns zeroes into heroes while many earthly cultures do the exact opposite. What can you do to create an atmosphere around you in which those who fall can rise again?

A Revolution of Kindness

Day 25 - Proverbs 25

The word kindness appears time and again throughout Proverbs. If there is one thing the world is lacking and the church so often is missing, it's kindness. Too often we are stern, harsh, and even brutal in our dealings with each other.

This is not God's way of dealing with us. He could employ that side of his character known as "sternness," but he chooses kindness instead. He knows that it is kindness alone that has the capacity to change a person or a situation (Romans 2:4). His divine kindness overwhelms our defenses and undermines our pretenses. It breaks down division and defuses hostility like nothing else.

God's sons and daughters should be the champions of kindness here on earth. As Proverbs 25 teaches, we should not be hasty in taking litigation (v. 8). We should not betray a confidence in order to win an argument (vv. 9–10). We should have a reputation for saying the right word to the right person at the right time in the right way (v. 11). We should employ kindness in our dealings with leaders, understanding that "gentle wisdom" has an extraordinary power to persuade. We should never say unkind, dishonest, or slanderous things about another (v. 18). We should not be insensitive in the presence of one who is grieving (v. 20). We should show kindness to our enemies. If they are hungry, win them over by buying them lunch (v. 21).

There is nothing quite like kindness. It is one of the strongest qualities of the culture of heaven, and it is meant

to be one of the clearest characteristics of those who follow Christ here on the earth.

God's kindness is what transforms us into kind people. Ask your Father to show you how truly kind he is, then list all the ways God has demonstrated his kindness to you.

Negative Words

Day 26 - Proverbs 26

Much of Proverbs 26 is about the power of words. If we are filled with the wisdom of heaven, we will use words carefully and prayerfully, understanding that language is powerful. We will be positive and prudent in our choice of words, ensuring that our words are healing not harmful.

When people are foolish rather than wise, their words will be frivolous (v. 4), silly (v. 5), untrustworthy (v. 7), hurtful (v. 9), stupid (v. 13), quarrelsome (v. 17), untruthful (v. 18), insensitive (v. 19), gossipy (v. 20), argumentative (v. 21), slick (v. 23), and hypocritical (v. 24).

Since the world is so full of people who are filled with earthly folly rather than heavenly wisdom, it is no surprise that so many people are badly hurt by words. How then do those who reign in life protect themselves from the harsh negativity of unjust and slanderous comments?

There is a beautiful promise to reassure us in verse 2: "An undeserved curse will be powerless to harm you." In other

words, when someone wishes and speaks ill of you for no just cause, then these words will be like arrows that fall short of where you are standing. They will not hurt you.

In fact, the text suggests that they may even return to harm those who spoke them. The curse, like a bird, will flutter over you for a moment and then fly back to the nest from which it came. The harm will return like a boomerang to the sender.

We are called to be wise in our use of words. But we are also called not to worry about those who speak negative words about us.

Spend some time in prayer thanking God that every curse spoken against you will not nest in your life. Then start blessing those who curse you. Note how the culture of heaven begins to invade your attitude toward them and your relationship with them.

Faithful Friends

Day 27 - Proverbs 27

If you lost absolutely everything—your house, your income, your security, even your family—would you have friends that would stand by you?

If you started to wander from the path of God's wisdom, choosing to yield to temptation, do you have friends who would challenge you in love and call you back on track?

We all need faithful friends—friends who will stick with us when everyone else walks out; friends who have the love and courage to correct us when we are making wrong choices.

In Proverbs 27, Solomon warns about false friends and true friends. False friends are insincere, flattering us when what we actually need is a rebuke (v. 6).

True friends, on the other hand, are not afraid to prick our consciences. Their wounds are born of faithful love. They have lasting healthy consequences if we heed them.

Furthermore, the discussions we enter into with our friends succeed in sharpening us, as a grinding wheel sharpens a blade (v. 17).

Let's learn to value "sweet friendships" (v. 9). They refresh the soul when the soul is tired and downcast. They awaken joy like the anointing oil of God's fragrant presence.

We should never give up on our friends. If we stick with them in their difficulties, they will be there for us in the day of our brokenness in a way even relatives won't (v. 10).

What kingdom friendships do you have that are faithful, truthful, and fruitful? Ask God to help you create and cultivate these kind of relationships.

Impaired Eyesight

Day 28 - Proverbs 28

What happens to our understanding of the ways of God

when we willfully choose to go down a path of sin? Suddenly what was so plain to us becomes obscure. What was clearly right and wrong becomes a matter for debate. What was just and unjust is an issue of interpretation. Our vision, once crystal clear, is now foggy. We no longer make right choices, and we no longer speak out with confidence against what we once knew was wrong.

Our choice to sin on any lasting scale has the capacity to bring a film over our eyes so that we no longer see things as God does. As Proverbs 28:4 says, those who turn their backs on what they know to be right will in the future no longer have the ability to tell right from wrong. Their own sinful life choices will mean that they justify behavior that they would never have tolerated before.

What are we to do to ensure that we don't fall into this spiritual blindness? Verse 4 says that we must "love the truth." The truth is a person named Jesus. Intimacy with him keeps us focused on his glorious beauty and love, protecting us from the inferior splendor of foolish delights.

We know there is a way that seems right, but its end is death. Folly does not always appear foolish in the beginning, but it lures those who follow it into dark places where they can no longer discern between good and evil.

But as we listen to God's voice and follow him, he will keep us on the path of life and fill us with every good thing.

What choices have you made that may be impairing your vision? Let God show you the end of those ways and then guide you to the steps his wisdom leads you to take.

The Leader as Seer

Day 29 - Proverbs 29

Every organization needs people with vision. If an organization lacks vision, it will lack clear direction. In aiming at nothing, it will successfully hit its target and achieve nothing. Whether it's in the boardroom of a business or the prayer room of a church, someone somewhere needs to have eyes to see where everyone should be heading.

One of the standout statements in Proverbs 29 is in verse 18 where Solomon teaches that where there is no prophetic vision, people start quickly wandering astray. In other words, where there is no clearly revealed direction, people create a free market economy where they do their own thing.

We must pause and remember here that Solomon was for a long time an extremely effective ruler because he had prayed for one gift more than any other: wisdom and knowledge to lead the people he was called to influence. This had given him the capacity to see what God saw and to draw his people toward that future reality. That is visionary leadership.

Leaders need to be intimate with the Father's heart. Only then do they begin seeing life through Wisdom's value system, enabling them to plan and respond as their Father would. Their connection to the Father enables them to see the end result of every action.

This place of intimacy births radical vision for how to reign in life. Time spent in the very presence of Wisdom releases plans that will shape nations into the Father's designs.

What vision is God showing you so that you do not wander astray? Draw near to him today and let him speak to you about your future plans.

The Epitome of Wisdom

Day 30 - Proverbs 30

Proverbs 30 describes four creatures that are very small but very wise (vv. 24–28). These four creatures are the feeble ant, the delicate rock badger, the leaderless locust, and the small lizard that is easy to catch. Each is singled out as the epitome of heavenly wisdom and as an example for human beings to follow.

The ant is wise because it stores up food in the summer that it will need in the winter. This illustrates the proactive wisdom of those who think ahead and strategize for future eventualities. This is a sign of true wisdom in the son and daughter of God.

The rock badger isn't a strong animal, so it climbs up to the highest crags and makes its hiding place there. This is a picture of the wise believer who reigns in life. We are not strong in ourselves but we hide in Christ, the Rock of Ages. There's no one higher than him.

The locust is a picture of wisdom because it moves with countless other locusts in an extraordinary unity and yet has no visible leader. This is a picture of wise believers who move

in a common purpose and direction, led by one who is invisible and yet very real—Jesus Christ.

The tiny lizard is also wise. It may be insignificant to look at, but it finds its way into significant places, not the least of which are kings' palaces. This is true of wise believers too. We may look insignificant, but God gives us proximity to significant people, not the least of which is himself, the King of kings!

Look again at the lesson of these four creatures—the ant, the badger, the locust, and the lizard. Which creature's characteristic do you want to grow in the most? Take time to meditate on that creature right now and ask the Holy Spirit to impart to you the wisdom his creation teaches.

The Beauty of Becoming

Day 31 - Proverbs 31:10–31

Proverbs 31:10–31 is both inspiring and terrifying. It can give us an enthralling picture of what we can become. And it can be wrongfully used as a measuring stick to show how far we are falling short of God's glorious design. The language and writing style used here implies that the perfections of this woman would exhaust the entire language. No person, male or female, can live up to this standard, that is, on their own and at the start of their journey.

But this is not a picture of what we look like at the start of

our race. We “ascend” (v. 29), going from glory to glory. We are transformed into his likeness as we live “in the wonder, awe, and fear of the Lord” (v. 30). We “become radiant” (v. 31) as we feed on wisdom from above and make daily choices that align with the revelation we receive from the Holy Spirit. God’s intimate love feeds our spirits and motivates “loving works of righteousness” (v. 31). These works “deserve to be admired” because they are the very works of our Bridegroom Jesus working through us.

There is no better Bridegroom than Jesus. He is full of grace and truth, gently leading his bride. Because of the work of Christ, you are that radiant bride. Jesus sees you as you are and loves you. He also sees you as you will become and says, “There are many valiant and noble ones, but you have ascended above them all!” (v. 29). Be emboldened by the magnificent adulation in his words to you today.

Whether you are man or woman, what parts of Proverbs 31:10–30 do you see the Holy Spirit working into your life so that you are becoming the radiant bride of Christ?

About The Passion Translation

The message of God's story is timeless; the Word of God doesn't change. But the methods by which that story is communicated should be timely; the vessels that steward God's Word can and should change. One of those timely methods and vessels is Bible translations. Bible translations are both a gift and a problem. They give us the words God spoke through his servants, but words can be very poor containers for revelation because they leak! The meanings of words change from one generation to the next. Meaning is influenced by culture, background, and many other details. You can imagine how differently the Hebrew authors of the Old Testament saw the world three thousand years ago from the way we see it today!

There is no such thing as a truly literal translation of the Bible, for there is not an equivalent language that perfectly conveys the meaning of the biblical text except as it is understood in its original cultural and linguistic setting. This problem is best addressed when we seek to transfer meaning, not merely words, from the original text to the receptor language.

The purpose of The Passion Translation is to reintroduce the passion and fire of the Bible to the English reader. It doesn't merely convey the original, literal meaning of words. It expresses God's passion for people and his world by translating the original, life-changing message of God's Word for modern readers.

You will notice at times we've italicized certain words or phrases. These highlighted portions are not in the original Hebrew, Greek, or Aramaic manuscripts but are implied from the context. We've made these implications explicit for the sake of narrative clarity and to better convey the meaning of God's Word. This is a common practice by mainstream translations,

including the New American Standard Bible and the King James Version.

God longs to have his Word expressed in every language in a way that would unlock the passion of his heart. Our goal is to trigger inside every English–speaking reader an overwhelming response to the truth of the Bible. This is a heart-level translation, from the passion of God's heart to the passion of your heart.

We pray this version of God's Word will kindle in you a burning desire for him and his heart, while impacting the church for years to come.

About the Translator

Dr. Brian Simmons is known as a passionate lover of God. After a dramatic conversion to Christ, Brian knew that God was calling him to go to the unreached people of the world and present the gospel of God's grace to all who would listen. With his wife Candice and their three children, he spent nearly eight years in the tropical rain forest of the Darien Province of Panama as a church planter, translator, and consultant. Brian was involved in the Paya-Kuna New Testament translation project. He studied linguistics and Bible translation principles with New Tribes Mission. After their ministry in the jungle, Brian was instrumental in planting a thriving church in New England (U.S.), and now travels full time as a speaker and Bible teacher. He has been happily married to Candice for over forty-two years and is known to boast regularly of his children and grandchildren. Brian and Candice may be contacted at:

Facebook.com/passiontranslation

Twitter.com/tPtBible

For more information about the translation project or any of Brian's books, please visit:

thePassionTranslation.com

StairwayMinistries.org